'The plan adopted by the US Bureau of Operations was to advance step by step to a position from which an invasion of the Philippines could be launched . . . It was believed in Washington that nothing short of intervention by the Japanese battle fleet was likely to frustrate the methodical fulfilment of this plan . . . Thus the only uncertain factor was the Japanese battle fleet. The general opinion was that Japan would not risk this force save in the last extremity.' p. 245 *The Great Pacific War, a History of the American–Japanese Campaign of 1931–33,* by Hector C. Bywater, *1925*

'The (Japanese) War Council had issued its decree: "At the first hint of peril to Yap or Guam, throw in your whole force."' *p. 271, Ibid.*

THE BATTLE OF THE
Philippine Sea
June 1944

W. D. DICKSON

LONDON

IAN ALLAN LTD

First published 1975

ISBN 0 7110 0517 6

Published by Ian Allan Ltd, Shepperton, Surrey and
printed in the United Kingdom by Morrison & Gibb Ltd
London and Edinburgh

Contents

Preface and Acknowledgements

The Battle of the Philippine Sea was the pivotal naval battle of 1944. For over twenty months the Japanese Navy had not made a major effort to interdict an American operation with their main surface forces. In this battle they committed their entire strength and were absolutely frustrated. On the Japanese side the principal results were the resort to suicide air attacks and the sacrifice of four of the remaining carriers (by then useless except as decoys) at Leyte Gulf. On the American side an acrimonious debate over tactics obscured the overwhelming nature of the victory and led Admiral Halsey to chase the four decoy carriers while the Japanese battleships and cruisers threatened one of the most startling reversals in naval history. Halsey was not going to be accused of fabian tactics, as Spruance had been. For these reasons the Battle of the Philippine Sea was one of the most important sea fights of the Pacific War and deserves a place in history next to Midway and Guadalcanal.

The battle also belongs in the record books along with Jutland and other 'biggest' battles. It was the 'biggest' carrier battle of the war and therefore quite likely of history. Twenty-four (USN 15; IJN 9) participated in the battle. Interestingly the number of carriers corresponds to the number of battleships dictated for each navy by the limitation treaties.

The sources consulted in preparation of this monograph were as follows:

1 HISTORY
A Official (USN)
1 'Battle Experience Supporting Operations for the Capture of the Marianas, June–August 1944', CONINCH Secret Information Bulletin Number 20.
2 'Naval Air Operations in the Marianas' Aviation History Unit

(USN) unpublished manuscript prepared by Lt W. G. Land and
Lt A. O. Van Wyen, both USNR.

3 'Initial Report on the Operation to Capture the Marianas Islands',
Commander Fifth Fleet Serial 00026 of July 13, 1944.

4 'Final Report on the Operation to Capture the Marianas Islands',
Commander Fifth Fleet Serial 00501 of August 3, 1944.

5 'Action Report of Operations in Support of the Capture of the
Marianas Islands', Commander Task Force 58 Serial 00388 of
September 11, 1944.

6 'Report of Operations of Task Group 58.1 in Support of Landings
in the Marianas, June 6 to June 27, 1944', Commander Task Group
58.1 Serial 0052 of July 14, 1944.

7 'Action Against the Japanese Fleet, June 18 to 22, 1944', Commander Task Group 58.2 Serial 00223 (undated).

8 'Action Report for Task Group 58.3 in *Forager* Operation including
Air Engagement Against the Japanese Fleet', Commander Task
Group 58.3 Serial 00116 of July 16, 1944.

9 'Operations in Marianas and Bonins, June 6–July 6, 1944, Action
Report on', Commander Task Group 58.4 Serial 0054 of July 13,
1944.

B *Official (IJN)*

1 'The *A-Go* Operation – May–June 1944', Japanese Monograph
No. 90, Military Intelligence Section Document No. 35211.

2 'The *A-Go* Operation Log – May–June 1944', Japanese Monograph
No. 91, MISD No. 35212.

3 Detailed Battle Report of *A-Go* Operations, Battles in Seas West
of Saipan from June 13 to June 22, 1944, including Section 2-B,
'Detailed Summary of Reconnaissance and Air Attacks June 15–22,
1944'. First Mobile Force Classified No. 1048 of September 5, 1944.

4 'The Campaigns of the Pacific War', US Strategic Bombing
Survey (Pacific) Naval Analysis Division.

5 'Interrogations of Japanese Officials', vols. I and II, USSBS
(Pacific) Naval Analysis Division.

C *Unofficial (USN)*

1 'New Guinea and the Marianas', vol. 8; History of US Naval
Operations in World War II; Morison, S. E., Rear Admiral
USNR (ret).

2 'The End of an Empire', vol. 4; Battle Report; Karig, Walter,
Capt USNR.

3 'The Fast Carriers', Reynolds, Clark.
4 'The Battles of the Philippine Sea', Lockwood, C. A., Adm USN and Adamson, H. C.
5 'History of US Submarine Operations in World War II', Roscoe, T.
6 'History of US Destroyer Operations in World War II', Roscoe, T.
7 'Mission Beyond Darkness', Bryan, J., Lt Cdr USNR and Philip Reed.
8 'How They Won the War in the Pacific'.
9 'Aircraft Carrier', Polmar, N.

D Unofficial (IJN)
1 'End of the Imperial Japanese Navy', Ito, M. and Roger Pineau and A. Y. Kuroda.
2 'Death of a Navy', D'Albas, A.
3 'Zero', Okumiya, M.; Horikoshi, J. and M. Caidin.
4 'Sunk', Hashimoto, M.

2 TECHNICAL
A USN
1 'US Warships of World War II', Silverstone, P.
2 'American Battleships, Carriers and Cruisers', Lenton, H.
3 'Supplement and General Index', vol. XV History of US Naval Operations in World War II, Morison, S. E.
4 'United States Navy Aircraft Since 1911', Swanborough and Bowers.
5 'History of Naval Fighter Direction', April, May and June 1946 issues of CIC magazine, a US Navy professional journal.
6 'Early Development of Shipboard Radar in The United States Navy', unpublished monograph of Lt (jg) Walter A. Hutchens provided by Lt Cdr R. Dulin USN, author of 'Battleship'.

B IJN
1 'Japanese Warships of World War II', Watts, A. J.
2 'Japanese Battleships and Cruisers'.
3 'Japanese Aircraft Carriers and Destroyers'.
4 'Japanese Aircraft of the Pacific War', Francillon, R. J.
5 'Tactical Planning in the Imperial Japanese Navy', unpublished monograph presented to the US Naval Institute by Minoru Genda (for Air Operations Officer for Admiral Nagumo).

This book follows the format of the previous volumes of this series. The first portion is a detailed account of the battle and the principal events leading up to it, while the second part is devoted to technical aspects. The preliminary moves of the two fleets are outlined in some detail to illustrate the complex preparations required for operations on the scale of *Forager* and *A-Go*. I have attempted to capture the complexity and flavour of carrier warfare as it was conducted during World War II by frequent use of actual dispatches. Where possible I have stated the situation as it existed and also as it was perceived by the principal participants, so the reader can better understand the environment where decisions, which we who have the benefit of hindsight may feel were incorrect, were made. Also because of the previously mentioned debate I have tried to quote the principals in full regarding their views on the controversial aspects of the battle and have saved my own comments for the concluding chapter. By doing this I hope that the text concerning the battle itself will not be considered a brief for either position.

In regard to the Japanese 'official' sources a word of explanation is appropriate. At the end of the war the Japanese destroyed a large portion of their official documents. Because of this the US Strategic Bombing Survey compiled a series of interrogations of senior Japanese officers and of other officers who had unique expertise. These were compiled and many were published in a 2 volume set known as 'Interrogations of Japanese Officials'. They are quite useful for a researcher but suffer from understandable deficiencies. First they are the recollection of the party being questioned and second there was such pressure to complete the project that there was no cross checking of discrepancies in testimony. When one interrogation contradicts another or the party being interrogated contradicts himself it is not evaluated. The correct answer is often a matter of speculation. The interrogators agreed that the Japanese were exceptionally cooperative and a short biography of each officer is included with an opinion of the Japanese officer's attitude toward the interrogators is given to assist the reader in evaluating his testimony. In addition to this project the Strategic Bombing Survey compiled an outline history of the war from the Japanese side using operations orders, dispatches, battle lessons and similar documents connected by explanatory text. Published as 'Campaigns of the Pacific War' this book contains an exceptionally detailed-by the standards of the book-section on the Battle of the Philippine Sea. The Military Intelligence Section of General MacArthur's staff also compiled a large number of documents either by translating captured documents or having persons who would know reconstruct logs and orders. These were known as the Japanese Monograph Series and two of them, Nos. 90 and 91, relate to *A-Go*. They seem to be among the best in the series which ranges from practically useless to very valuable.

In the text I have generally used Royal Navy usage in referring to Japanese Naval tactical and administrative units since their navy more nearly followed the British practice than the American.

In addition to the sources cited above I would like to thank Captain William Harting, USAF who read the text and provided valuable comments. Lt Cdr R. O. Dulin USN (co-author of *Battleship*) has provided much information regarding technical aspects, particularly with regard to gunnery and radar. D. C. Allard of the US Navy's History office and the Japanese War History Office have both answered numerous inquiries and have been very helpful.

Glossary

Abbreviations, Acronyms, Nicknames and Japanese Navalese
All military organizations use acronyms, nicknames, abbreviations and initials in describing equipment, commands etc. Perhaps no organization in the world (even including the Wehrmacht) surpasses the US Navy in such usage. The Japanese were not unlike other military in this respect. They used Roman letters in abbreviating their organizational units; for example 1S in a Japanese table of organization meant First Squadron (*Ichi Sentai* and 1SF meant First Squadron (Flying) (*Ichi Koku Sentai*). The following is a list of those used in this book and the US Navy's phonetic alphabet in use in 1944.

A–*ABLE*
ANGELS–CIC code for altitude
A6M–*Mitsubishi* fighter–also Zeke or Zero
ASP–Anti-Submarine patrol by aircraft
ASW–Anti-Submarine Warfare
Avenger–Grumman TBF/TBM (General Motors) torpedo plane

B–*BAKER*
BAF–Japanese shore based aircraft (Base Air Force) *Konkyo Koku Kant Kantai*
BANDIT–CIC Code–Identified enemy aircraft
BATDIV–Battleship Division USN
BB–Battleship USN (IJN *Senkan*)
BETTY–G4M Japanese shore-based bomber
B5N–*Nakajima* torpedo plane—also Kate
BOGEY–CIC Code–unidentified radar air contact
B6N–*Nakajima* torpedo plane—also Jill or *Tenzan*
B-24–USAAF heavy bomber

Butai–IJN Force

C–*CHARLIE*
CA–Heavy Cruiser USN (IJN *Junyokan Ito*)
CAP–Combat Air Patrol (see *Shotai*)
CARDIV–Carrier Division USN
Chutai–IJN literally 'Company' intermediate formation of aircraft
CL–Light Cruiser USN (IJN *Junyokan Nito*)
CIC–Combat Information Centre
COMSUBPAC–Commander Submarines Pacific
CORSAIR–F4U fighter
CORTDIV–Escort Division (DEs)
CTF–Commander Task Force
CTG–Commander Task Group
CV–Fleet Aircraft Carrier USN (IJN *Koku Bokan*)
CVL–Light Fleet Aircraft Carrier USN
CVE–Escort Aircraft Carrier
CAN–USN slang for destroyer (see also Tincan)

D–*DOG*
Daitai–literally 'Battalion' large formation of IJN aircraft
DD–Destroyer (IJN *Kuchicukan*), slang in USN–'Tincan' or 'Can'
DE–Destroyer Escort
DF–Destroyer Flotilla IJN (Equivalent of USN DESRON)
DESRON–Destroyer Squadron USN
DESDIV–Destroyer Division USN
DG–Destroyer Group IJN (Equivalent of USN DESDIV)
Dauntless–SBD Dive Bomber
Deckload Strike–The maximum number of aircraft an aircraft carrier can launch from its deck in one strike. Usually about $\frac{1}{3}$ of the VF, $\frac{1}{2}$ of the VB and VT
D4Y–*Yokusuka* dive bomber, also Judy and *Suisei*
D3A–*Aichi* dive bomber, also Val

E–*EASY*
E14Y–*Yokusuka* submarine based seaplane, also Glenn
E13A–*Aichi* scout plane, also Jake

F–*FOX*
FDO–Fighter director officer

F4U–Chance-Vought fighter, also Corsair
FISH–CIC code enemy torpedo plane also USN slang for torpedoes
F6F–Grumman fighter also HELLCAT
FMF–First Mobile Force (Fleet) IJN (*Dai Ichi Kido Butai* (*Kantai*))

G–*GEORGE*
G4M–*Mitsubishi* land based bomber, also Betty
Glenn–*Yokusuka* seaplane E14Y

H–*HOW*
HAWK–CIC code–enemy dive bomber
HELLCAT–F6F Fighter
HELLDIVER–SB2C Dive Bomber
Hey Rube–CIC code–All aircraft return to base
HF/DF–High Frequency Direction Finder
Hikotai–Squadron of aircraft IJN

I–*ITEM*
I-Boat; Large Japanese ocean going submarine (cruiser submarine)
IFF–Device which shows characteristic 'blip' on radar–'Identification
    Friend or Foe'

J–*JIG*
JAKE–USN designation for *Aichi* E13A
JILL–USN designation for *Nakajima* B6N
JUDY–USN designation for *Yokusuka* D4Y
JIN–*Nakajima* torpedo plane, shore based, also Irving
Junyokan–Cruiser *Ito* (1st class) Heavy; *Nito* (2nd class) Light

K–*KING*
Kantai–IJN Fleet
KATE–USN designation for *Nakajima* B5N
KdF–Designation used in Japanese tables of organization to identify
    the commander of a fleet; for example *KdF* Mobile Force would
    mean Commander Mobile Force
Kido Kantai–Mobile Fleet IJN (*Kido Butai*–Mobile Force)
Koku Bokan–IJN Aircraft Carrier
Koku Kantai–Air Fleet
Koku Sentai–Airctaft Carrier Squadron abbreviated SF. Also means
    Air Flotilla

Kokutai–Naval Air Group, for example 601 *Kokutai*
Kushu Butai–Air Attack Force

L–*LOVE*
LCT–Landing craft, Tank
LST–Landing ship, Tank–USN slang 'Large Slow Target'

M–*MIKE*

N–*NAN*
NAG–Naval Air Group IJN (*Kokutai*)

O–*OBOE*
OS2U–USN floatplane

P–*PETER*
PBM–Martin flying boat
PB47–Coronado flying boat
PB2Y–Land based long range patrol aircraft (same as B-24–Liberator)
P1Y–*Yokusuka* torpedo plane–shore based
POINT OPTION–A moving point and vector given to pilots
    launched from an aircraft carrier on an extended mission from
    which they can calculate the predicted position of the carrier at
    any time

Q–*QUEEN*

R–*ROGER*
RADAR–Radio Detection and Ranging
RAT–CIC code–enemy fighter
RO-boat–Small Japanese ocean going submarine

S–*SUGAR*
S–IJN Squadron of battleships or cruisers (*Sentai*)
SBD–Douglas dive bomber, also Dauntless
SB2C–Curtiss dive bomber, also Helldiver
SG–IJN Supply Group
Senkan–IJN Battleship
SF–Flying Squadron (Aircraft Carrier Squadron)–IJN (*Koku Sentai*)

Shotai–IJN literally 'Section' smallest tactical unit of aircraft in the IJN; for example a *Shotai* of VF would be the Japanese equivalent of a CAP section

SONAR–SOund Navigation And Ranging

ss–USN designation for submarines

SUBPAC–Submarine Force Pacific

SUBSOWESPAC–Submarine Force SouthWest Pacific

SUBRON–Submarine Squadron

Suisei–D4Y Judy dive bomber

T–*TARE*

TALLY-HO–CIC code 'Enemy in sight'

TBF/TBM–Avenger torpedo plane

Tenzan–B6N Jill torpedo plane

TF–Task Force USN

TG–Task Group USN

TINCAN–USN slang for destroyers, also CAN

Tokubetsu Kogeki Tai–Air Strike Unit (Raid) literally Special Attack Unit

U–*UNCLE*

V–*VICTOR*

vb–Dive Bomber–with suffix number–dive bomber squadron (e.g. vb7)

vf–Fighter–with number suffix–fighter squadron

vt–Torpedo plane–with number suffix–torpedo squadron

vcs–Cruiser based scout plane–number suffix–squadron

vp–patrol aircraft–with number suffix–patrol squadron

vo–Observation float plane–number suffix–squadron

vf (n)–Night fighter–number suffix–squadron

vs–Scout (not ASW as today) aircraft–number suffix–squadron

VAL–D3A dive bomber

W–*WILLIAM*

WINDOW–Aluminium strips cut to the wave length of radar and dropped to create electronic disturbance on the receiver. CHAFF is similar

X–*XRAY*

Y–*YOKE*

Z–*ZEBRA*
ZEKE–A6M Fighter
ZERO–A6M Fighter

PART I
THE BATTLE

Introduction

'With the losses we have sustained, it is necessary to revise completely our strategy of a Pacific war. The losses of battleships commit us to the strategic defensive until our forces can again be built up. However, a very powerful striking force of carriers, cruisers and destroyers survives. These forces must be operated boldly and vigorously on the tactical offensive in order to retrieve our initial disaster.' Preface to Admiral Kimmel's estimate to the Secretary of the Navy dated December 10, 1941.

The Carrier War in the Pacific up to April 1944

The Japanese attack on Pearl Harbor opened the Pacific War. It also indicated the scale and importance aircraft carrier operations would assume in the Pacific theatre. In that attack, six Japanese aircraft carriers (*Akagi, Kaga, Hiryu, Soryu, Shokaku, Zuikaku*) neutralized the US Navy's Battle Force, Pacific Fleet. After Pearl Harbor the Japanese carrier force returned to Japan. In January 1942 that force commenced a series of operations which would not be matched until the US Navy's Fast Carrier offensive of 1944–45. Supporting operations in Rabaul, Kavieng and Java, attacking Darwin and neutralizing the Japanese western flank in the Indian Ocean operations, the Japanese carriers operated almost continuously from January 5, 1942 until April 22, 1942, covering nearly 180° of latitude in operations. It was one of the most admirably executed operations of the war and the results obtained indicated a high degree of personnel training and technical excellence, wholly unexpected by Western naval experts.

During the same period the American carriers were not idle and, if the overall results were not as spectacular as those obtained by the Japanese carriers, the effect on the US carrier force cannot be overemphasized. From January to April 1942, carriers *Lexington* (cv–2), *Yorktown* (cv–5), *Hornet* (cv–8), and *Enterprise* (cv–6) conducted strikes on the periphery of the Japanese Empire and penetrated its inner defences on occasion, attacking such widely separated targets as New Guinea, the Marshalls, Wake Island, Marcus Island and, in the famous Doolittle raid, Tokyo itself. For psychological reasons, the latter operation was probably the most important single carrier operation of the first six months of the war in the Pacific.

These operations culminated in the battles of Coral Sea and Midway. In the first battle, Fifth Aircraft Carrier Squadron (S.F.), composed of *Shokaku* and *Zuikaku* and a covering group, which included light carrier *Shoho*, was supporting a Japanese attempt to capture Port Moresby. This force was met by carriers *Yorktown* and *Lexington*. The Japanese lost the carrier *Shoho* and abandoned their attempts to capture Port Moresby in the first carrier battle between US and Japanese forces (*Hiryu*'s sinking of HMS *Hermes* was the first carrier v. carrier battle of the war). Carrier *Shokaku* was heavily damaged and Fifth S.F.'s air groups were so severely handled that both ships were scratched from the Midway operation. The US lost carrier *Lexington* and *Yorktown* was heavily damaged, apparently out of action for some time. Both sides greatly exaggerated the results. The American boasting was generally restricted to the press, while the Japanese reaction was within the Navy and more particularly among the pilots of the First and Second S.F. Their reaction was jubilant. If the lowly regarded pilots of Fifth S.F. could sink two first line enemy carriers (as the Japanese assumed they had) and not lose either of their ships (the loss of the *Shoho* occurred before the battle between the big carriers), then First and Second S.F. should have no trouble handling anything the Americans threw at them. This arrogance would have serious consequences.

The Midway Operation was designed to draw the US Fleet out for the final decisive battle in the Central Pacific. The Nagumo Force, composed of *Akagi*, *Kaga*, *Hiryu* and *Soryu* with their screening ships would spearhead the attack on Midway, the invasion would take place successfully, and the US Pacific Fleet would sortie to its certain destruction. The central fallacy in their plan was the fact, unknown to the Japanese, that the Americans had broken the Japanese Naval Codes and knew the Japanese plan in intimate detail. As a result the US Navy was able to place its three available carriers, *Hornet*, *Enterprise* and *Yorktown* (the latter ship was available because of the perhaps unmatched efforts of the Pearl Harbor Shipyard), near Midway. With a combination of intelligence, phenomenal luck and courage of the American aviators, all four Japanese carriers were destroyed at the cost of *Yorktown*.

The Guadalcanal campaign involved some of the most violent sea fighting in history. From August 1942 through November 1942 the US Navy and the Imperial Japanese Navy fought six major battles involving heavy losses on both sides. Two of these battles, Eastern Solomons and Santa Cruz, were fought by carrier aircraft. In August the Nagumo Force, now built around *Shokaku* and *Zuikaku*, covered a Japanese reinforcement convoy. *Ryujo* (a CVL) was offered as a lure to the American Carrier Force, built around *Saratoga* and *Enterprise*. The Americans took the bait and overwhelmed *Ryujo*. *Shokaku* and *Zuikaku* counterattacked and hit *Enterprise*, though not fatally. An American attack hit *Shokaku*. The Japanese troops landed, so the battle was a relative standoff. In October, *Shokaku*, *Zuikaku*, *Zuiho* and *Junyo* (*Hiyo* had engineering difficulties and could not participate), covering another Japanese convoy to Guadalcanal, were intercepted by an American force composed of *Hornet* and *Enterprise*, plus screening ships (though the IJN outnumbered the USN 4 to 2 in carriers the air groups were much less desperate. IJN had 212 total: 87 VF; 68 VB; 57 VT; USN had 171 total: 70 VF, 72 VB, 29 VT). Air Groups on both sides attacked with resolution. *Shokaku* was heavily damaged, but so was *Enterprise*, and *Hornet* was lost. The Battle of Santa Cruz was a tactical victory for the Japanese and marked the end of carrier v. carrier fighting in 1942. The intensity and frequency of carrier battles (four in six months) in 1942 indicated that this type of action would continue with increasing ferocity. In fact, the next battle would not take place for twenty months. There were several reasons for this. After Santa Cruz, *Enterprise* was the only operational US carrier in the Pacific and she could not be risked except in dire circumstances. More important, however, was the Japanese carrier pilot situation. When the war began the Japanese had about 3500 pilots and a like number of aircrew personnel in the Naval Air Corps. Of these, approximately four hundred pilots, plus air crews, were assigned to the first line carriers. Most of these pilots, particularly those assigned to *Kaga*, *Akagi*, *Hiryu* and *Soryu*, had extensive flying experience and might have been the best group of naval aviators ever assembled. The general policy was to keep the best pilots with the first line carriers and to train new aviators on a need basis. By the end of October 1942 the bulk of the original 400 was gone. This meant that the superb pilots of 1941 were being replaced with less experienced and, often, inexperienced men.

The American offensive from January 1943 to October 1943

proceeded up the Solomons and along the New Guinea coast neutralizing Rabaul in the process. The operations always took place within range of shore based aircraft and the air operations were almost exclusively conducted by that type of aircraft. During this period the Japanese air groups were painfully built back to strength. The carrier force was now composed of two squadrons: First (*Shokaku, Zuikaku, Zuiho*) at Truk and Second (*Junyo, Hiyo, Ryuho*) at Singapore. With the American attacks on the Gilberts and increasing pressure on Rabaul, these air groups were committed to the defence of Rabaul and decimated while the carriers returned to Japan to train new air groups.

At the same time American carriers of the new *Essex* and *Independence* classes began arriving in the Pacific and the long awaited and much debated Central Pacific campaign began with the attack on the Gilberts. The Gilberts and Marshalls occupied the fast carriers throughout April 1944 in a series of operations which left little doubt that the US Navy had now surpassed the Japanese Navy in carrier operations.

Japanese Carrier Doctrine and Operational Planning

'The Japanese Navy thought always of the US carriers. They talked about how many were building, and how many were in the Pacific and that these must be sunk; but it was always the carriers they talked about.' Admiral Weneker, German Naval Attaché to Japan during the war.

'So we felt that if we could deal a serious blow to your surface Task Force, that would widen the gap between your landing attempts and also shorten the distance between the stepping stones by which you made the advance toward Japan.' Admiral Soemu Toyoda, C in C, Combined Fleet.

By the middle of 1941 the Japanese had developed definite ideas about the use of aircraft carriers in combat. Prior to that time they felt that carriers presented contradictions that were nearly unsolvable. On the one hand coordination of attacking formations suggested a concentration of all the carriers in a force, while, on the other, the vulnerability of aircraft carriers suggested a dispersed disposition. Their solution was simple; in attacking land targets their carriers would concentrate in a single formation for maximum coordination, but when facing enemy carriers the Japanese would disperse their ships in squadron size units, attempting to 'encircle the enemy'. Midway seemed to confirm their thinking. Their carriers were concentrated to attack an enemy land base when they were surprised by an enemy carrier force. Santa Cruz further reinforced their tactical thinking. In that battle *Shokaku*, *Zuikaku*, and *Zuiho* operated separate from *Junyo*, with battleships and cruisers ahead of each carrier group as a defensive vanguard. While the former ships were being worked over by US carrier aircraft, *Junyo*, undetected throughout the battle, contributed heavily to the sinking of uss *Hornet*. In seeking to keep the enemy off balance, the Japanese Navy favoured gambit and surprise tactics. To insure success in such operations absolute knowledge of the enemy's movements is required. The Japanese had recognized this before the war and had adopted multi-phase air searches as their standard technique to insure that enemy movements were always known. During early operations they relaxed their reconnaissance requirements and at Midway they paid the price for this laxity. After Midway reconnaissance was the only area of carrier operations in which the Japanese remained superior to their American counterparts in technique right up to the end of the war.

One of the strange paradoxes of the Pacific war, was the effect constant attrition of Japanese Naval Aviation had on American high level thinking concerning the desire of the Japanese Navy's leaders for a fight. The highly respected journal *Foreign Affairs* carried an article which stated that it was contrary to Japanese Naval tradition to fight for outlying bases and that nothing short of an attack on the Japanese mainland could bring the Japanese Navy out. *Time* carried a similar article, however the military affairs correspondent for *Newsweek*, Admiral Pratt, former Chief of Naval Operations, said that the Japanese would fight when they thought it was opportune to do so, and warned against any relaxation of pressure on the Japanese and complacency. Perhaps influenced by the *Foreign Affairs* article, Admiral Nimitz was quoted in the June 21, 1944 (in a statement made before the battle) *New York Times* as having said, 'I don't know anything more we can do to provoke these people into a fleet action.' The unacceptable answer, as actual Japanese planning shows, was for the USN and USAAF to stop shooting down Japanese aircraft long enough for the Japanese Navy to build up its air groups with adequately trained aviators in sufficient numbers to man the carriers.

As early as May 1943 Admiral Koga had issued the first version of 'Z' Operation Plan which would commit the carriers along with the battleships and cruisers to the defence of the Aleutians, Wake,

Marshalls, Gilberts, Nauru, Ocean and Bismarks, with the fleet based at Truk. The Gilberts and Marshalls were removed from the vital defence line in September 1943 and on March 8, 1944 Koga issued the final revision of 'Z' Operation Plan which called for using the fleet in defence of the Central Pacific. The Japanese Navy was even slower than the US Navy in officially recognizing the aircraft carrier as the new 'capital ship'. On March 1, 1944 the Navy was re-organized and a new administrative fleet formed in recognition of this fact. The First Mobile Fleet (*Dai Ichi Kido Kantai*) would contain most of the carriers, battleships, cruisers and modern destroyers, and would constitute the principal weapon for attacking the American carrier force.

In March Combined Fleet began study of an operation so daring in concept that it deserves comment though it never got beyond the planning stage. To be known as '*U*' (pronounced 'EW') Operation Plan, it involved a surprise attack by First Mobile Force on the American Task Force in its anchorage at Majuro. Its outline was as follows: First Mobile Force would concentrate in the Inland Sea in late April and at that time or in early May take a route north of the Bonins, Marcus and Wake to a position northeast of Majuro where it would surprise the US carrier force in its advance anchorage and, with the cooperation of land based air forces staged through Marcus and Wake, destroy it. Five or six submarines would land four torpedo equipped amphibious tanks each, which would cross the reef and attack the carriers. The last part involves a bit of derring-do (and in fact the tanks had development problems) and the entire plan had a very high degree of risk, but it shows just how anxious the Japanese were for a fight.★ The plan was in its early stages of development when Admiral Koga was killed in an aircraft accident and it was shelved, never to be completed.

The date of the Admiral's death was March 31, 1944. For about a month Combined Fleet was commanded by a caretaker, Vice Admiral Shiro Takasu, who was formally relieved on May 2, 1944 by Admiral Soemu Toyoda who served in that capacity throughout the operations described in this book. He raised his flag in light cruiser *Oyodo* in Tokyo Bay that day and received orders from Admiral Shimada, Chief of the Naval General Staff stating that

★ Admiral Pratt's article in NEWSWEEK referred to earlier also warned that the Japanese best chance of slowing or turning the tide lay in a Pearl Harbor type attack and that one was very likely in the offing.

First Mobile Fleet and First Air Fleet (land based air) would be hurled against the enemy at the first opportunity. Admiral Toyoda issued *Combined Fleet Ultra Secret Operation Order 76* of May 3 which outlined 'A' (pronounced 'AH')-*Go*, the basic order governing Japanese participation in the battle described in this book. This directive provided that the entire strength of the Japanese Navy would be used should the American target be the Western Carolines or Palau, but in the event the Marianas were chosen then shore based air would be the only force committed. This was because of the fuel situation in the fleet due to US submarine activity. Upon the order 'Start *A-go* Operation' Base Air Force would be deployed in the Western Carolines, Southern Philippines and Western New Guinea areas while First Mobile Force would concentrate in the southern Philippines and be put on six hour standby. Part of First Mobile Force would be sent to Ulithi or Palau as a decoy to lure the enemy while submarines reconnoitered the area south of the Carolines. This latter portion will be important when we consider the '*Na*' line. When 'Prepare for *A-Go* Operation Battle' was issued Base Air Force would maintain contact with and attack the US Task Force while First Mobile Force sortied and conducted daylight air attacks on the enemy carriers while operating outside the range of American carrier aircraft. This order was followed by a message to the fleet exhorting the men to '. . . . destroy the enemy who enjoys the luxury of material resources'.

In preparation for these operations the Japanese played a series of war games to consider the best tactics they might employ. The tactics mentioned above were considered. The Japanese never favoured what they called 'grouping' their carriers and Midway, as mentioned previously, convinced them this aversion was well founded. Their favourite tactic was what they referred to as 'encircle-ment' and involved splitting their carriers into two or three groups which would envelop the enemy in a pincer-like action. They found that with their inferior force the risk of defeat in detail was great using 'encirclement' tactics in their games, since none of the three Japanese carrier squadrons (except perhaps First S.F.) was a match for a typical US Task Group. The Battle of Midway had suggested a new tactical concept when using carriers and from this they developed a new disposition which they referred to as the 'straight line thrust' or 'vertical depth disposition'. In this disposition the battleships and cruisers formed a vanguard in advance of a main body composed of aircraft carriers, screened by destroyers only. The vanguard would be accompanied by a squadron of small carriers and would shield the main body, furnish scouting, offer a tempting lure and also act as an early warning picket line should the attackers choose to ignore the lure. This tactic was favoured by the Japanese for use in *A-Go* though the time of the decision is unknown and there are indications it was not finally made until as late as June 17; but a meeting of Mobile Force staff on May 20 seems the most likely date. In conjunction with all their basic tactics the Japanese were disposed to use decoys. This is mentioned because of the misconception which arose during the war concerning the 'encirclement' tactic and decoy tactics, which were distinct concepts in Japanese tactical thinking.

The principal limiting factor in Japanese planning at this time was the fuel situation. The Borneo petroleum was such a high grade that it could be pumped directly out of the ground into ships' bunkers, but it turned out to have such impurities that unprocessed it fouled boilers and contained elements which increased the fire hazard when it was in use. Therefore it was ordered that oil would be processed before it was used by Mobile Force. When the *A-Go* plan was distributed, at a meeting of the staffs of Combined Fleet, Mobile Force and Base Air Force between May 8–11, 1944 in the Marianas, the question of an American attack on the Marianas was raised and soon Combined Fleet reversed itself on the question of unprocessed oil. Thus by early June First Mobile Force would be capable of giving battle in the Marianas.

Though the Japanese high command had a sober view of their chances of success, the aviators had remarkably high hopes. This is understandable only because of the enthusiasm of youth, for the quality of the 1944 Japanese naval aviator bore no relationship to that of 1942. The average period of training for pilots before the war was three and a quarter years. By contrast the pilots of Naval Air Group 601 (*Taiho, Shokaku, Zuikaku*) had about six months' training while groups 652 (*Junyo, Hiyo, Ryuho*) and 653 (*Chitose, Chiyoda, Zuiho*) had two and three months respectively. The average Japanese naval aviator had about 275 hours total flying time. The commanders of the air groups were correspondingly less experienced. In the October 1942 Battle of Santa Cruz the air group commanders were both 1927 *Eta Jima* (Japanese Naval Academy) graduates. In this battle Lt Cdr Tarui of Group 601 and Lt Cdr Yamagami of Group 653 were 1936 graduates and Lt Cdr Iwami of Group 652 finished his naval academy course in 1934 – drop of nearly ten years of air group leaders in just 18 months in the experience level of fighting. To compound further their lack of training, the advance base chosen by First Mobile Force, Tawi-Tawi, did not have an airfield, therefore the aviators were laid off nearly a month just before the battle. US submarines and the fuel situation in the Empire forced the carriers to remain in Tawi-Tawi anchorage most of the period of May 11–June 13. In 1942 the Japanese practice had been as stated earlier regarding replacements. The effect was that student pilots never received practical instruction since veteran pilots were not rotated into the training command. The same disastrous situation held true with the aircrew personnel. Operation of communication equipment was erratic and the airborne radars (though few in number this was their best electronic equipment vis-a-vis USN equipment) were 'totally unusable'. The introduction of new aircraft types, B6N (Jill) and D4Y (Judy), which were very 'hot' machines, requiring experienced aviators, complicated the problem.

Almost as important for Japanese chances of success as the poor level of pilot training was their general attack tactics which had changed little from 1942. Essentially they relied on a straight thrust with little or no evasion, at high altitude in massed formations with fighter cover above and behind and on the flanks. The idea behind this doctrine was simple – punch through the combat air patrol with a sufficient number of attack aircraft and the vulnerable American carriers could be taken. It had worked in 1942 and at this time the Japanese had no reason to believe it would not work again. Spectacular advances in American radar equipment and doctrine changes had rendered such tactics impractical, in fact, suicidal. Even had the Japanese pilots been more skilful it is highly doubtful that they could have successfully run the CAP gauntlet which American radar provided. In 1942 a raid might be intercepted at 25 miles range and on some occasions dive bombers had started their dives before they were hit. In this battle most Japanese aircraft were met at about 60 miles and had to fight off interceptors for 15 minutes before they reached the American ships. The task may have been impossible using these tactics. The Japanese used pathfinders in the conventional fashion. When the raid was forming up one or two aircraft, usually three place machines, such as Jill or Kate, proceeded immediately to the target's position to lead the raid over its intended victim. They also used 'Window' in this battle, but very sparingly. 'Window' is a radar jamming method which involves the dropping of strips of aluminium at high altitude which, while drifting to the earth, will appear on radar screens as potential targets. Skilful operators can often distinguish 'Window' from other targets, but when used liberally and in conjunction with many small raids its use was, in 1945, effectively disrupting.

US Navy Carrier Doctrine and Operational Planning

'Enemy Task Force action will give our own task forces a chance to close the enemy, bring his force into action, and perhaps score a crippling victory.' Commander Task Force 58 Operation Plan 7-44 of May 10, 1944.

In 1942 the US Navy faced the same problems as the Japanese and, not surprisingly, came up with quite similar solutions, though there were important differences. On the one hand, carriers were most effective when they could coordinate their attacks, therefore concentration was desirable, while on the other hand their vulnerability meant that dispersal was the preferred method of employment. When the US Navy had few carriers they were usually operated in separate formations which remained within mutual support distance (an important difference from the Japanese doctrine of 'encirclement') but outside visual range of one another. This had the desired effect. At Midway *Yorktown* (cv–5) was the only US carrier attacked (and sunk). The same held true for *Enterprise* at Eastern Solomons, where she was the only US carrier hit, and at Santa Cruz where *Hornet* (cv–8) was overwhelmed and sunk when the Japanese might have bagged both US carriers had they split their effort. In fact, in the latter battle they did damage both US carriers, but *Enterprise* was hit too late in the day with too little force to be put out of action. As the carrier offensive developed the question of multiple carrier formations developed into a question of how many carriers could operate in one screen. The number of carriers available made single carriers impractical because the number of screening ships available was far too small for formations of fifteen or more. As many as six carriers operated in one formation in this battle and other operation in 1944.

In this battle the most important aspect of US carrier doctrine would be the highly developed fighter direction teams. Generally each Task Group maintained two eight plane divisions on standing combat air patrol (CAP). The fighter directors, after observing the progress of a raid on radar and evaluating it, would vector a number of fighters of the standing CAP to an interception point, making course adjustments as the fighter force approached the target on the radar scope. The fighter directors gave the CAP estimates of the composition (numbers only), altitude ('angels'), course and speed of the raid so that the fighters would be at a proper altitude at the time of contact ('tally-ho'). Generally, rigid control of altitude, course and speed of the CAP was maintained by the fighter director officers (FDO) until 'tally-ho'. At 'tally-ho' the CAP commander was charged with first advising the FDO of the composition, course and speed of the incoming raid so reinforcements could be sent if required and second with destruction of the raid. The aircraft which were committed to a particular interception were immediately replaced by eight more aircraft in the Standing CAP so the FDO always had a reserve of well-fuelled, well-armed fighters to throw in if any raiders broke through the initial interception.

American air search technique and equipment had not been spectacular in 1942 (even at Midway) and in this area the Japanese Navy still surpassed the USN. After Santa Cruz the role of search was gradually less emphasized because of the absence of moving targets which had to be found to be attacked. In June 1942, at Midway, USS *Enterprise* (CV-6) carried four squadrons of aircraft: VF-6, 27 F4F; VB-6, 19 SBD; VS-6, 19 SBD; VT-6, 14 TBD (79 total), while in June 1944 the same ship embarked three squadrons and a night fighter detachment as follows: VF-10, 31 F6F; VB-10, 21 SBD; VT-10, 14 TBF; VF (N), 3 F4U (69). Thus by 1944 the VS (Scout Bomber) aircraft had been integrated into the VB (Dive Bomber) squadrons. This probably reduced administrative workloads, but the down-grading of the scout function would have a real effect on the American ability to find Japanese ships in this battle and also in the October fight off Cape Enganyo, Luzon. In fact, in this battle almost all US carrier based scouting was conducted by F6F and TBF since they (and 3 F4U) were the only aircraft in Task Force 58 equipped with radar (24 F6F, 3 F4U, 37 TBF were radar equipped). In spite of the reasons for the decline in American scouting it is perplexing to read the aggressive pronouncements of the American carrier admirals when discussing the Japanese carrier force (aptly 'Mobile Force') and their failure to develop an effective doctrine for finding that force. The reader will note the difference in scope of

Japanese air searches and those conducted by the Americans. When one remembers the numerical inferiority of the Japanese force the scale of American air searches borders on negligence.

As mentioned earlier, there were doubts throughout the American high command, with Admiral King as a notable exception, that the Japanese fleet would fight before the home islands were threatened. For example, Admiral Turner's General Operation Plan 1–44 says:

'It is believed that these units of the Japanese Fleet will not interfere with our operation against (the Marianas) except for "hit and run" raids on detached units of our forces, but will conserve their strength until the time when they can go into action in waters nearer their main bases.'

Admiral Mitscher's Oplan had a more balanced assessment:

'For the first time in more than 18 months the enemy has a large carrier force in fighting condition. His 3 CVs, 2 XCVs and 4 CVLs which are ready for combat carry planes equivalent to those carried by 4 *Essex* (CV) and 3 *Independence* (CVL) class carriers.
'If the enemy uses all his carrier based planes in conjunction with the land planes based in the Marianas, he will still have fewer aircraft available for attacking our ships than we will be able to employ against him. Enemy Task Force action will give our own task forces a chance to close the enemy, bring his force into action, and perhaps score a crippling victory.',

but his action report says, 'the prevailing opinion in the fleet was that the Japanese Navy would not come out to defend the Marianas'. The two principal advantages that the Japanese had, longer range aircraft and proximity of air bases to the Marianas were recognized in Mitscher's Oplan:

'By steaming at 25 knots from their bases in the southern Philippines, Japanese carriers would be in position to strike our forces within 50–58 hours after departure from their bases. In spite of our superiority in all types of ships such an action would not mean undue risk to the enemy's carriers. His carrier planes have greater ranges than our corresponding types. The enemy could launch his air groups some 250 miles from our ships. There is a definite possibility of longer range carrier strikes than the enemy had delivered in the past. If such an attack were successful, the enemy might then send in his battleships and cruisers to attack our transports.

32

'It is believed that there is no way to estimate Japanese searches other than by saying that when the Task Force comes within 600 miles of any of the Japanese bases named above (Truk, Guam, Tinian, Marcus and Chichi Jima) it is in an area searched regularly by enemy aircraft.'

The likelihood of the Japanese using 'outranging' and shuttle tactics was also forseen and a dispatch concerning that possibility forwarded to Spruance on June 15.

The Task Force/Task Group concept in effect meant that Task Force 58 consisted of four powerful carrier 'fleets' and a battleship 'fleet' which could operate with great flexibility either in one concentrated fleet as in the battle or with each Task Group on independent missions as in the Bonins raids discussed in the text. The carrier groups could operate at relatively long ranges from one another and still offer some degree of mutual support, though clearly not as much as they offered when operating in close proximity.

This brings us to the most controversial point in the battle; whether the carriers should have steamed westward on the night of June 18–19 thus exposing the beachheads (though not many of the transports since as will be seen the bulk of them had been sent eastward on the 17th) to a possible Japanese flank attack. Admiral Spruance, over the objection of Admiral Mitscher, chose to remain close to the Marianas rather than take that risk. The merits of that decision and of the alternative offered by Mitscher will be discussed in the conclusion.

American attack aircraft loading practice was also still behind Japanese concepts. Midway had been a spectacular victory for American dive bombers but was a false indicator of their importance vis-a-vis torpedo bombers because of the embarrassed condition (full deck load of armed and fuelled aircraft on board) of the Japanese carriers. Because of this and the island offensive American torpedo pilots had little experience in using their intended weapons and as will be seen, many were loaded with bombs on June 20 rather than torpedoes, which was unquestionably more devastating. In the Japanese Navy torpedo planes carried torpedoes when attacking ships.

The real difference in the two fleets lay not in doctrine but in training and here more than any other area (except perhaps in radar) the USN had the clear edge. Like their Japanese counterparts, but with a factual basis, American aviators were absolutely confident of their superiority. In contrast to the Japanese aviators, US pilots had about 300 hours before carrier assignment and about two years' training before entering the combat zone. An average US pilot had about 525 hours flight time.

Pearl Harbor forced the US Navy to use aircraft carriers as the main offensive weapon and put a temporary halt to the battleship-carrier debate in the navy. American carrier performance ended the debate. The residue of the struggle was a lingering bitterness between line officers ('black shoes') and aviators ('brown shoes'). On the one hand the senior line officers represented vested interest since they had advanced to their positions during the period of primacy of the battleship, cruiser and destroyer and saw it all evaporate at Pearl Harbor. The aviators, whose rise had been through air squadrons and who felt, rightly so in most cases, that the line officers threw up obstacles to proper utilization of carriers during the between war years, took advantage of the opening created by Pearl Harbor and moved to take over the high command of the entire navy. Admiral Frederick Sherman, the leading spokesman of the 'Air Navy' suggested that all planning should originate from aviators and all major flags in the navy, and that in all staffs the chief of staff, operations officer and plans officer, should be aviators. The reaction amongst line officers was predictable. Men whose entire experience in the Navy had been in air squadrons suddenly knew more about the operations of ships and fleets than officers whose entire careers had been spent in that area. Spruance's chief of staff's reaction to the promotion of one aviator is illustrative:

'He was a flier? Well, that's astounding, the way these aviators go. They can command air squadrons based on tenders, and maybe have a tour on a carrier as commander of an air squadron, and then if they're lucky they'll get command of a deep draft ship. It will be the first really seagoing experience of their lives, to command a tanker or a supply ship or a tender, and that will qualify them for command of anything, although they've never been through the process of a ship at all. They've been aviators all their lives, and then they suddenly come to command rank and they've got to get some seagoing experience. So they put them in a tanker for a year and then they give them command of a 50,000 ton carrier, and they terrify everybody else in the same ocean.'

The controversy eventually led to the rule that all aviator admirals would have a line officer chief of staff and vice versa. This came later. In the meantime, with feelings running high, the aviators were anxious to show that they were the only people competent to handle carriers and looked for evidence to support their thesis.

CHAPTER ONE

Preliminary Moves—April 30-June 17 1944

'The Combined Fleet will direct its main operations in the area extending south of the Central Pacific to the north coast of New Guinea.' Combined Fleet Ultrasecret Operation order No 76 of May 3 1944.

'This force will assist in the capture, occupation and defence of SAIPAN, TINIAN and GUAM . . . by protecting the *Joint Expeditionary Force* during and after occupation by these forces from enemy air and surface forces.' Commander Task Force 58 Secret Operation Order 7-44 of May 24, 1944.

April 30–May 11, 1944; Position of Forces in early May

On April 30 Task Force 58 (TF 58) was on course east for Majuro and a well deserved rest following a 43-day sweep through the Southwest Pacific. At this time Task Force 58 was composed of 5 CV, 7 CVL, 6 BB, 9 CA, 5 CL and 52 DD. En route a cruiser group bombarded Satawan on April 30 and Admiral Lee's battleships hit Ponape the next day. Task Group 58.1 (TG 58.1) with Lee's battleship group and the cruisers which struck Satawan arrived at Eniwetok and Task Groups 58.2 and 58.3 reached Majuro on May 4. Task Group 58.1 would arrive at Majuro before May 10. Carriers *Wasp*, *Essex* and *San Jacinto* were at Pearl Harbor, departing on May 3 accompanied by 2 CL (AA) and 2 DD arriving at Majuro on May 8. Cruiser *Indianapolis*, which would serve as Admiral Spruance's flagship in the forthcoming operations sortied from San Francisco on May 1, followed on May 5 by battleship *Washington*, three old battleships and eight destroyers, arriving at Pearl Harbor on May 6 and May 11 respectively. Battleship *Massachusetts*, in company with carriers *Yorktown*, *Princeton* and *Monterey* and seven destroyers (TG 58.7) left Majuro on May 6 for Pearl Harbor, arriving May 11. With one exception, the fast carriers conducted no major operations until the sortie for the Marianas.

Task force 52, Bombardment Group 1 and Task Group 51.1 had completed their assembly in Hawaii by May 10 and Task Force 53 and Bombardment Group 2 had begun their assembly at Guadalcanal, Purvis Bay and Tulagi in the Lower Solomons.

During this period Seventh USAAF hit Truk every day with a heavy bomb group while Thirteenth USAAF added to the effort on May 6, 9, and 19. Photographic reconnaissance was conducted on May 7 when ten USAAF B-24s escorted six USN PB4Y photo aircraft to Guam.

In the early part of May the principal units of the Imperial Japanese Navy were distributed as follows: First Aircraft Carrier Squadron (1 S.F.), First, Third, Fourth, Fifth, Seventh Squadrons and most of Second and Tenth Flotillas were at Singapore. Carrier *Zuikaku* had just come out of drydock at Singapore on the 6th. Second S.F. and 3 S.F., battleship *Musashi* and some destroyers were in the Inland Sea. The two carrier squadrons in Japan had taken their air groups on board on May 5-6. These groups had been training in the Kure–Iwakuni area prior to that date.

May 11–May 16, 1944—The Japanese Fleet concentrates

At 0300 on May 11, First, Third, Fourth, Seventh Squadrons and Second Destroyer Flotilla at Lingga (south of Singapore) sortied for Tawi-Tawi, First Mobile Force's (FMF) advance base for *A-Go*. The same day the ships in the Empire designated for *A-Go* departed the Inland Sea, stopping at Okinawa on May 12 for fuel, and then proceeded on to Tawi-Tawi. The next day (May 12) First S.F., Fifth Squadron and Tenth Destroyer Flotilla left Singapore for Tawi-Tawi.

The day the first major Japanese units started for Tawi-Tawi Admiral Kincaid issued his OPLAN (Operation Plan) 6A–44 which estimated that the Japanese Fleet was about to concentrate in 'the Celebes Sea, using anchorages in the vicinity of Tawi-Tawi'. Based on this estimate submarine *Bonefish* (SS–223) was ordered to check that area for enemy activity. This was the first move by US submarines during an operation in which they would play a prominent role. *Bonefish* was approaching Tawi-Tawi, north of Borneo at 0400 on May 14 when she ran across three Japanese tankers, escorted by three destroyers. She got into position to attack and sank destroyer *Inazuma*. The Japanese estimated the cause of *Inazuma*'s loss as mines. On May 16 *Bonefish* tried unsuccessfully to look into Tawi-Tawi.

On the Japanese side May 14, coincidentally the same day *Bonefish* reached Tawi-Tawi, marked the opening of Japanese

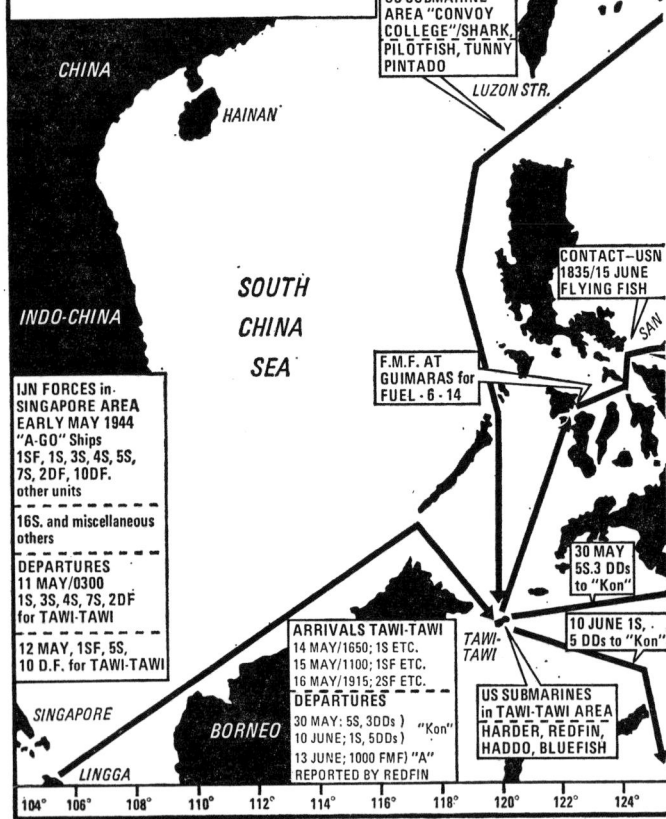

DIAGRAM 1
MOVEMENTS of PRINCIPAL UNITS
of the
IMPERIAL JAPANESE NAVY
EARLY MAY 1944 – 16 JUNE 1944
and
AMERICAN SUBMARINE DISPOSITIONS,
AIR SEARCHES, and T.F. 58 DISPOSITIONS
on 15 – 16 JUNE

FORMOSA

US SUBMARINE
AREA "CONVOY
COLLEGE"/SHARK,
PILOTFISH, TUNNY
PINTADO

LUZON STR.

CHINA

HAINAN

CONTACT–USN
1835/15 JUNE
FLYING FISH

SOUTH
CHINA
SEA

INDO-CHINA

SAN

F.M.F. AT
GUIMARAS for
FUEL · 6 · 14

IJN FORCES in
SINGAPORE AREA
EARLY MAY 1944
"A-GO" Ships
1SF, 1S, 3S, 4S, 5S,
7S, 2DF, 10DF.
other units
– – – – – – – –
16S. and miscellaneous
others
– – – – – – – –
DEPARTURES
11 MAY/0300
1S, 3S, 4S, 7S, 2DF
for TAWI-TAWI
– – – – – – – –
12 MAY, 1SF, 5S,
10 D.F. for TAWI-TAWI

30 MAY
5S.3 DDs
to "Kon"

10 JUNE 1S,
5 DDs to "Kon".

ARRIVALS TAWI-TAWI
14 MAY/1650; 1S ETC.
15 MAY/1100; 1SF ETC.
16 MAY/1915; 2SF ETC.
– – – – – – – –
DEPARTURES
30 MAY: 5S, 3DDs)
10 JUNE; 1S, 5DDs) "Kon"
13 JUNE; 1000 FMF) "A"
REPORTED BY REDFIN

TAWI-
TAWI

US SUBMARINES
in TAWI-TAWI AREA
HARDER, REDFIN,
HADDO, BLUEFISH

SINGAPORE

BORNEO

LINGGA

104° 106° 108° 110° 112° 114° 116° 118° 120° 122° 124°

38

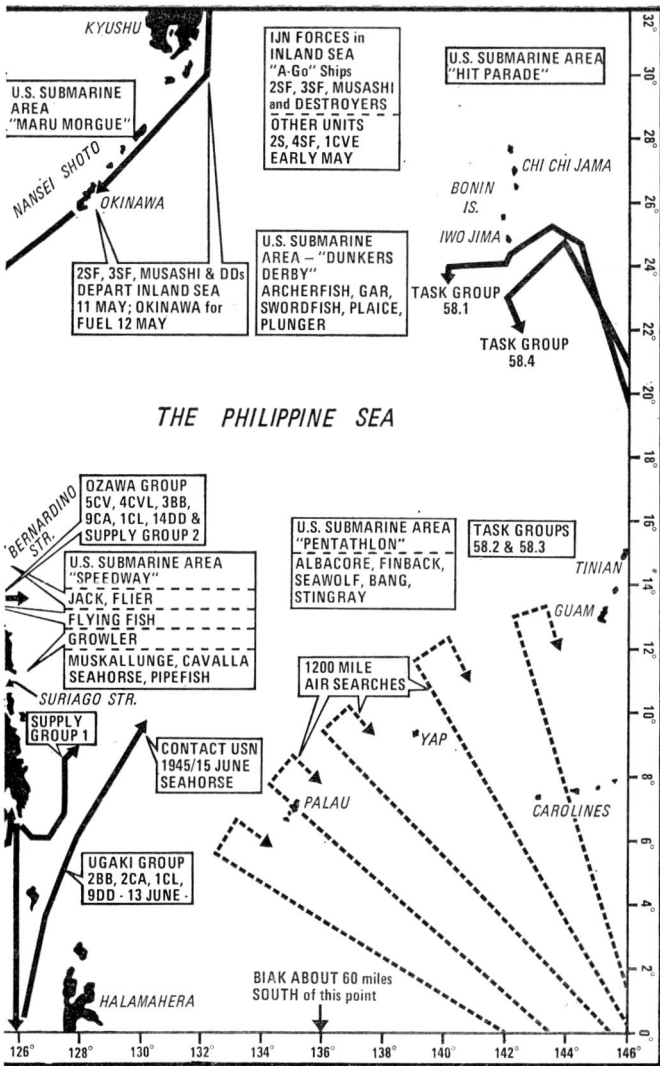

KYUSHU

U.S. SUBMARINE
AREA
"MARU MORGUE"

NANSEI SHOTO

OKINAWA

IJN FORCES in
INLAND SEA
"A-Go" Ships
2SF, 3SF, MUSASHI
and DESTROYERS
OTHER UNITS
2S, 4SF, 1CVE
EARLY MAY

U.S. SUBMARINE AREA
"HIT PARADE"

CHI CHI JAMA

BONIN
IS.

IWO JIMA

2SF, 3SF, MUSASHI & DDs
DEPART INLAND SEA
11 MAY; OKINAWA for
FUEL 12 MAY

U.S. SUBMARINE
AREA — "DUNKERS
DERBY"
ARCHERFISH, GAR,
SWORDFISH, PLAICE,
PLUNGER

TASK GROUP
58.1

TASK GROUP
58.4

THE PHILIPPINE SEA

BERNADINO
STR.

OZAWA GROUP
5CV, 4CVL, 3BB,
9CA, 1CL, 14DD &
SUPPLY GROUP 2

U.S. SUBMARINE AREA
"PENTATHLON"
ALBACORE, FINBACK,
SEAWOLF, BANG,
STINGRAY

TASK GROUPS
58.2 & 58.3

TINIAN

U.S. SUBMARINE
AREA
"SPEEDWAY"
JACK, FLIER
FLYING FISH
GROWLER
MUSKALLUNGE, CAVALLA
SEAHORSE, PIPEFISH

GUAM

SURIAGO STR.

SUPPLY
GROUP 1

CONTACT USN
1945/15 JUNE
SEAHORSE

1200 MILE
AIR SEARCHES

YAP

PALAU

CAROLINES

UGAKI GROUP
2BB, 2CA, 1CL,
9DD - 13 JUNE

HALAMAHERA

BIAK ABOUT 60 miles
SOUTH of this point

126°   128°   130°   132°   134°   136°   138°   140°   142°   144°   146°

submarine operations which were completely frustrated during the entire operation, An element of Admiral Takagi's Advanced Expeditionary Force (AEF) was sent to the area south of the Carolines with the principal duty of gaining intelligence of the enemy situation forming a picket line (known by the *Kana*★ designation *Na*) which was complete by May 20.

Far to the east TF 52 began invasion rehearsals at Maalae Bay, Maui and Kahoolawe.

At 1650 May 14 the first segment of the Singapore detachment arrived at Tawi-Tawi. The remainder of the Singapore force entered Tawi-Tawi on the 15th at 1100. This latter movement was observed by *Bonefish*, but not before she was detected. That night, after she had effected her escape, her important find was reported to COMSUB-SOWESPAC (Commander Submarine Force South West Pacific) as one carrier, three battleships, one heavy cruiser and destroyers heading for Tawi-Tawi.

As the Japanese Fleet concentrated at its advance base the only major operation conducted by TF 58 during thr month of May got underway. On May 15 a Task Group under the command of Admiral Montgomery sortied from Majuro. Designated Task Group 58.6 this force consisted of the following ships:

CV – *Essex, Wasp*
CVL – *San Jacinto*
CA – *Boston, Baltimore, Canberra*
CLAA – *San Diego, Reno*
DD – *Owen, Miller, The Sullivans, Stephen Potter, Tingey, Hickox, Hunt, Lewis Hancock, Marshall, Bradford, Brown, Cowell.*

The force was followed by a replenishment force of two oilers escorted by three destroyer escorts (DE).

The next day 2 S.F., 3 S.F., *Musashi* and their destroyer screen completed the Japanese concentration at 1915.

Destroyer Division 94 (DESDIV 94) had departed Blanche Harbor on May 12 based on an aircraft sighting of a Japanese submarine. By the morning of the 16th the destroyers arrived at the scene and began

★ '*Kana*' Japanese phonetic alphabet as opposed to '*Romanji*' which is the use of Chinese characters for Japanese words.

searching. Four more destroyers (DESDIV 93) arrived and the search continued until 2145 when sonar contact was obtained. Though contact was lost temporarily it was regained at 2213 and about midnight *Haggard* (DD–555) and *Franks* (DD–554) delivered successful attacks on submarine *I–176* which was on a supply mission to Bougainville. The location of this kill was 156° 29′ E, 4° 01′ S.

May 17–May 26—Montgomery's raids on Marcus and Wake and the start of *England*'s adventures

Task Force 53 completed its assembly at Guadalcanal, Tulagi and Purvis Bay together with Bombardment Group 2 and Minesweeper Group 2 on May 17.

First and Second Aircraft Carrier Squadrons conducted underway exercises on May 18 (presumably these included operating their aircraft though the sources are silent on this point). The operations of American submarines prevented much needed flight training and the lack of an airfield at Tawi-Tawi curtailed air operations for the period FMF remained at that base. The reason Tawi-Tawi was selected in spite of the obvious disadvantages of lack of an airfield and accessibility to submarines was its access to the Western Carolines and Marianas, the anticipated operations area for *A-Go*.

On May 18 Light Carrier *Bataan* and destroyers *Haraden* and *Halligan* left Majuro for Pearl Harbor, arriving May 22.

A SOWESPAC (South West Pacific Command) aircraft detected a Japanese submarine en route from Truk to the by-passed garrison at Buin. Escort Division 39 (CORTDIV 39) composed of *England* (DE–635), *George* (DE–697) and *Raby* (DE–698), was ordered out of Purvis Bay in the Eastern Solomons on May 18 and set course to intercept. The three ships formed a line abreast scout line with 4000-yard spacing. It was estimated that they would reach the submarine's projected track in the afternoon of May 20. They did not have to wait long. At 1325 on May 19 when they had reached 158° 17′ E/ 05° 10′ S the sonar operator on *England* reported an 'underwater object' and after evaluating the target *England* conducted five hedge-hog attacks. At 1433 on the fifth attack a muffled explosion was heard, followed shortly by a violent explosion. Soon oil and debris gushed to the surface marking the end of submarine *I–16*.

Having refuelled on May 18, Montgomery's Task Group conducted a night-fighter sweep of Marcus in the early hours of May 19. The previous day a unit designated Task Unit 58.6.4 composed of *San*

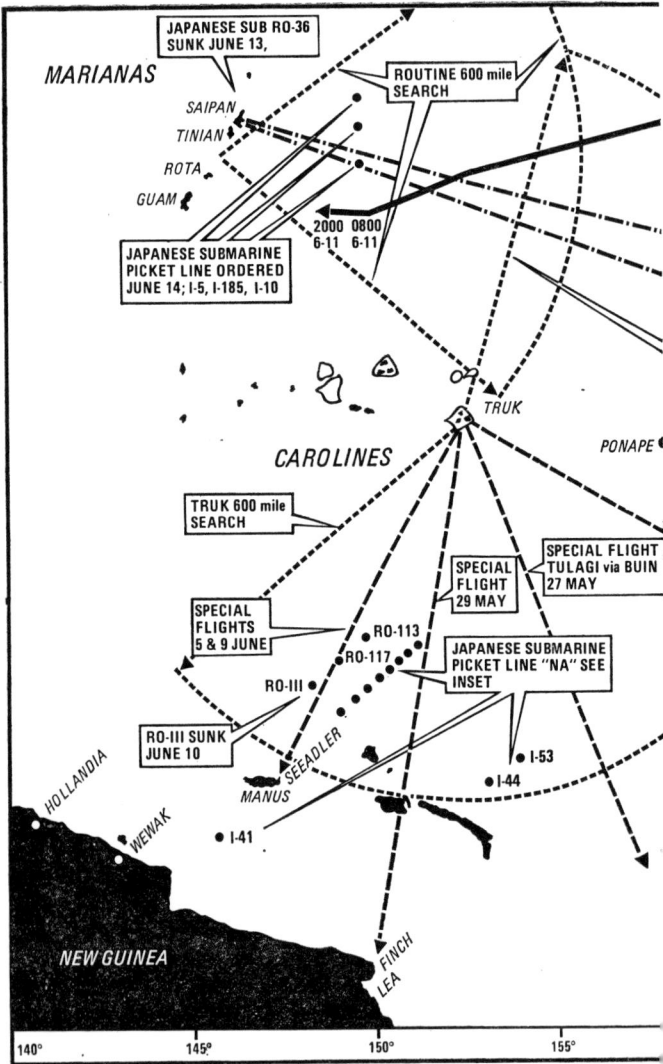

MARIANAS

JAPANESE SUB RO-36 SUNK JUNE 13,

SAIPAN
TINIAN
ROTA
GUAM

ROUTINE 600 mile SEARCH

2000 0800
6-11 6-11

JAPANESE SUBMARINE PICKET LINE ORDERED JUNE 14; I-5, I-185, I-10

TRUK

PONAPE

CAROLINES

TRUK 600 mile SEARCH

SPECIAL FLIGHT 29 MAY

SPECIAL FLIGHT TULAGI via BUIN 27 MAY

SPECIAL FLIGHTS 5 & 9 JUNE

RO-113
RO-117

JAPANESE SUBMARINE PICKET LINE "NA" SEE INSET

RO-III

RO-III SUNK JUNE 10

SEEADLER

MANUS

I-53

I-44

HOLLANDIA
WEWAK

I-41

NEW GUINEA

FINCH
LEA

140°   145°   150°   155°

42

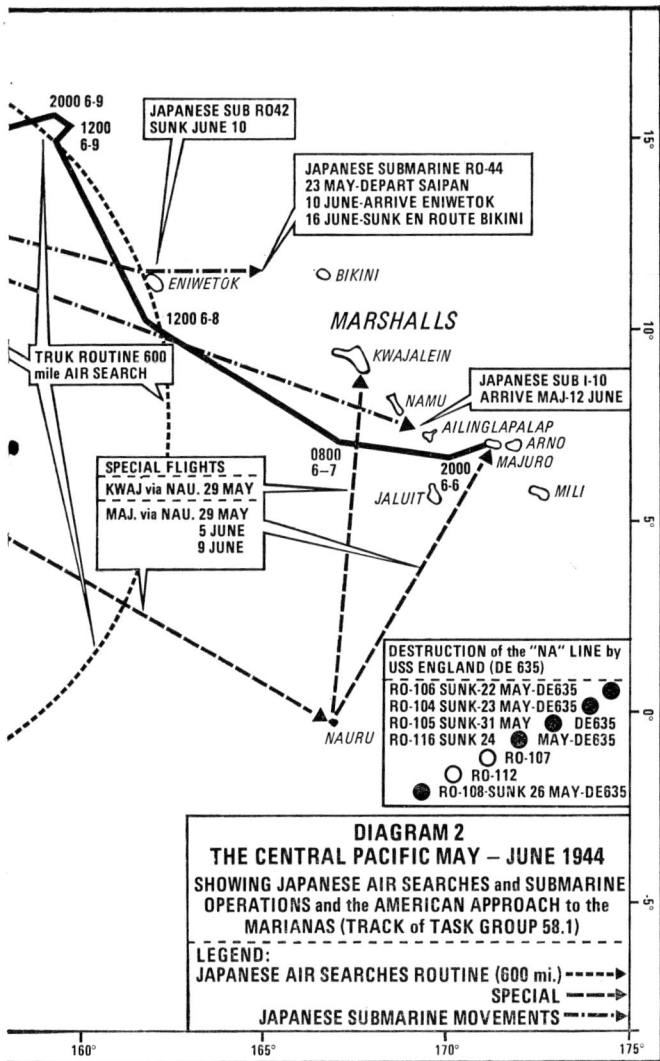

2000 6-9
1200 6-9

JAPANESE SUB RO42
SUNK JUNE 10

JAPANESE SUBMARINE RO-44
23 MAY-DEPART SAIPAN
10 JUNE-ARRIVE ENIWETOK
16 JUNE-SUNK EN ROUTE BIKINI

○ BIKINI
ENIWETOK

MARSHALLS

1200 6-8

KWAJALEIN

NAMU

TRUK ROUTINE 600
mile AIR SEARCH

JAPANESE SUB I-10
ARRIVE MAJ-12 JUNE

AILINGLAPALAP
○ ARNO
MAJURO

0800
6-7

2000
6-6

JALUIT

○ MILI

SPECIAL FLIGHTS
KWAJ via NAU. 29 MAY
MAJ. via NAU. 29 MAY
5 JUNE
9 JUNE

DESTRUCTION of the "NA" LINE by
USS ENGLAND (DE 635)
RO-106 SUNK-22 MAY-DE635
RO-104 SUNK-23 MAY-DE635
RO-105 SUNK-31 MAY   DE635
RO-116 SUNK 24   MAY-DE635
○ RO-107
○ RO-112
RO-108-SUNK 26 MAY-DE635

NAURU

DIAGRAM 2
THE CENTRAL PACIFIC MAY – JUNE 1944
SHOWING JAPANESE AIR SEARCHES and SUBMARINE
OPERATIONS and the AMERICAN APPROACH to the
MARIANAS (TRACK of TASK GROUP 58.1)

LEGEND:
JAPANESE AIR SEARCHES ROUTINE (600 mi.) ------►
SPECIAL ———►
JAPANESE SUBMARINE MOVEMENTS —·—·—·►

160°   165°   170°   175°

15°
10°
5°
0°
-5°

Jacinto, San Diego, Hickox, Hunt, Lewis Hancock and *Marshall* had been detached to sweep north in search of enemy picket boats, rejoining at 0900 on May 21, after sinking one sampan and destroying a mine in an otherwise uneventful search. On May 19-20, aircraft dropped 150 tons of bombs on Marcus destroying two small boats in the harbour, damaging the buildings on the island and shooting down the only aircraft encountered, a G4M(Betty). Four *Wasp* F6Fs accounted for the intruder. The attacking aircraft, in the meantime, met intense flak over Marcus losing four of their number while one quarter of the participants were damaged. The report of a raid of 94 USN aircraft was received by Combined Fleet Headquarters (TG 58.6 conducted 255 air sorties on May 19) and at the same time a reconnaissance aircraft operating from Tinian sighted a US Task Group estimated at two aircraft carriers, four battleships, and eight other ships 150 miles southwest of Marcus. This activity caused Admiral Toyoda to execute '*To*' Operation, a contingency plan for the defence of the Empire (Imperial HQ Naval Staff Directive No. 383 DTG May 201035).* In addition to alerting home defence units '*To*' required increased security measures in the Bonins, East Carolines, and Marianas, increased reconnaissance from Iwo Jima and Tinian. American strikes continued on May 20 as Montgomery sent 118 aircraft in attacks, finally calling off further operations because of poor wind conditions.

On the same day Admiral Toyoda issued the command 'Start *A-Go* Operations'. The effect of this signal was as follows: forces in the area of anticipated operations were to increase their patrol activities. Base Air Forces were to reconnoitre American advance bases at Tulagi, Majuro, Kwajalein, Eniwetok and the Admiralty Islands and to strengthen their routine patrols. Fifth Base Air Force (5 BAF) was to start its deployment on the 23rd with its completion anticipated by the 26th. First Mobile Force was put on six hour alert. On special orders the battleship *Fuso*, Fifth Squadron and two destroyers could be detached and sent to the Ulithi-Palau area as a decoy force hoping to lure the Americans into the centre of the Japanese concentration. Whether such a force would have constituted sufficiently tempting bait to attract the American task force is doubtful, however, in view of the great weight given to Japanese decoy tactics by Admiral

---

* DTG–date time group; a common method of serializing communications used in most navies in which the date, here May 20 and time 1035 are combined for a serial number.

Spruance in the battle, the fact that Commander Mobile Force was given the option to employ gambit tactics is of interest.

The Japanese submarine dispositions ordered on May 14 had been completed by May 20. North of New Ireland three picket lines were formed of two, seven and three boats, respectively, east to west, and an additional boat was ordered to guard the New Guinea–Admiralty Island passage. The principal objective of this scout line ('Na') was to detect the advance of American forces from the Solomons in the direction of Biak, Palau and Yap. This was in keeping with the Japanese hope that the next US thrust would be in that area.

Upon receipt of 'Start *A-Go*' Admiral Ozawa issued broad instructions stating that in the forthcoming operations FMF would attack with disregard to damage suffered, and individual units were declared expendable for the overall success of the enterprise. Individual initiative was to overcome any difficulties in communications.

The rehearsals at Maalaea Bay, Maui and Kahoolawe being held by TF 52 were completed on May 20 but not without incident. LST–485 lost an LCT over the side in heavy sea during the night and 19 sleeping sailors and Marines were killed. Upon their return to Oahu, LST–353 blew up while loading ammunition, destroying six LSTs and three LCTs and killing 163 men while 396 were injured. This disaster caused but one day's delay in departure for TF 52 because of energetic staff work and the transfer of two LSTs from Admiral Halsey's South Pacific Command

The day after receipt of 'Start *A-Go*' Admiral Ozawa held a meeting on flagship *Taiho* to review plans for the forthcoming operations. Though no record of this meeting survives the operational policies which were discussed have. Upon orders FMF would sortie, secretly if possible, to a position east of the Philippines and absorb the decoy force (presumably if it survived). Fifth Base Air Force and the vanguard force would determine enemy movements. Then, in co-ordination with 5 BAF, FMF would attack and destroy the American Task Force. It is interesting that the Japanese considered the possibility of a flank attack by American carriers. The units of Naval Air Group 652 (NAG 652) assigned to 2 SF were to be held in reserve until American movements were fully known. Units were expected to press the attack and surface action under favourable conditions was to be encouraged. The carrier aircraft would transfer to shore bases if the tactical situation dictated. Three tactical dispositions were available for use. The first of these described as 'defence in depth' provided for splitting the FMF into a main body and a vanguard. This is virtually the tactic employed by the Japanese and will not be discussed further at this point. The second tactic provided that FMF split into three groups approximately* as follows:

A Force: 1 S.F., 3s, 5s, 10 DF less 4 DG
B Force: 2 S.F., *Mogami*, *Fuso*, *Nagato*, 4 DG and 27 DG
C Force: 3 S.F., 1s less *Nagato*, 4s, 7s less *Mogami*, 2DF less 27DG

This force would advance in a three pronged 'encirclement', the favourite Japanese attack disposition. The availability of this disposition to the Japanese, together with the option of using a decoy force should be kept in mind, particularly in view of American experience fighting Japanese carriers in 1942, when we come to Admiral Spruance's decision on the night of June 18–19. Lastly the carrier groups could concentrate in one massed disposition similar to the one employed by the US carriers. Whether the decision to employ the 'defence in depth' tactic was made at this time is not known though (as mentioned in Chapter One) it was favoured by the Japanese from the beginning.

On May 22, TD 53 began rehearsal exercises at Cape Esperance. In the Central Pacific Admiral Montgomery's group refuelled that morning and at 1105 detached the oiler unit which returned to Majuro.

Because of the poor radio communications between Tokyo Bay and Tawi-Tawi, Admiral Toyoda got his flagship, the light cruiser *Oyodo*, under way at 1300 on May 22 for the Inland Sea.

Earlier that day the adventures of CORTDIV 39 commenced instalment number two, again starring USS *England*. Manus based aircraft detected a submarine and CORTDIV 39 was ordered to investigate. At 0350, May 22, *George* obtained a radar contact at 14000 yards followed by a similar contact at 15000 yards from *England* (both DEs had the same contact). As they approached the contact *George* opened her searchlight shutters and though she failed to gain visual contact, *England*'s lookouts were more fortunate seeing the Japanese submarine at less than a mile just as she submerged. *George* now missed with hedgehogs as her sonar operator got a good sound

---

* The Task Organization table in Mono 90 contains many obvious typographical errors and this organization was constructed from that table and is only approximate.

contact which he quickly lost. *England* now gained contact at 2500 yards and on her second run hit *Ro–106* with a hedgehog salvo punching the first hole in the '*NA*' line.

While *England* continued her one-ship war against Advance Expeditionary Force, American submarines continued to harass FMF. Third Aircraft Carrier Squadron was conducting underway exercises near Tawi-Tawi on May 22 when *Puffer* (ss–268) fired a spread of six torpedoes at light carrier *Chitose* and though two hit, both were duds, and no damage was sustained. Heavy cruiser *Tone* was sent to search for the submarine, but had no luck.

Admiral Montgomery duplicated his attack of May 19–20 on May 23 except the target was now Wake. The results were substantially similar to the Marcus raid and one US aircraft was lost. Combined Fleet received prompt notice of this attack as a raid of '185 aircraft in three waves'. In fact, 354 sorties were flown in five waves and a total of 148 tons of bombs were dropped. Taking note of the movement of the US Task Group away from the Empire, Toyoda cancelled '*To*' operation (DTG May 241800).

On May 23, the same day Japanese submarine *Ro–44* departed Saipan for Eniwetok on a reconnaissance mission, *England* and her consorts went to work in earnest on the *NA* line. Near dawn *Raby*'s radar detected *Ro–104* on the surface. She charged the disappearing 'blip' and for half an hour conducted a series of fruitless hedgehog attacks. The Japanese submarine commander manoeuvred his boat skilfully and succeeded in confusing *Raby*'s sonar operator by pinging on his own sonar. *George* now made five attacks, interrupted by one dry run by *England*, failing to get a hit. On her first live run *England* hit the unfortunate *RO* boat at 0834. Shortly after this kill another submarine was detected, but it got away (it was probably *RO–105*). Commander CORTDIV 39 (Commander Hamilton Hains) deduced correctly that he was in the middle of a Japanese submarine scout line but he was low on fuel and ammunition. He decided to return to Manus for fuel. An examination of the chart of the Japanese submarine disposition reveals the extraordinary fortune of this decision, for from the position of the destruction of *RO–104* to Manus was almost the axis of the *NA* line. At 16000 yard spacing the three DEs now headed for Manus. They did not have to wait too long. Shortly after midnight on May 24 *George* had a radar target at 14000 yards. When *Ro–116* dived, *England*'s sonar quikcly picked her up at 0150 and after two unsuccessful attempts *England* sank her fourth Japanese submarine. Following this success, CORTDIV 39 continued south-ward toward Seeadler Harbour for much needed fuel and hedgehog ammunition, still in scouting formation. This time *Raby* was first to get contact at 14000 yards followed shortly by *England*. At 4100 yards *Ro-108* submerged, but she was quickly detected on sonar and on her first salvo *England* dispatched the southern anchor of the now demolished *NA* line. The time was 2323. CORTDIV 39 arrived at Manus on the afternoon of the 27th and after refuelling and replenishment their ammunition stores sortied with *Spangler* (DE–696) late on the 28th to join *Hoggatt Bay* (CVE–75) and destroyers *Hazelwood* (DD–531) and *McCord* (DD–534). *England's* adventures had not ended.

The crucial fuel situation of FMF was further aggravated when submarine *Gurnard* (SS–254) sank fleet oiler *Tatekawa Maru* of FMF Supply Group outside Davao Gulf on May 24.

Battleships *Washington* and *North Carolina* in company with three light cruisers, seven destroyers and a large minelayer got underway from Pearl Harbor on May 24 to arrive at Majuro on May 30.

At Tawi-Tawi a Filipino coastwatcher got a good look at FMF and passed his findings on to US intelligence, reporting the presence of six carriers, ten cruisers and battleships and about 40 other ships on May 25.

Admiral Montgomery's Task Group arrived at Majuro on May 25 and TG58.6 was dissolved. At Pearl Harbor Admiral Spruance broke his flag in heavy cruiser *Indianapolis*, his choice for flagship during amphibious operations. That ship departed the next day accompanied by destroyers *Selfridge* and *Ellet* making Majuro on June 1.

May 27–June 5, 1944 'Kon' Operation to the sortie of Task Force 58

The American invasion of Biak on May 27 was considered sufficiently important to detach units allocated to '*A-Go*' to this threatened quarter. The extent of this reaction will be discussed more fully later. However, at this time, twenty-one land based aircraft of the 23rd Air Flotilla were dispatched to Sorong.

On the same day Biak was attacked, a reconnaissance aircraft of 5 BAF departed Truk, flew southeast to Buin, refuelled and then continued on to reconnoitre the Tulagi area. One carrier (*Saratoga* class), two converted carriers, four battleships, five cruisers, three destroyers and fifty small ships, together with seven large transports,

16 medium transports, 23 small transports and 40 'sea trucks' (presumably amphibious tractors) were reported in the Florida–Lunga area. This was the first of many similar reconnaissance missions conducted by the Japanese during the period covered in this volume. The extent and quality of their aerial scouting, both strategic and tactical, will soon become apparent.

Admiral Ozawa called another meeting on flagship *Taiho* on the 27th to discuss tactics.

The movement of Task Force 52 from Pearl Harbor to Eniwetok began on May 29. Carriers *Yorktown*, *Monterey* and *Princeton* with their screen of seven destroyers departed Pearl Harbor the same day for Majuro, followed the next day by *Bataan* and two destroyers. Both groups arrived at Majuro on June 3.

The situation on Biak caused Combined Fleet to order certain air forces stationed in the Marianas and Carolines to be transferred to the western part of New Guinea. There were 70 fighters, 16 bombers and four reconnaissance aircraft allocated to this transfer. Battleship *Fuso*, Fifth Squadron (*Myoko*, *Haguro*), and part of Destroyer Group 10 and 27 were also detached from FMF for the repulse of the Biak invasion force. These forces were added to the Southwest Area Fleet (Seventh Fleet), commanded by Rear Admiral Naomasa Sakonju. The Seventh Fleet was composed of 16th Squadron (heavy cruiser *Aoba*, light cruiser *Kinu*), three destroyers (*Shigure*, *Uranami*, *Shikinami*) and formed the nucleus of the Japanese forces now preparing to meet the Biak threat head-on. Combined Fleet quickly drafted necessary orders for the operation how designated '*Kon*'.

Japanese reconnaissance aircraft had a very fruitful day on the 29th. Naval Air Groups 121 and 151 (NAG 121 & NAG 151) checked Majuro in the Marshalls and Finschaven in New Guinea. These missions revealed important Allied concentrations in the Central and South Pacific and also demonstrate the thoroughness of Japanese scouting. The missions originated from Truk. The Majuro aircraft refuelled at Nauru then flew on to Majuro finding a major portion of Fifth Fleet, reporting seven fleet carriers, two converted carriers, three battleships, six cruisers, eighteen destroyers, two transports and six oilers. Actual American forces at Majuro at this time were 6 CV, 5 CVL, 1 CVE, 7 BB, 8 CA, 10 CL, 62 DD, 10–15 SS and many auxiliaries. Thirteen of the ships were reported as underway (2 CV, 3 CA, 8 DD). The types identified were 2 *Essex*, 1 *Enterprise*, 2 *Casablanca* and 1 *Iowa*. The aircraft which went to Finschafen found sixteen transports and three destroyers. Two aircraft were lost 200°/450 miles from Truk and 135°/500 miles from Palau respectively, cause unknown. A Japanese Army aircraft source unknown checked Humboldt Bay finding four cruisers, two submarines, thirteen destroyers and twenty-eight transports.

As related earlier CORTDIV 39, plus *Spangler*, had left Seeadler late in the afternoon of May 28 to renew its private war on AEF. Destroyer *Hazelwood* made a depth-charge attack (most Pacific Fleet destroyers lacked ahead thrown weapons at this time) on a disappearing radar contact shortly before 0200 May 30. She got a probable hit but was unable to dispatch the submarine though she did maintain contact until the DEs arrived in their familiar scouting line. *George* and *Raby* attacked with the former getting three probable hedgehog hits while *Raby* failed to score at all. The Japanese submarine commander had not only skilfully evaded the two DEs and destroyer all day by manoeuvring, but now he resorted to some theatrics to shake his tormentors. The destroyers heard three explosions indicating the sub might have blown up from damage suffered in the earlier attacks. Apparently she had fired torpedoes set to explode after a short run to throw the American ships off, because sonar contact was soon regained. By dawn *England* and *Spangler* rejoined on a 5000 yard circle around the contact area. *Spangler* made a hedgehog attack which failed. Word was now received that enemy aircraft might be in the vicinity. Before leaving Commander Hains gave *England* a chance. At 0735 a hedgehog salvo destroyed *RO–105*. In less than two weeks *England* had demolished the NA line sinking five of the boats in the main line and one supply submarine, the most spectacular score for any ASW ship in any theatre on either side during the war. More important than the scoreboard, however, was the gutting of the Japanese submarine portion of 'A-Go' even before the 'execute' was issued by Commander Combined Fleet. To the readers who are familiar with Japanese submarine operations of 1942 (cv *Yorktown* finished off by *I–168*, cv *Wasp* sunk by *I–19* and several other major ships hit) and in view of the successes of American submarines in these operations the contribution of *England* and her sisters cannot be overemphasized. *England*'s adventures prompted Admiral King to signal, 'There'll always be an *England* – in the US Navy!' Admiral King's hope was outweighed by postwar economies as the little ship was broken-up in November 1946, $2\frac{1}{2}$ years after the Admiral's pronouncement.

Task Force 53 completed its rehearsals at Cape Esperance, Guadalcanal. The tractor groups left Ironbottom Sound for Kwajalein the same day (May 31) while the transport groups of TF 52 departed Pearl Harbor; destination Eniwetok.

The '*Kon*' force was now concentrated at Davao with the planned counterattack scheduled for June 4. In addition to the surface forces mentioned previously, large minelayers *Itsukushima* and *Tsugaru* with LST 127 had joined '*Kon*'s' ranks along with 2500 amphibious troops. The air strength now available for '*Kon*' consisted of 2 VF and 2 VB at Sorong, 10 VF at Babo, 6 VF at Kau, 18 VF, 12 VB at Washin. Seventy-six aircraft (48 VF, 8 VS, 20 VB) were to transfer from Yap to Washin via Davao to arrive June 2. Though the Japanese reaction to the increasing Allied pressure at Biak was well executed in view of their limited resources, it had the effect of further reducing the numbers of shore based aircraft available for '*A-Go*' which in all Japanese planning was to be the decisive effort. It was the classic dilemma of trying to remain flexible in a rapidly changing situation while at the same time trying to stick to carefully laid plans, in this case compounded by a rapidly deteriorating supply position. (The reader should keep these crucial factors in mind when analysing the Japanese moves throughout the period covered by this book.)

The aircraft of 5 BAF were now ordered to assume '*A-Go*' dispositions in the Palau area, further shifting the main strength of that force away from the Marianas. Captain Fuchida (who led the Pearl Harbor attack and was now Admiral Toyoda's Air Staff Officer) estimated that the Japanese naval air strength on airfields in the Marianas on June 1 as about:

SAIPAN No. 1	100 A6M VF	TINIAN No. 4	80 A6M VF
SAIPAN No. 2	50 D4Y VB	GUAM No. 1	100 A6M VF
TINIAN No. 1	80 G4M VB/VT	GUAM No. 2	60 P1Y VT
TINIAN No. 2	50 D4Y VB		—
	20 JIN VF (N)		540 Total

Though the figures seem high it indicates how much '*Kon*' and the assumption of '*A-Go*' dispositions were based on the belief that the Palaus would be the area of the 'decisive battle' dislocated Japanese shore-based air strength by the time of the battle. Reconnaissance, probably from Truk, found eight destroyers, ten small ships, 18 transports, one oiler and ten other ships at Kwajalein plus many aircraft on the field. Two destroyers and a similar number of transports were sighted at Ruon while a *Saratoga* class carrier, one battleship, one cruiser, one transport and forty small ships were reported in the Admiralty Islands.

On June 2, aircraft from 5 BAF (23rd Air Flotilla–54 aircraft) attacked Allied forces in the Biak area losing twelve of their number, while inflicting superficial damage to LST–467.

Another of Truk's checks of Eniwetok was flown on June 2. An aircraft of NAG 151 found two cruisers, one destroyer, 17 transports, one tanker and about twenty aircraft. Additional reconnaissance of American advance bases was planned as soon as possible by NAG 121 and NAG 151.

The 'Kon' surface unit sortied on June 2 and was apparently seen the next day by an American Liberator (Navy PB4Y) at 1310 when 330 miles southeast of Davao at position 04° 18′ N, 128° 30′ E on course 150, speed 20 reported as 2 BB, 3 CA, 1 CL, 9 DD. Submarine *Rasher* sighted two Japanese task groups of two cruisers and two destroyers and two heavy cruisers (*Atago* or *Nachi* class), three light cruisers, two destroyers and one unidentified craft in the vicinity of 04° 30′ N, 128° 00′ E en route to Halmaheras. Various air sightings indicated a Japanese concentration in the vicinity of Halmaheras. The Japanese force turned back, having lost any chance of surprise, and Admiral Toyoda temporarily suspended 'Kon' at 2200 on June 3.

Supply Group 2, composed of *Genyo Maru*, *Azusa Maru* and two destroyers departed Tawi-Tawi for its 'A-Go' standby position 130 miles east of the northern end of Mindanao.

Commander Combined Fleet issued dispatch operation order No. 114 (DTG 031420) ordering Air Group 2 of 5 BAF to concentrate in the Halmahera area with advance bases at Sorong and Babo with rear bases at Washin and Kau. This same day (June 3) 5 BAF and Japanese Army Air Force aircraft (32 VF, 9 VB, 10 JAAF aircraft) again struck Allied shipping near Biak inflicting minor damage while losing eleven of their number. By now the Japanese had about 200 aircraft in the 'Kon' theatre. The aviators were now hit from an unexpected quarter. A large number of the pilots and aircrewmen contracted malaria and were unable to participate in 'Kon' or 'A-Go'.

Fifth Base Air Force continued its attacks on Biak forces the next day finding Allied cruisers at sea. Twenty-eight fighters and six bombers attacked the ships damaging light cruiser *Nashville* (CL–43) with a near miss.

The transport group of TF 53 now moved out of Ironbottom Sound for Kwajalein, followed on June 5 by the old battleships and nine destroyers of the shore bombardment groups.

On June 5, five BAF long range air reconnaissance aircraft got their last look at TF 58 in its Majuro anchorage. The next time that force would be seen by the Japanese would be in battle. The aircraft, which had come by the now well travelled Truk–Nauru–Majuro route, arrived at 1050 and gave a very accurate report: 'Regular aircraft carriers, six (all either *Essex* or *Enterprise* class), half of them have 60 small fighters on the flight deck; converted carriers, eight (among them two of the *Independence* class); battleships, six; cruisers, eight or more; destroyers, 16 or more; tankers, 10; there were many other ships'. The actual ship count in Majuro on June 5 was 7 CV, 8 CVL, 1 CVE, 7 BB, 9 CA, 10 CL, 71 DD, 16 DE, about 10–15 submarines and many auxiliaries. A similar check of the Admiralty Islands found one aircraft carrier, two battleships or cruisers and three destroyers. In fact no carriers were in the Admiralties at this time.

Supply Group 2 which had now reached its standby position, as ordered on June 3, was now diverted to an anchorage in Surigao Strait (Point 'J').

American aircraft had confirmed the Japanese concentration at Tawi-Tawi and Commander Submarine Force, South West Pacific had ordered his boats to positions as follows:

A Tawi-Tawi:
   Harder, Redfin, Bluefish
B Southeast of Mindanao:
   Hake, Bashaw, Paddle

while Commander Submarine Force Pacific Fleet placed his boats at the following positions:

A Luzon Strait:
   Tunny, Pilotfish, Pintado
B San Bernardino Strait:
   Flying Fish
C Surigao Strait:
   Growler
D West of the Marianas from 20° to Palau:
   Albacore, Seahorse, Bang, Finback, Stingray, Muskallunge, Pipefish, Cavalla.

On June 5 USS *Puffer* which had missed carrier *Chitose* on May 22 sank two of Admiral Ozawa's most valuable auxiliaries, aircraft stores ships, *Ashizura* and *Takasaki*. (Their primary function was replenishment of aircraft carriers, carrying a broad range of aviation items including bombs, torpedoes, machine gun ammunition, aviation gasoline. *Ashizuri* was equipped with aircrew quarters and shops for repairing damaged aircraft also – valuable ships indeed.) The position was 6° 33′ N, 120° 13′ W in the Sulu Sea and the Cause was attributed to mines by the Japanese. USS *Bluefish* reported 2 CV, 6 CA, 2 possible BB and 10 medium and small vessels in Tawi-Tawi on the 5th.

June 6-June 13: From the American Sortie to the Japanese Sortie

The same day, having concentrated at Majuro, Task Force 58 got underway, formed into four task groups, received its aircraft and proceeded to its refuelling rendezvous, set for the night of June 9–10. The force split the distance between Truk and Wake and headed for the Marianas.

If USS *England* seemed to have a particular dislike for Japanese submarines, USS *Harder* (SS-257) would soon demonstrate a similar disdain for Japanese destroyers. Proceeding toward Tawi-Tawi, she had reached a position off oil-rich Tarakan on June 6 when her radar detected the approach of a tanker convoy, three oilers, with a destroyer screen. Discovered in the moonlight while attempting a surfaced approach, she fired three torpedoes from her stern tubes at destroyer *Minatzuki*, which was charging in for a depth charge attack. Two hit and the destroyer broke up and sank, carrying all but 45 of her 150 man crew with her. When the chase was resumed another screening destroyer subjected *Harder* to an intensive depth charge attack, which was so vigorous that *Harder* fired six torpedoes at her tormentor. All missed. The destroyer captain succeeded in his purpose since the tankers got away. Entering Sibutu Passage *Harder* sighted a third destroyer at noon on the 7th. The setup was nearly perfect, when the destroyer apparently sighted the periscope since it now charged directly for *Harder*'s position. *Harder* fired three torpedoes. Two hit and the *Yugumo* class destroyer *Hayanami*, one of Japan's most modern, on ASW patrol, headed for the bottom. The time was 1242. *Harder* was harassed by about six other Japanese destroyers before she could break off the action.

June 7. Fifth Squadron (*Myoko*, *Haguro*) and part of Destroyer Group 10 (*Kazegumo*, *Asagumo*) departed Davao Gulf for Batjan. The force commander reported that destroyer *Kazegumo* had hit a mine and sunk. The 'mine' was USS *Hake* (SS–256), as US submarines continued their attrition of FMF destroyers.

The transports and tractor groups of TF 52 arrived at Eniwetok on the 7th and 8th, while TF 53 completed its concentration at Kwajalein on the 8th.

Two cruisers and a like number of destroyers were seen entering Davao at 0230 by submarine *Hake*. Admiral Sakonju's 16th Squadron (CA *Aoba*, CL *Kinu*) had rendezvoused with Destroyer Group 19 (*Shikinami*, *Uranami*) and DG 17 (*Shiratsuyu*, *Shigure*, *Samidare*, *Harusame*) on the 7th, west of New Guinea, and the admiral transferred his flag to destroyer *Shikinami*. The destroyers now headed for Biak, after embarking troops at Sorong, while the cruisers went to Ambon. In spite of air cover provided by 23rd Air Flotilla, an American air attack sank destroyer *Harusame* and damaged three other ships. Next day the Japanese destroyers encountered an Allied cruiser/destroyer force: CA HMAS *Australia*; CLs *Phoenix*, *Boise*; DDs *Fletcher*, *Jenkins*, *Radford*, *La Vallette*, *Hutchins*, *Daly*, *Bache*, *Beale*, *Abner Read*, *Ammen*, *Mullany*, *Trathen*, HMAS *Arunta* and HMAS *Warramunga*. The Japanese destroyers were chased away, after they had set their troop barges adrift.

First Mobile Force Battle Report entry for this day indicates how Admiral Ozawa's staff viewed the deteriorating situation at Tawi-Tawi. The discovery of the concentration at Tawi-Tawi by the Americans was obvious and the intensity of the enemy submarine activity was such (four destroyers attacked in three days) that FMF would have to move to Guimaras on the 13th. Supply Group 2 was ordered to leave Surigao Strait, its *A-Go* stand-by area, for Guimaras on the island of Panay immediately.

June 9. At 0930 a reconnaissance aircraft of 5 BAF checked Majuro finding ten transports and two destroyers, since TF 58 had departed three days earlier. A similar mission against the Admiralty Islands at 0900 revealed 1 battleship, 3 cruisers, 20 transports and about 135 aircraft.

Task Group 51.1 (Reserve Troops) which had left Pearl Harbor arrived at Kwajalein, while TF 52 and TF 53 departed for the Marianas.

That night TF 58 had reached its refuelling rendezvous and commenced replenishment, finishing before dawn.

Commander Dealey (USS *Harder*) had not read Admiral Ozawa's log concerning American submarines but he had helped write two chapters and was about to add a third. After sinking *Hayanami*, *Harder* picked up six British intelligence agents on the northeast coast of Borneo. When *Harder* was about 40 miles from Tawi-Tawi she was seen by a patrol aircraft. The aircraft dropped a bomb as the submarine submerged. Fortunately it missed. Two patrolling destroyers followed the aircraft but were unable to flush the submarine and they soon abandoned the search. That evening Dealey sighted two destroyers in a scouting line at Sibutu Passage. He fired a spread of torpedoes which dispatched *Tanikaze*. Dealey reported sinking the second destroyer in the same salvo, but no evidence of this second loss appears in the Japanese official records. The next day (June 10 at 1800) he sighted a powerful Japanese force leaving Tawi-Tawi. *Harder* was seen and a Japanese destroyer charged. Dealey fired three torpedoes and he reported heavy explosions, however there is again no indication in Japanese official documents that any other Japanese ship in that area was hit by torpedoes that day. In any case, after he broke contact, Dealey reported three battleships, four cruisers, six–eight destroyers steaming south.

June 10. Dealey's contact had departed Tawi-Tawi at 1600 under orders from Commander Combined Fleet to reinforce *Kon* forces and was composed of part of First Squadron (BBs *Yamato*, *Musashi*), light cruiser *Noshiro* (Commander DF 2 on board) and two destroyers; destination Batjan. Commander, First Squadron, Vice Admiral Ugaki assumed command of *Kon*. This transfer was favoured by Admiral Ozawa. Thus while the US Fifth Fleet was on its way to the Marianas, Japanese attention was focused in the Southwest Pacific.

Submarine *Ro–44* now reached Eniwetok but the bulk of the US fleet had departed. Her sister, *Ro–42* was sunk near Eniwetok by USS *Bangust* (DE–739). *Ro–111* was caught by an American hunter-killer group composed of *Hoggatt Bay* (CVE–75), and Destroyer Division 41; *Taylor* (DD–468), *Nicholas* (DD–449), *O'Bannon* (DD–450) and *Hopewell* (DD–681) and was disposed of by *Taylor*.

A check of Hollandia by a Japanese Army Air Force aircraft revealed three cruisers, three destroyers and 44 transports. Two Saipan based aircraft failed to return to their base. Whether these were operational losses or combat losses is unknown.

The situation at Tawi-Tawi had become desperate. The Japanese intensified their anti-submarine patrols forming an anti-submarine unit around two destroyers, a mine-sweeper and three subchasers, together with a few aircraft to attempt to break up the American submarine concentration. This is in contrast to the ASW resources available to the Allies and points up the disastrous proportions the Japanese destroyer situation had reached at this stage of the war.

June 11. A Japanese convoy composed of 12 merchant ships and 16 fishing boats, escorted by one torpedo boat and 9 patrol craft left Saipan for Yokohama on the 11th. This little group would soon find itself in range of the aircraft of Task Force 58.

On the morning of June 11, after topping off destroyers, TF 58 Combat Air Patrol (CAP) shot down two snoopers as that force moved into strike range of the Marianas. Destroyer pickets now advanced 20 miles to the west of the disposition. The original plan had been to sweep the Japanese airfields in the early morning hours of June 12. This was also doctrine and Mitscher hoped to catch the Japanese off-guard as the force had reached a position just 200 miles east of Guam (13° 45′ N, 148° 50′ E) by 1300 on the 11th. Mitscher moved the first sweep up to that afternoon sending 208 F6Fs and 8 TBFs against Saipan and Tinian. The attackers estimated that they destroyed 36 Japanese aircraft, while losing eleven of their number (all Hellcats). Six of the pilots were killed.

Now Commander Combined Fleet received word that an enemy task force had attacked the Marianas. Patrol aircraft sighted enemy carrier-type aircraft east of Guam and at 1150 a carrier group was seen 170 miles east of that island. Reports were received that enemy carrier-type aircraft subjected all four major islands of the Marianas to air raids between 1300 and 1500. It was estimated that fifty American aircraft had been shot down. As mentioned above only eleven were lost but many more were hit by the intense anti-aircraft fire encountered. The Japanese reported the loss of 35 aircraft the first day. So effective were the American raiders that Admiral Nimitz reported, 'Control of the air had been effected by the original fighter sweep on June 11.'

When TF 58 had reached a point somewhat over 100 miles east of Guam it split into two groups with TG 58.1 continuing on toward Guam while the other three groups (TG 58.7 had not been formed at this time) turned northwest toward Saipan and Tinian.

Destroyers *Yamagumo* and *Nowake* departed Tawi-Tawi for *Kon* operations this day. *Harder* reported 3 or 4 battleships, six cruisers and destroyers at that base.

June 12. In the early hours of June 12, 5 BAF began operations which were designed to reduce the US carrier force to a size FMF could handle. Ten G4M (Betty) from Truk (probably from NAG 755) conducted night torpedo attacks against the northern task groups between 0315 and 0415. Their method of attack was as follows: pathfinder aircraft circled the American groups at about 5000 metres dropping flares and as the attack commander sighted silhouetted ships the main body would move in for their attacks. No hits were obtained and one G4M was shot down.

Cruiser-submarine *I-10* sent her reconnaissance aircraft over Majuro, but the ships she sought were now far to the west. The aircraft, an E14Y (Glenn) was lost in recovery operations.

Japanese Combined Fleet knew the whereabouts of the ships *I-10* sought. The reports came in: 0420–0930 Saipan attacked by nearly 500 aircraft in four waves; Guam by 700 aircraft in nine waves between 0240 and 1730; Tinian reported 175 aircraft in four waves between 0730 and 1500 while six aircraft were seen over Rota at 1000. It was estimated that 65 American aircraft were destroyed while the airfields on the three major islands were all temporarily out of action. Though Admiral Toyoda did not execute *A-Go* at this time all units were advised that response to the American attacks were to be governed by that operation order. Attacks were to be restricted until the enemy's intentions were known. Japanese reconnaissance and captured documents on US aviators shot down over the Marianas now give Combined Fleet a fair picture of the force attacking the Marianas. This estimate was as follows:

Group 1: 2 CV, 1 CVL, 1 BB – 90 miles east of Saipan at 0550.
Group 2: 2 CV – 90 miles northeast of Saipan at 0550.
Group 3: 5 CV – position not given at 0640.
Group 4: 2 CV, 2 CVL, 3 BB – 90 miles SE of Saipan at 1230.

Supply group east of Saipan. Invasion force location still unknown. Enemy submarines seem to be concentrating in the Marianas, Carolines, Southern Philippines areas.

The American plan was to destroy enemy aircraft, bomb airfields and destroy enemy shore installations. To accomplish this purpose each carrier group was assigned one or more of the major islands in the Marianas as follows: TG 58.1 – Guam and Rota; TG 58.2 – Tinian;

TG 58.3 – Saipan; and TG 58.4 Saipan and Pagan. On this day TG 58.1 sent 468 sorties against Guam and Rota, losing 15 of their number and reporting the destruction of 40 enemy aircraft in the air or on the ground. Group 58.2 sent 401 sorties against its appointed target, Tinian. Opposition was much lighter and these strikes lost only 4 aircraft and claimed 14 enemy aircraft. Task Groups 58.3 and 58.4 launched 465 missions. They lost only seven of their planes and claimed 24 Japanese aircraft destroyed. In addition to attacks on the Marianas, Task Group 58.4 found the Japanese convoy which had left Saipan the day before, now 160 miles north-northwest of Saipan and in three attacks on the 12th and 13th sank ten of the merchant ships, the torpedo boat (*Ootori*), three of the subchasers and some of the fishing boats. Admiral Clark's air groups, which were hitting Guam, found another convoy 130 miles west of Guam and hit it on the 13th damaging one of the ships. Amazingly, in view of the massive US concentration, the convoy got through to Saipan.

June 13. By now, there could be no doubt that the Marianas were the target selected by the Americans so Admiral Toyoda alerted all his forces (Dispatch Operation Order No. 146) 'Prepare for *A-Go* Operation Battle'. This order required that the Japanese First Mobile Force should sortie immediately, which it did at 1000, and proceed to an area east of the Philippines to be in position to attack the enemy task force. If possible the sortie was to be kept secret. It was impossible. USS *Redfin* (SS–272) sighted the Japanese fleet at 1100 and reported that six carriers with aircraft on deck, four battleships, eight cruisers and six destroyers accompanied by two oilers, two transports and two destroyers were headed north (320°/18 knots) out of Tawi-Tawi at 0100. *Kon* was suspended 'temporarily' (Combined Fleet Dispatch Operation Order 147) and First and Fifth Squadrons, together with their destroyers, now at Batjan, were ordered to rejoin FMF near its refuelling rendezvous in the Philippine Sea. Units of 5 BAF in Halmahera were ordered to concentrate in the Western Carolines while the 23rd Air Flotilla was to remain in the New Guinea area to support local forces in that area pending completion of *A-Go*. Supply Group 1, at Davao, was put on 30 minutes alert and old battleship *Fuso* transferred most of her fuel to the oilers of that force, emphasizing the scarcity of fuel oil in the Japanese fleet. The same day, pointing up another problem in the Japanese fleet, a B6N crashed on *Taiho*, destroying two A6M, two D4Y and two B6N.

Submarine *Ro–44* finished her reconnaissance of Eniwetok and departed for Bikini. *Ro–36* was sunk off Saipan by USS *Melvin* (DD–680) while the former was conducting scouting and weather reporting operations near that island.

The Japanese received reports that air attacks were continuing throughout the Marianas and that these were followed by a gunnery bombardment of Saipan and Tinian. (TG 58.1 – 339 sorties v. Guam and Rota; lost 4; claimed 7 enemy a/c: TG 58.2 – 126 sorties v. Tinian; lost 2; claimed 8 enemy a/c: TGs 58.3 and 58.4 – 413 sorties v. Saipan; lost 4; claimed 5 enemy a/c.) The former attacks cost Torpedo Squadron 16 its commander, Commander R. H. Isley, who was killed in a rocket attack on Saipan. The latter operation was conducted by Admiral Lee's Fast Battleships and the new ships failed miserably in this strange assignment. Unlike the old battleships of Admiral Turner's force, which were trained for shore bombardment, Lee's ships were trained for AA defence and surface battle and though 2432 sixteen inch and 12544 five inch shells were fired no important results were achieved. That night TG 58.2 and 58.3 retired to the northeast of Saipan.

A Truk-based reconnaissance aircraft had sighted a large carrier group 400 miles north of that island between 0630 and 0930 while an Iwo Jima plane spotted a group composed of 2 CV and 2 BB 170 miles north of Guam. A carrier and ten other ships were seen 70 miles east of Guam.

On the day of the Japanese sortie, US Naval Intelligence estimated Japanese dispositions as follows:

2 The Japanese probably suspected, but did not yet know that an amphibious operation was about to commence.
3 It is believed that the Japanese Fleet was disposed about as follows:
   A Halmahera. One division of new battleships, one division of cruisers, and at least one squadron of destroyers.
   B Tawitawi. Three of four battleships, one, possibly three divisions of carriers, one, possibly two divisions of cruisers, about twenty destroyers, and some auxiliary vessels.
   C Operating northwest of New Guinea against MacArthur's forces in Wewak were one, possibly two, divisions of cruisers, possibly one battleship, and some destroyers.
   D There were supposed to be three replenishment forces, of which two were believed to be in the Philippines and one en

route to the Philippines. One replenishment force possibly was operating in the Surigao Area awaiting rendezvous orders.

E In the Empire and the north were three battleships, approximately seven heavy and light cruisers, two or three CVEs, plus destroyers and a considerable number of submarines.

F In the Marianas and Western Carolines were many Japanese submarines.

4 Of the three carrier divisions operating in the Philippines two were not definitely located.

5 The Japanese had air bases in the Marianas, Western Carolines, Philippines and Iwo Jima.

The same intelligence sources estimated the following Japanese Nava Air Strength as of May 18:

CARRIER Divisions (in Philippines Area)

CARDIV 1 (*Shokaku, Zuikaku, Taiho* – 27 VF, 27 VB, 18 VT, 3 Recce each)

CARDIV 2 (*Hitaka, Hayataka* – 27 VF, 18 VB, 6 VT each; *Ryuho* – 27 VF, 6 VT)

CARDIV 3 (*Chitose, Chiyoda, Zuiho* – 21 VF, 9 VT each)

EMPIRE (COMBAT UNITS) 250 VF, 120 VB, 80 VB(L), 55 VB(M), 10 F/B, 35 F/P

MARIANAS 186 VF, 48 VB, 82 VB(L), 15 VB(M), 6 F/B, 16 F/P

CAROLINES 42 VF, 12 VB, 6 VB(M), 6 F/B

PALAU and YAP 52 VF, 24 VB, 9 VB(M), 2 F/B, 11 F/P

PHILIPPINES, D.E.I.* and NEW GUINEA (Land Based) 70 VF, 16 VB, 61 VB(M), 2 F/B, 68 F/P.

A remarkably accurate analysis.

June 14–June 18: The neutralization of the Bonins to the first contacts between main forces

June 14. On June 14 Admiral Tagaki, Commander Advance Expeditionary Force, ordered submarines *I–5, I–10,* and *I–185* from his few remaining boats to deploy in a line east of Saipan for participation in *A-Go*. He feared that to move them to the west of the Marianas might interfere with the operations of FMF. Of course the possibility of getting mixed up with friendly forces is an important consideration in submarine deployment, but the decision here

---

* *D.E.I.*—Dutch East Indies, now Indonesia.

effectively eliminated the remaining Japanese submarines from further operations, though not from further attrition.

Two Japanese oilers, accompanied by two other auxiliaries and an escort of 2–4 destroyers, were seen leaving Davao at 1100 by a US submarine, while *Bonefish* confirmed that Tawi-Tawi was now empty.

At 1300 First Mobile Force arrived at Guimaras for refuelling. Fleet oilers *Azusa Maru* and *Genyo Maru* transferred 10,800 tons of black oil to Ozawa's ships between 1700 and 0700, June 15.

Reports of American activity in the Marianas continued to come in to Admiral Toyoda's headquarters. American battleships, now Turner's professionals, were reported to be bombarding Saipan and Tinian while carrier aircraft attacks on Tinian, Guam and Rota were noted.*

With the information provided by *Redfin*, Admiral Spruance decided to neutralize his northern flank before FMF arrived. He had clearly established aerial superiority in the Marianas and the remaining threat from shore based air came from the Japanese ability to shuttle aircraft in from other areas. Many of these were within the range of the USAAF and, as noted previously, were the object of constant attention by that service, but the Bonins were not. Accordingly he told Admiral Mitscher to detach TG 58.1 and TG 58.4 (at 2000 June 13) to strike the Bonins on June 16 and for TG 58.1 to return in time for an June 18 rendezvous. Task Group 58.4 was to retire to Eniwetok. Both group commanders were reluctant. Clark feared he might miss the battle which seemed imminent, while Harrill tried to beg off, claiming his ships were low on fuel and only after a personal confrontation with Clark, who flew over to *Hornet* upon learning of Harrill's near insubordination, did Harrill agree to carry out his orders. After a heated discussion, Harrill agreed to go with Clark, whose own reticencead been cured by the lure of a dangerous mission and the assurance that he would return in time for any carrier battle. Because of the personalities involved, Admiral Mitscher advised Clark and Harrill to 'cooperate', though, under ordinary circum-

---

* Short summary of American Air Operations June 14

T.G.	Target(s)	No of sorties	Losses	Enemy a/c dest.
58.2	Guam and Rota	80	2	13
58.2	Saipan	78	1	0
58.3	Saipan	190	1	5
58.2	Tinian	34	1	0

stances (in any Navy) Harrill, Clark's senior, would have been put in tactical command. The decision to establish this unusual command relationship was, in retrospect, very wise and shows he had insight into the personalities of his subordinates.

On the 14th TG 58.2 and 58.3 refuelled their destroyers to ensure that they would be available throughout the expected battle. The Task Groups operated southwest of Tinian and continued their attacks on the Marianas. Both groups reported shooting down some enemy search aircraft and it was assumed, by the American commanders, that the presence and make-up of the American Carrier Forces were known in some detail.

June 15. At 0552 Admiral Kincaid signalled, 'Land the Landing Force'.

The first Japanese formation to enter the Philippine Sea was Supply Group 1 which had departed Davao on June 14. While proceeding north in the early hours of June 15 destroyer *Shiratsuya* sank with heavy loss of life in a collision with fleet oiler *Seiyo Maru* at 0345. The destroyer was manoeuvring to avoid an imagined American submarine.

Admiral Toyoda now decided that the Marianas were going to be the area desired for battle and at 0855 issued the following message:

'On the morning of the 15th a strong enemy force began landing operations in the Saipan–Tinian area. The Combined Fleet will attack the enemy in the Marianas area and annihilate the invasion force. Activate *A-Go* Operation for decisive battle.'

At 0900, FMF left Guimaras, passing through the Visayen Sea toward San Bernardino, under the cover of Philippine-based aircraft. A coast watcher sighted the Japanese at 1100 in the Sibuyan Sea, reporting 3 CV, 2 AK and 16 other warships. At 1830 another coast-watcher gave a very good count of FMF (3 BB, 9 CV, 10 CA, 11 DD, and 2 PC) entering San Bernardino. This intelligence was not received by Admiral Spruance until June 17.

After receiving word (COMFIFTHFLT 142355) that TG 58.1 and 58.4 should restrict their strikes on the Bonins to the 16th to ensure timely rendezvous on the 18th, Admiral Clark charged into launch position at 1430 on the 15th when his group was 135 miles from Iwo Jima and 142 miles from Chichi Jima. Ten Japanese aircraft were shot down and seven were destroyed on the ground at Iwo. Twenty-one float reconnaissance aircraft were eliminated at Chichi. Three freighters were damaged at Chichi. A total of three US aircraft were lost and two aviators were killed. Destroyers *Boyd* (DD–544) and *Charette* (DD–581) caught merchant ship *Tatsutagawa* and sank her. Harrill, whose intended retirement to Eniwetok had been cancelled by Admiral Spruance, trailed astern and did not launch any attacks on the 15th.

Admiral Toyoda estimated that FMF could be in a position to attack the Americans by June 19 at the latest. He knew that the Americans had now commenced landing operations on Saipan, while their aerial bombardment of the entire archipelago continued. He received word that a surface group had hit Tinian that night and he knew of Clark's strike on the Bonins. At 1717 he gave the 'Execute "*A-Go*" Operations'* stating, 'The destiny of our Empire lies in the outcome of this battle. Each member will fight to the end . . . Move out for Operation *A*.' His plan was to concentrate his land-based aircraft at Iwo-Jima, Marcus, Truk, Yap, Palau and the Marianas (for the latter, as the tactical situation permitted) with land based air attacks to commence June 18. His patrol aircraft continued to give him a good picture of American operations in the Marianas and Bonins estimating the US forces in the Marianas as follows: 2 CV groups near Saipan; 1 CV group near the Bonins; one or two CV groups 450 miles north of Truk, 2 convoys with CVEs north of Truk and the main troopship convoy at Saipan.

Naval Air Group 551 stationed at Truk sent eleven B6N (torpedo bombers Jill) against the American force at Saipan reporting four transports, one cruiser and one battleship sunk. In fact no hits were obtained.

Japanese First Mobile Force was seen entering the Philippine Sea at 1835 by *Flying Fish* (SS–229), reported as 3BB, 3CV, cruisers and destroyers on course 080° at 20 knots, and just over an hour later (1945) *Seahorse* (SS–304) sighted Admiral Ugaki's force well to the east of Mindanao, reporting, 'Six ships, 10–11N, 129–35E, Course 045°, SOA** 16.5 knots, *Seahorse* trailing', but not before the Japanese jammed her transmissions.*** Her message was finally transmitted in

---

* The Japanese Operation Order contemplated various contingencies and various stages of readiness up to the final 'Execute'.

** SOA – Speed of Advance.

*** Japanese Mono 90 has the following interesting quote regarding this, 'At 2038 (1938 USN) hours, while we were advancing, we found out by intercepting enemy signals that an enemy submarine had discovered the movements of our Task Force and had sent back a message to that effect'.

clear at 0400 June 16. The boat developed engine trouble and was unable to trail as she had advised. Both of these important sightings were received by Admiral Spruance, and their separation (a coincidence unrelated to tactics) noted. It was assumed, correctly, that the Ugaki group was the same force identified at Batjan, so it was known that tactics were not necessarily the reason for the split.

At dusk Reeves' and Montgomery's groups, while 40 miles west of Saipan recovering aircraft on a southeasterly course, detected enemy raids, estimated as eight Bettys with fighter escort, *San Jacinto* (CVL-30), newest addition to the Fast Carrier Force, dispatched her CAP which shot down seven of the intruders breaking up the attack, which had apparently originated from Guam. At 1912 a bigger raid from Yap composed of three D4Y (Judy dive-bombers), 10 P1Y (torpedo-bombers) escorted by six A6M (Zeros) attacked Reeves' group, picking *Lexington* and *Enterprise* as their targets. About a dozen of the aircraft broke through and launched their weapons and though there were several near misses with torpedoes, the only damage suffered was in the screen when the carriers fired AA weapons into their own screening ships, killing two and wounding 58 officers and men. Seven of the attackers were shot down by two night fighters and Task Group AA, and four others (unaccounted for by AA or CAP) failed to return, bringing the total losses from this raid to eleven attackers.

COMSUBPAC, Admiral Lockwood, now placed submarines off Saipan as lifeguards and sent boats to scout Truk, Woleai and Palau. His submarines were ordered to continue their routine patrols except for the Marianas area and to destroy enemy ships and furnish advance warning of the approach of enemy task forces.

Noting the advance of the Japanese Fleet, Admiral Spruance requested that Admiralties and Wakde PB4Ys (Liberators) extended their searches to 1200 miles.

That evening Admiral Ozawa issued his battle plan in the following tactical estimate:

1 The strength of the enemy:
  A *In the area of the Marianas Islands.*
    The enemy is divided into approximately five groups, centred around fifteen aircraft carriers, seven of which are the regular type and eight of which are the type converted from cruisers.

It is believed that practically all of the American task force strength has come to make an attack.

At present a group of supply ships are located in an area four hundred nautical miles east of the Archipelago and one group of LSTs has been observed to be commencing landing operations in the vicinity of the Archipelago. The arrival of a large-scale invasion fleet within the near future is almost inevitable. We have only observed part of the CVEs or escort carriers which are east of the Archipelago, but there is a good possibility that they will come in extremely large numbers to attack, both before and after the decisive battle in the vicinity of the Archipelago.

B *In the area around the Admiralty Islands.*

We cannot rely too heavily on this report because it was made by a fighter 'plane, but approximately eight carriers and all other types of ships, including battleships and transports, are said to be lying in wait in this area.

2 Our calculations of the strategy of the enemy.

The objective the enemy is to accomplish one or more of the following:

A The invasion and occupation of strategic bases in the Mariana Archipelago.

B Together with the above operation, to strengthen invasion operations in western New Guinea and to invade and occupy strategic areas in the western Caroline Islands.

C To draw out our task force strength for a decisive battle.

3 An estimated study of the distribution of enemy forces in the region around the Mariana Archipelago both before and after the decisive battle between task forces:

A It is quite possible that the enemy knew the plans of our task force. (Reason: Because of the interception of signals by enemy submarines they knew about our departure from Tawitawi on the thirteenth and our departure from Guimaras on the fifteenth, and it would not be difficult for them to assume what our intentions were. Therefore, judging from the strategic speed employed by the Americans formerly, they probably know that our task force is going to attack in the vicinity of the Archipelago between the eighteenth and nineteenth.)

B From looking at the distribution of enemy forces up to the fifteenth we see that most of the task force striking power has been distributed along the Archipelago. However one force is always maintained in the rear for purposes of supply or as a reserve force. In attacking and occupying an Archipelago it is necessary to maintain re-inforcements. So it is thought that the distribution of the enemy is generally as follows:

(1) In the vicinity of the Archipelago: at the most they will probably distribute their forces so as to be centred around two-thirds, or ten, of their aircraft carriers. Moreover, judging from the present conditions of the invasion battle, the distance travelled west by them will not be great but it is presumed to be, at the most, 300 nautical miles.

(2) They will probably station between one-third and one-half of their forces to the west of the Archipelago, and the remainder will aid in the land fighting and act as reserve strength.

(3) From the present battle conditions there is little possibility that they will remove all of their forces away from the invasion battle line and deploy them temporarily to the east of the Archipelago.

(4) It is very improbable that they intend to send part of their task force far to the west to make a flank attack on our advancing task force, or to make a surprise attack, because they would be entering an area within the limits patrolled by our land-based aircraft.

(5) Our air bases extend far to the southwest part of the Archipelago; however, since we are weak in the north, the enemy will probably attack the southern islands and try to cut aircraft and other supply lines while, at the same time, employ one element of the task force to attack in the north'

(6) It is very possible that the enemy will employ a great number of escort carriers in the vicinity of the Archipelago to reinforce the battle on land.

II Things which should be considered in the tactical directions of task forces.

   1 From the standpoint of the manoeuverability of a task force and, especially from the standpoint of fuel supplies, great delays in time schedules are not to be permitted.

   2 It is necessary to choose a time when the distribution of those of our fighting power which can participate in a decisive battle in the battle area has the most potentialities and, especially, when our land-based air power has great potentialities. This

necessitates a consideration of present fighting strength and of the capacity of reinforcements.

3 The strength of endurance of the forces defending the Marianas.

From the above considerations, we see that it is not possible to delay the engagement of our task force in a decisive battle beyond the nineteenth, we must, rather, consider how we can hasten the enegagement.

III Decision. Tactical policies which should be adopted by the task force. As previously planned, the main, tactical objective will be to shell the enemy task force in the vicinity of the Mariana Archipelago on the nineteenth and thereafter, to carry out Operation 'A', launch into battle of pursuit and completely annihilate the enemy.

1 We must be on guard against any surprise movements of the enemy after the sixteenth and must maintain the required observation of the enemy. In the south, the scouting of the enemy will be left to our land-based air power. Their main objective shall be to watch for a northerly frontal attack.

Especially, when one considers how the enemy is deployed, it is quite possible *that the eighteenth shall be the day of the decisive battle*. Therefore, we must sufficiently patrol and search out the enemy.

2 At dawn on the nineteenth we shall arrive at a point 300 miles west of the Archipelago and, while taking in aircraft, we shall make tactical moves, so that we shall be able to attack the enemy task force power (regular aircraft carriers) in the vicinity to the east of the Archipelago.

3 Our attack will consist of battle plan one, which depends on a long, longitudinal array of forces, and battle plan two for daylight aerial warfare. We shall reserve the 652 Air group as reinforcements against surprise attacks of the enemy and it shall carry out strict patrols in the north.

4 We shall strengthen the reconnaissance of the enemy by our land-based aircraft, both the day before and the day of the battle, and we shall strengthen our defensive contacts with the enemy. We shall distinguish between regular aircraft carriers and escort carriers, and we shall demand that each unit concerned put forth its utmost strength in the decisive battle.

5 The disposal of aircraft in accordance with the results of the battle. Based in general, on the plan for directing combined fleet tactics.

A When we have obtained very good results, the entire force shall pursue and annihilate the enemy.

B If the results are not good, we shall retreat temporarily, reorganize our forces and resume the attack.

June 16. A special night search of radar equipped TBFs was launched to search sector 230°–295° to 325 miles at 0100 by Task Force 58.

Because of inclement weather, the Japanese flew no long-range air searches from their carriers this day, however 3 ACS flew off anti-submarine patrols at 0930 and 2 ACS launched 2 D4ys (Judy) to find Supply Group 1 at 1453. At 1000 Supply Group 1 had joined Admiral Ugaki's force and this combined force steamed on toward its rendezvous with the remainder of FMF, refuelling en route. This important rendezvous took place at 1700. The entire Japanese force (First Mobile Force and Supply Group 1) then turned north by east and began refuelling operations. Supply Group 2 trailed astern.

Reports of enemy attacks continued to come into Admiral Toyoda's flagship *Oyodo* in the Inland Sea; 0500, 200 CV aircraft attacked Guam, 0715 Guam bombarded by 3 CV, 3 BB, 12 CA, 12 DD and an *Iowa* class battleship was reported sunk near Guam by a submarine (without foundation), 50 CV aircraft raided Tinian disabling the airfield until 1800, 20 CV aircraft bombed Saipan while about 200 landing craft were operating near Saipan harbor. Many transports were seen near Tinian. Patrol aircraft from Truk sighted 2 CV task groups 330 miles north of that island and a third group 350 miles southwest of their base.

The weather near the Bonins was so bad by now that further strikes against Chichi Jima were called off, however a 54 plane sweep of Iwo, launched at 1330, destroyed another 63 Japanese aircraft. One US plane was lost in the raid and another battle damaged machine was destroyed in a deck landing accident upon return to its ship. By 1710 all aircraft were recovered and Clark set course southwest to refuel his destroyers in the heavy sea. When this was complete he set course for the rendezvous. Task Groups 58.2 and 58.3 fuelled to the west of the Marianas.

The American carrier strikes in the Bonins were noted by Admiral Ozawa, who, in the Japanese tradition, was taught to look for flanking attacks. In view of the invasion operations he estimated that such an attack by the Americans was unlikely. The importance of this appreciation of American dispositions will become apparent later.

During the forenoon watch Admirals Spruance and Kincaid held a conference on board the latter's flagship and arrived at the following decision: five heavy cruisers and three light cruisers together with twenty-one destroyers (CRUDIV 6, CRUDIV 12, DESRON 45, DESDIVS 1, 12, 106) would join TF 58 leaving seven old battleships, three cruisers and five destroyers at Saipan, in addition to the CVE groups; six radar equipped PBM (Martin flying-boats) aircraft were to move from Eniwetok to Saipan for 600 mile night aerial searches; those transports which could be moved without endangering the invasion would go to a position 200 miles east of the Marianas until the Japanese threat had passed and the invasion of Guam, which had been scheduled for June 18 would be postponed indefinitely (to be launched July 21). Task Groups 58.2 and 58.3 refuelled to the west of the Marianas so the carriers could search as far to the west as practicable. All fast carrier operations were to be restricted to the neutralisation of Guam and Rota, and searches.

Admiral Mitscher, who felt that the Japanese were about to 'fight or feint', issued this tactical estimate to his ships:

'Believe Japanese will approach from a southerly direction under their shore based air cover close to Yap and Ulithi to attempt to operate in the vicinity of Guam. However, they may come from the west. Our searches must cover both possibilities. Will ask CTG 58.4 and CTG 58.1 to search north and west of us tomorrow.'

A special strike was sent against Guam to crater the runways and destroy aircraft.

Mitscher's analysis is very interesting in view of the following question put to Admiral Ozawa, after the war, and the admiral's response:

'Q. When you first approached the Marianas the night of the 18th–19th with your plan of attacking by air and then bringing the fleet in during the final approach, was the intention to come in straight toward Saipan, or to come from the south or from the north in a flanking attack? In other words were you going to go in straight or come from the side to get the transports?

70

A. The plan was to go direct. It would take too much fuel to take the longer route, which had been considered, but we planned to go in straight and we did not change that plan during the approach. Perhaps a little southerly sag in the line of approach for the sake of air cover, but in the main plans agreed to were straight approach.'

One G4M (Betty bomber) and four B6N (Jill) of NAG 551, from Truk, attacked the American forces, claiming one cruiser sunk and two hit. There is no verification of this attack in USN records.

Ro-44 was cruising on the surface toward Eniwetok, when she was sighted by lookouts on USS *Burden R. Hastings* (DE-19). When she failed to respond to recognition signals the DE sank her.

June 17. USS *Cavalla* (SS-244) had been ordered to relieve *Flying Fish* at San Bernardino. She was proceeding to that station when, at 0510 June 17, she sighted two fleet oilers, one ship of unknown type and three destroyers at 13° 29′ N, 130° 45′ E on course 120° speed 15 knots. She reported this interesting find to her headquarters and was advised, 'Destruction those tankers of great importance. Trail, attack, report.' Unable to close, Commander Kossler followed them, assuming correctly that they would eventually lead to the Japanese fleet. The force *Cavalla* had found was Supply Group 2, which was trailing First Mobile Force and Supply Group 1 which were southeast of SG 2's position refuelling. First Mobile Force continued fuelling on a westerly course on the morning of the 17th until 1300, then turned northeast toward the Marianas. *Cavalla* would continue to follow the Japanese fleet. Supply Group 1 continued westerly to join Supply Group 2, then both groups turned northeast and proceeded to their standy position (14° 40′ N, 134° 20′ E). After sending out anti-submarine patrols at 0535 the Japanese launched two long range searches to the east and south at 0540. The former was composed of 9 D4Y (Judy) from 1 ACS which reconnoitered ahead to 350 miles, while the latter was a five plane group sent to the same range to the south. The former group produced no results and returned at 1115. The southern group lost one aircraft and reported several contacts:

0725 Unidentified cruiser 342°/64 miles from Peleliu.
0830 Surfaced submarine which promptly submerged 218°/23 miles from Peleliu.

Two destroyers were deatched to search for the downed aircraft. First ACS was ordered to determine the location of SG 2 and at

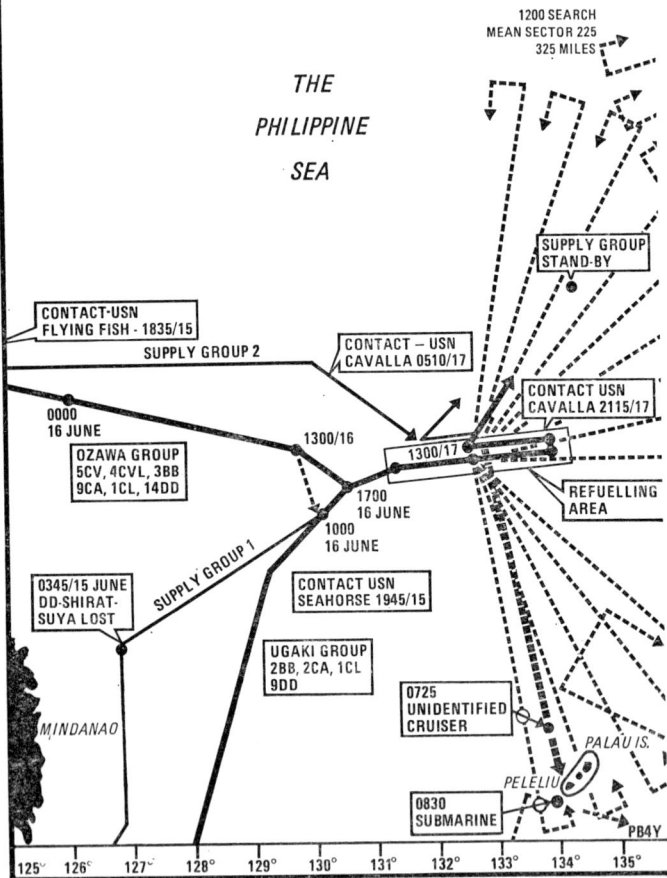

DIAGRAM 3
MOVEMENT of FORCES
16 – 17 JUNE 1944

THE
PHILIPPINE
SEA

1200 SEARCH
MEAN SECTOR 225
325 MILES

SUPPLY GROUP
STAND-BY

CONTACT-USN
FLYING FISH - 1835/15

SUPPLY GROUP 2

CONTACT – USN
CAVALLA 0510/17

CONTACT USN
CAVALLA 2115/17

0000
16 JUNE

1300/16

1300/17

REFUELLING
AREA

OZAWA GROUP
5CV, 4CVL, 3BB
9CA, 1CL, 14DD

1700
16 JUNE

1000
16 JUNE

0345/15 JUNE
DD-SHIRAT-
SUYA LOST

SUPPLY GROUP 1

CONTACT USN
SEAHORSE 1945/15

UGAKI GROUP
2BB, 2CA, 1CL
9DD

0725
UNIDENTIFIED
CRUISER

MINDANAO

PALAU IS.

PELELIU

0830
SUBMARINE

PB4Y

125° 126° 127° 128° 129° 130° 131° 132° 133° 134° 135°

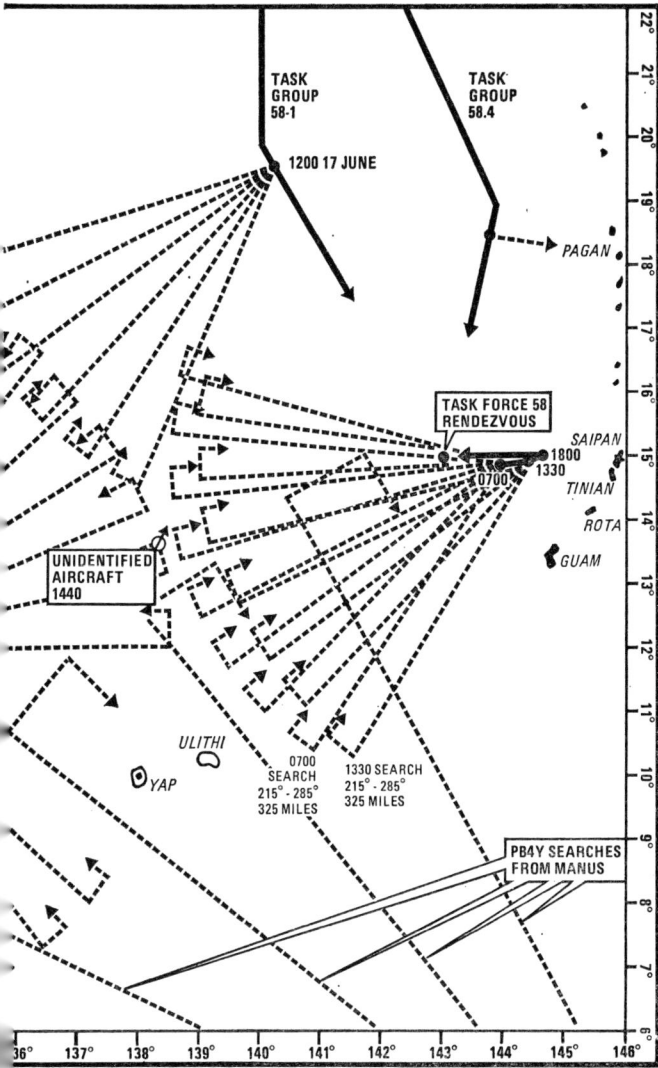

TASK GROUP 58-1

TASK GROUP 58.4

1200 17 JUNE

PAGAN

TASK FORCE 58 RENDEZVOUS

SAIPAN
1800
1330
0700
TINIAN
ROTA
GUAM

UNIDENTIFIED AIRCRAFT 1440

ULITHI

YAP

0700 SEARCH 215° - 285° 325 MILES

1330 SEARCH 215° - 285° 325 MILES

PB4Y SEARCHES FROM MANUS

22°
21°
20°
19°
18°
17°
16°
15°
14°
13°
12°
11°
10°
9°
8°
7°
6°

36°   137°   138°   139°   140°   141°   142°   143°   144°   145°   146°

1000 launched two D4Ys (Judy), which found the tanker group at 1230. Ozawa sent a courier aircraft (a DY4) to Peleliu with the following tactical appreciation:

TOP SECRET 17085

From: Commander First Mobile Force
To: Combined Fleet HQ, Fifth Base Air Force, Central Pacific Fleet.
TEXT: The First Mobile Force, being at location 'E' on the evening of the seventeenth and having finished supplying operations, will advance to a general location west of Saipan by dawn of the nineteenth, going via point 'O'★ at 15.0° N, 136.0° E. In the meantime, this fleet shall guard against westerly advances of the enemy and their movements from the north. The objective is first to shell regular aircraft carrier groups and then, by employing all fighting power, to annihilate the enemy task forces and their invading forces. The following are the requests made of land-based air units:

  1 It is requested that, from the evening preceding the decisive battle, you shall maintain a constant reconnaissance of the regular aircraft carriers of the enemy in the vicinity of the Mariana Islands. If this is impossible, notify us immediately of the condition and deployment of regular aircraft carriers as of noon.

  2 We request intensified patrolling of the area west of the Marianas by each base on the day previous to the decisive battle. Special attention shall be paid to carry on reconnaissance in the sector from 160° to 210° from Iwo Jima.

  3 If the forces of the Yawata unit are not deployed on time, it is believed we shall be forced to delay the decisive battle by one day. Please notify us of such a probability.

En route, the aircraft, which was launched at 1100, encountered two carrier type aircraft at 1410, 053°/630 miles from Peleliu and an unidentified plane at 030°/500 miles from the same island. The time of the second sighting was 1440.

A night search was launched by US TG 58.3 at 0200, thirty minutes

---

★ Translator notes that the point might have been designated 'C' rather than 'O'.

late, because American formation was further east than originally anticipated when it finished fuelling into the wind. Both groups (58.2 and 58.3) remained on a westerly course at 23 knots until 0430 to make up the distance lost in fuelling, recovering the uneventful search at 0700. At that time dawn searches by 8 fighter escorted TBFs (Avengers) from *Enterprise* were launched to cover 215°–285° to 325 miles, when that ship was at 14° 40′ N, 144° E, while Clark's and Harrill's groups were ordered to search between 15° N and 20° N and as far west as possible and to keep the area east of 138° and south of 20° covered. Generally, American searches were conducted by two or three aircraft for each 10° sector, a dive bomber or torpedo plane accompanied by one or two fighters. This allowed for better coordination in attacks on enemy ships or aircraft and increased the probability that the message would get through. The only thing sighted by this search was an AK in sinking condition at 14° 27′ N, 142° 10′ E.

Mitscher recommended the following tactical disposition and movements for Task Force 58 in the forthcoming battle:

A Present status:
  1 Task Group 58.2 is 12 miles south of Task Group 58.3.
  2 Task Group 58.3 will be in Lat. 15° N, Long. 144° 30′ E at 1600 today (June 17).
  3 A search was launched at 1330 distance 325 miles, between bearings 215°–285°. This search is to be recovered about 1830 in vicinity Lat. 15° N, Long. 144° 30′ E.
B Recommended disposition upon the joining of forces from Task Force 51:
  1 Task Group 58.2 composed of carriers, CruDiv 13, DesRon 52, DesDiv 1; 12 miles south of Task Group 58.3.
  2 Composition of Task Group 58.3: CruDiv 12, carriers, DesRon 50 and DesDiv 90.
  3 Task Group 58.7 composed of battleships, CruDiv 6, DesDiv 12 (16 torpedoes each), DesDiv 89, and DesDiv 106; stationed 15 miles west of Task Group 58.3
C 1 If battle is joined before Task Groups 58.1 and 58.3 join us, Task Group 58.2 will be designated battle line carriers.
  2 When Task Groups 58.1 and 58.4 join, propose to put Task Group 58.1 12 miles north of Task Group 58.3 and Task Group 58.4 12 miles south of Task Group 58.2.

3 As soon as Task Group 58.1 and 58.4 join, propose to have *San Juan* join Task Group 58.2 and *Reno* join Task Group 58.3 so that one CL (AA) will be with each carrier group.
4 If battle is joined after Task Group 58.1 and 58.4 join us, Task Group 58.4 will become battle line carrier group.
5 After first air battles have been fought and we have control of the air, recommend CruDivs 10, 13 and 12 and DesDivs 11, 1 and 90 be released from carrier groups to join Task Group 58.7.
6 After initial air battle, or before if it became feasible, recommend Task Group 58.1 take station about 50 miles to north-northwest of Task Group 58.3 in order to hit Japs from northern flank and cut them off from escaping to the north.

D Recommend movement tonight; at 1800 course 310° until reaching Lat. 16° N, then course 270° until daylight launch. It is hoped this will permit us to flank the enemy, keep outside of 400 miles range of Yap and to keep as far from other shore-based air flown in to Rota and Guam as practicable, and still be in position to hit enemy carrier groups (down wind from us).

E As soon as things quiet down a bit, one Task Group at a time should be refuelled in vicinity of Marianas, during which time it can assist Task Force 51 on Guam, Rota, or Saipan as directed.

Mitscher's plan was to make good distance to the west during the night when flight operations were at a minimum – and head easterly toward the next day's rendezvous while operating aircraft. Until contact was made this was the proposed pattern of operations.

Task Group 51.1 arrived at Saipan on this day. This was the Reserve landing force.

At 0800 Admiral Harrill's group (58.4) launched a 35 plane raid against Regan, which damaged some buildings, but had no important results. That afternoon destroyers *Converse* (DD–509) and *Dyson* (DD–572) of Clark's TG 58.1 picked up some survivors from the Japanese convoy hit on June 12–13. They had no useful information. More important, Admiral Harrill's group called off refuelling to insure that they arrived at the rendezvous on time.[*] This decision by Harrill would have an effect on the operations of June 20.

---

[*] TG 58.4 Action report says 'During morning of the 17th destroyers were topped off from heavy ships'. Other sources disagree with this.

Admiral Spruance appraised his tactical situation, recognizing that:

'Enemy forces probably consisting of 5BB, 9CV, 8CA and a number of destroyers were at sea east of the Philippines for the purpose of attacking our amphibious forces engaged in the capture of Saipan. The task of Task Force 58 was to cover our amphibious forces and to prevent such an attack. The enemy attack would probably involve a strike by carrier based aircraft, supported and followed up heavy fleet units. The possibility existed that the enemy fleet might be divided with a portion of it involving carriers coming in around one of our flanks. If Task Force 58 were moved too far from Saipan before the location of the enemy was definitely determined, such a flank attack could inflict heavy damage on our amphibious forces at Saipan. Routes of withdrawal to be northward and to the south-westward would remain open to such a flanking force. The use of enemy airfields on Guam and Rota was available to the enemy except as our carrier-based aircraft were able to keep those fields neutralized.'

With this analysis in mind he issued his battle plan at 1415:

'Our air will first knock out enemy carriers, then will attack battleships and cruisers to slow or disable them. Battle line will destroy enemy fleet either by fleet action *if the enemy elects to fight* or by sinking slowed or crippled ships if enemy retreats. Action against the enemy must be pushed vigorously by all hands to insure complete destruction of his fleet. Destroyers running short of fuel may be returned to Saipan if necessary for refuelling.'

'Get the carriers'; that was what the American carrier sailors wanted to hear, but a careful reading of Admiral Spruance's battle plan should have made it clear to them that Admiral Spruance viewed their role as a shield first and sword second: *'If enemy elects to fight . . .'*

Admiral Mitscher advised his carriers of the make-up of deck load strikes to be launched when the Japanese fleet was found:

'Proposed plan for strike on enemy surface forces: Make deck load launch from CVS consisting of 16 VF, 12 VB, and 9 VT. Second deck load 16 VF and available VB and VT. Second deck load prepared for launch as second wave unless situation indicates delay advisable.

Augment VT from CVLS as practicable. Arming VT: half torpedoes, VB half GP,* half SAP. Later strikes include AP as targets indicate.'

At 1330 afternoon searches were launched from Task Groups 58.2 and 58.3 in accordance with Admiral Mitscher's battle plan outlined above, when those groups had reached 14° 45' N, 144° 13' E, covering to 325 miles. This search was unproductive but several enemy scout planes were shot down in the vicinity of Task Groups 58.2 and 58.3.

Upon joining TF 58, Admiral Spruance signalled Mitscher:

'Desire you proceed at your discretion, selecting dispositions and movements best calculated to meet the enemy under the most advantageous condition. I shall issue general directives when necessary and leave details to you and Admiral Lee.'

At this time the battleships were taken out of the carrier task groups and a separate Battle-Line Task Group (TG 58.7) formed along the probable line of approach of the Japanese, so the confusion of forming a battle force in combat would be avoided, should the necessity arise. Though unorthodox, the loss in anti-aircraft fire-power in each task group was considered to be offset by the offensive advantages gained.

Admiral Nimitz signalled Admiral Spruance:

'On the eve of a possible fleet action, you and the officers and men under your command have the confidence of the naval service and the country. We count on you to make the victory decisive.'

The CVE groups now relieved TG 58.2 and 58.3 in their air support roles. Clark's and Harrill's groups now en route to the fleet rendezvous sent 12 aircraft in air searches to 350 miles and found nothing. Clark felt that if his group and Harrill's headed southwestward they could catch the Japanese fleet in a trap, forcing them into a position of having to fight regardless of the tactical situation. He discussed the idea with Admiral Davison, who was in *Yorktown* as an observer. Davison liked the plan so Clark checked with Harrill, who said no. With Harrill's refusal Clark felt that the risk was too great with his group (2 CV, 2 CVL, 3 CA, 2 CLAA, 12 DD; 135 VF, 77 VB, 53 VB) acting alone so he continued with Harrill toward the fleet rendezvous. Whether Clark's plan would have been approved by Spruance is

---

* GP – General Purpose bomb; SAP – Semi-armour piercing bomb; AP – Armour Piercing bomb.

doubtful, but the plan certainly had interesting possibilities. It is doubtful, as the next two days would show, that Clark's and Harrill's groups would remain undetected for long. The strikes on Iwo Jima and Chichi Jima had made Ozawa sensitive about his northern flank, as noted previously, and as the reader has seen, constant bombardment of Japanese airfields throughout the theatre of operations had not eliminated their very efficient shore based reconnaissance aircraft. A review of the intelligence received throughout the period June 11–17 by Combined Fleet confirms this. Of course, the fact that the Japanese might have known of any independent movements of Clark and Harrill is not conclusive against such operations, but is a factor in considering the chances of their success.

Truk now sent five B6N (Jill) with one J1N (Irving torpedo-bomber) as a pathfinder against the American forces. They hit Captain Carter's tractor group (TG 53.16) of TF 53 at 1750, hitting LCI–468 with a torpedo, killing 15 and wounding three. The ship was so badly damaged that it had to be scuttled. Three of the Japanese aircraft were lost, but the survivors reported sinking a transport and hitting a destroyer.

At 1930 31 A6M (Zero), 17 D4Y (Judy) and 2 P1Y (torpedo-bomber and 2 P1Y from Yap struck at the ships unloading at Charon Konoa (Saipan), hitting LST–84 with a bomb. After this attack they ran across the escort carrier task groups and struck them, getting near misses on *Gambier Bay* (CVE–73) of TG 52.11 and *Coral Sea* (CVE–57) of TG 53.7. *Fanshaw Bay* (CVE–70) was hit on her after aircraft elevator killing eleven men. The latter ship was forced to retire to Eniwetok for repairs. Forty-six FM–2 (Wildcats) were sent out to intercept these raiders, but failed to make contact. Two from *White Plains* (CVE–66) of TG 52.14 were improperly identified and fired upon by friendly ships after being attacked by a four plane section of CAP. Fortunately no one was hurt, but one of the aircraft landed in such a damaged condition that it crashed through the barrier and destroyed five other aircraft. The Japanese attackers reported that they had hit an American Carrier Task Force 30 miles east of Tinian, sinking two or three CVs and leaving another ship burning. It seemed to the Japanese high command that 5 BAF was performing its appointed tasks quite well at this point.

Japanese shore-based search aircraft found four or five CVEs, 5 or 6 BBs, 4 to 6 cruisers, 30 DDs and 60 transports near Saipan and Tinian and six CV, eight BB and 18 cruisers and destroyers north of Rota.

The dismaying report that Saipan Airfield No. 1 (Aslito) had fallen into American hands was received by Admiral Toyoda this day. At the time this report was received Toyoda also received word that air raids continued on all four major islands. (These were now being conducted by the CVE groups.)

At 2115 *Cavalla* found the Japanese Fleet, which had completed fuelling and was headed for battle, at position 12° 23′ N, 132° 26′ E, zigzagging on base course 080°, speed 19 knots reported as fifteen or more large combatants. Actually the Japanese force was about sixty miles further east and north of the position (about 13° N, 133° E) given by *Cavalla*. By 0345 June 18 Admiral Mitscher had received this report, 24 minutes after Spruance. Again, *Cavalla* could not close, so she simply trailed the Japanese. Her persistence would be rewarded. Spruance's and Mitscher's analysis of *Cavalla*'s reports are interesting in the divergence of conclusions reached. Commander Fifth Fleet reasoned:

'It appeared from the *Cavalla* reports, however, that the entire enemy force was not concentrated in one disposition that if the force sighted by the *Cavalla* was the same as that sighted by the *Flying Fish* in San Bernardino Strait, a speed of less than 10 knots had been made good; and that the position of the *Cavalla* contact indicated a possible approach to the Marianas by this task group via the southern flank.'

Of course there was another obvious explanation of the slow advance of FMF, refuelling which was, in fact, the reason. The proximity of fleet oilers should have suggested this. Mitscher's staff felt:

'At this speed the enemy would be approximately 660 miles from Saipan at dawn and 500 miles from our 0530 position. We could scarcely hope to locate and strike the enemy on the morning of the 18th. However, by steaming directly for the enemy's possible 1500 position, we could possibly locate the enemy during the afternoon search, and perhaps, if he maintained his course and speed, hit him with one strike late in the afternoon.'

Two more Japanese submarines were lost on the 17th. *RO-114* was sunk by destroyers *Melvin* (DD-680) and *Wadleigh* (DD-689), while *RO-117* was found by a PB4Y (Liberator) of Eniwetok based VB-109 and destroyed by that aircraft.

Admiral Mitscher now advised his carrier groups that until further notice no attacks on shore targets would be conducted and to stand by for attacks on enemy surface forces. He advised Admiral Spruance that he intended to rendezvous about noon with Task Groups 58.1 and 58.4 on the 18th at 15° N, 143° E. The three task groups (58.2, 58.3, and 58.7) set course northwest until midnight, then west along latitude 16° N. Fighter couriers were sent to Clark's and Harrill's groups to advise them of Mitscher's decision to concentrate before heading west.

PBMs were to search 255°–295° to 600 miles from Saipan that night.

Meanwhile, in the Japanese Fleet the possibility of action the next day was recognized and search plans, make-up of strike groups, flight deck spottings and similar orders were issued.

CHAPTER TWO

The Battle of the Philippine Sea, June 18-20 1944

June 18. First Contacts Between Main Forces

'Our land based search planes cannot cover the sector north and west of Marianas. Our Task Force must depend on its own searches for timely warning of the approach of enemy ships in that area.' Intelligence Annex CTF 58 OPLAN 7-44 of May 16, 1944.

'I humbly relay the message which has been received from the Emperor through the Chief of Staff, Imperial General Headquarters, Naval Section: "This operation has immense bearing on the fate of the Empire. It is hoped that the forces will exert their utmost and achieve as magnificent results as in the Battle of Tsushima." ' This message was sent from Admiral Ozawa to all hands at 0008.

As related earlier, Admiral Mitscher's flagship received *Cavalla*'s report at 0345 on June 18. Upon receipt of the same report Admiral Lockwood ordered submarine group 'Pentathalon' to form a picket line across the projected line of advance of the Japanese Fleet. This placement would provide the opportunity for one of the more spectacular successes of the battle. The boats in that group were *Finback* (ss–230), *Bang* (ss–385), *Stingray* (ss–186), *Albacore* (ss–218) and *Seawolf* (ss–197).

First Mobile Force had reached 13° 50' N, 134° 20' E at 0600 when first stage air reconnaissance was launched. These aircraft, 14 B5N (Kate) from 3 S.F. and two E13A (Jake) of Fifth Squadron, were to cover sector 350°–110° to a range of 425 miles. FMF was on course 060° at speed 20 knots at this time. It seems likely that this search would have discovered any movements attempted by Clark and Harrill. As it was they discovered four American scout aircraft searching in front of Task Force 58. One was seen by aircraft No. 5

at 073°/410 miles from FMF (Grid KI–TSU–4–TE*) at 0840 and three by aircraft No. 1 at 0855 bearing 060°/425 miles (Grid TSU–SHI–1–A) from the Japanese Fleet. The latter group of aircraft was on an easterly course. Task Force 58 launched regular dawn air searches at 0535 to search sector 195°–275° to a range of 325 miles (*Enterprise*–8 VT 235°–275°). Task Groups 58.1 and 58.4 would cover areas north of these searches. Task Group 58.3 was at 15° 52′ N; 141° 49′ E at the time of these launches. These searches found three Japanese aircraft searching ahead of FMF between 0755, at which time TG 58.4 aircraft destroyed a Judy at 15° 19′ N; 138° E, and 0850 when a Jake was destroyed at 12° 35′ N; 138° 09′ E. At 0930 TG 58.4 aircraft splashed a Betty at 16° 38′ N; 141° 09′ E. Thus in the forenoon watch of June 18 main forces made first contact with one another at approximately the same time. It was the last time for two days that the US commander would know as much about his enemy's movements as his enemy knew of his. Two E13A (Jake) from Fifth Squadron and one B5N (Kate) from 3 S.F. failed to return from the Japanese air searches.

At 1200 FMF launched seven D4Y (Judy) from First SF and two E13A (Jake) from 5 Squadron to search sector 340°–100° to a range of 420 miles. Ozawa's force had now reached 14° 40′ N; 135° 40′ E and, simultaneous with the search launch, changed course to 030°. This second search, with the assistance of 5 BAF, produced the first ship contacts in the battle and gave the Japanese a tactical edge they would not relinquish for two days. First however three lesser sightings were received. At 1450 an American flying boat (identified as a PB2Y (Coronado) – probably a PB4Y (Liberator) – was seen at HO–RO–1–TA at 2000 metres altitude by No. 13 aircraft. Forty minutes later No. 3 aircraft saw two American carrier aircraft on a westerly course at RE–SHI–11–CHI. At 1545 1 ACS launched eight fighters and sent them on a vector of 140° to 120 miles in an attempt to catch the PB2Y. It is interesting that the Japanese would send fighters on such a long range interception based on a scout plane report. They did not find the flying-boat. At 1549 No. 17 aircraft sighted two carrier aircraft at NU–RO–3–SU. With this increasing frequency of contacts between the scouting aircraft of the two fleets

* During the war the Japanese used a grid coordinate method of contact reporting known as the *CHI-HE* map grid code. It involved two Kana characters for the major coordinates and a number-*Kana* combination for the minor coordinates.

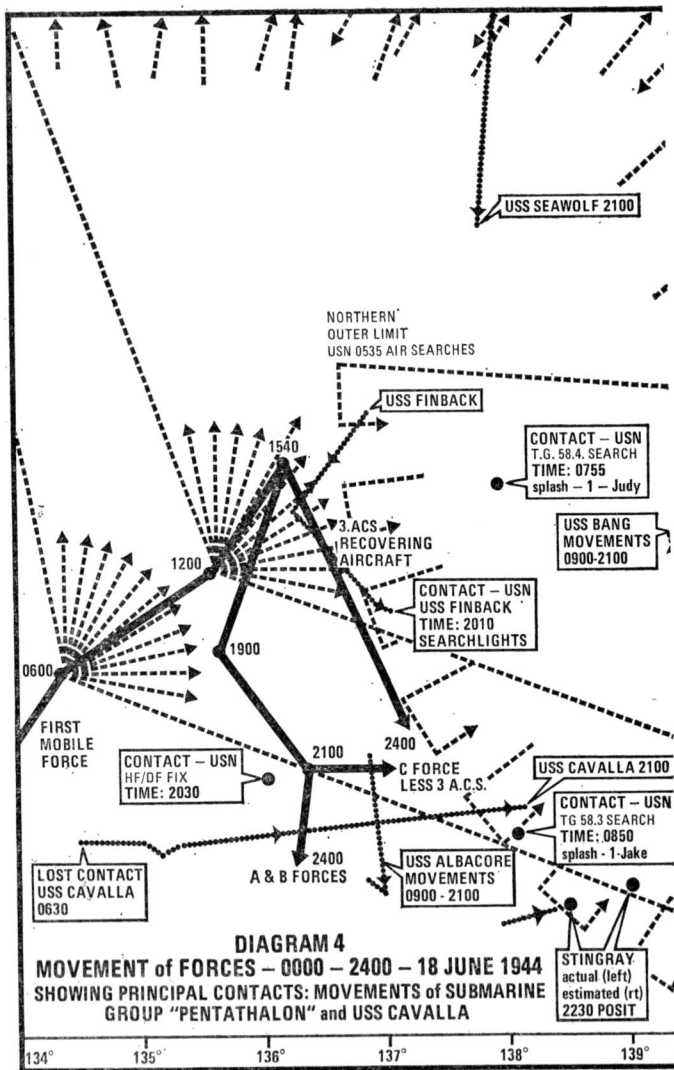

USS SEAWOLF 2100

NORTHERN
OUTER LIMIT
USN 0535 AIR SEARCHES

USS FINBACK

1540

3.ACS
RECOVERING
AIRCRAFT

1200

0600

1900

FIRST
MOBILE
FORCE

CONTACT – USN
HF/DF FIX
TIME: 2030

2100   C FORCE
LESS 3 A.C.S.

2400

2400
A & B FORCES

LOST CONTACT
USS CAVALLA
0630

CONTACT – USN
T.G. 58.4. SEARCH
TIME: 0755
splash – 1 – Judy

USS BANG
MOVEMENTS
0900-2100

CONTACT – USN
USS FINBACK
TIME: 2010
SEARCHLIGHTS

USS CAVALLA 2100

CONTACT – USN
TG 58.3 SEARCH
TIME: 0850
splash - 1-Jake

USS ALBACORE
MOVEMENTS
0900 - 2100

STINGRAY
actual (left)
estimated (rt)
2230 POSIT

DIAGRAM 4
MOVEMENT of FORCES – 0000 – 2400 – 18 JUNE 1944
SHOWING PRINCIPAL CONTACTS: MOVEMENTS of SUBMARINE
GROUP "PENTATHALON" and USS CAVALLA

134°   135°   136°   137°   138°   139°

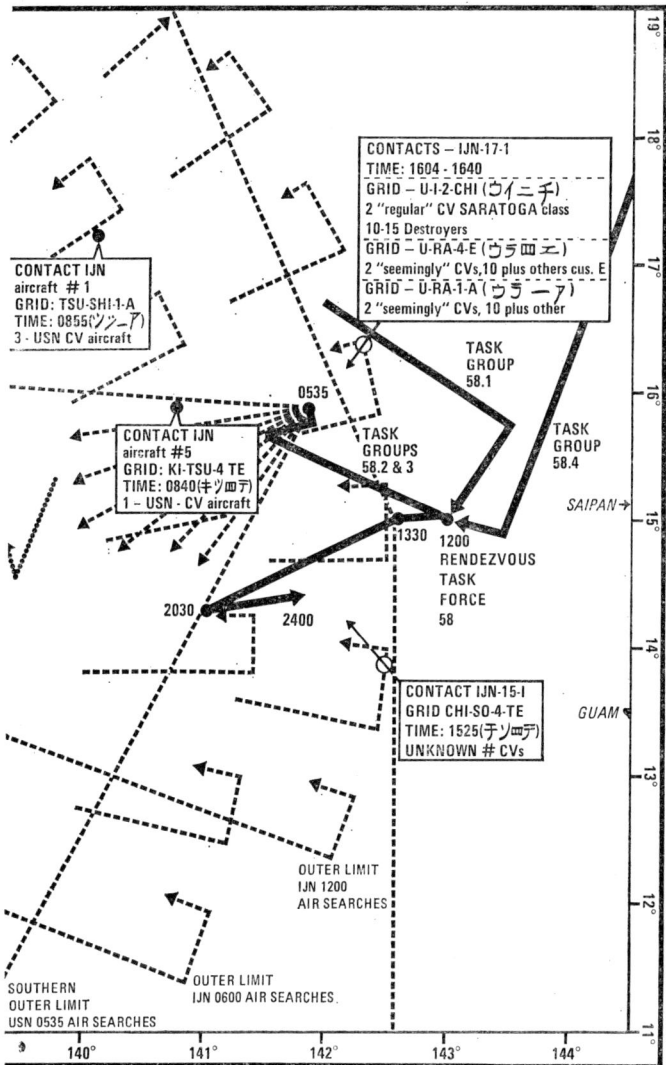

CONTACTS – IJN-17-1
TIME: 1604 - 1640
GRID – U-I-2-CHI (ウイニチ)
2 "regular" CV SARATOGA class
10-15 Destroyers
GRID – U-RA-4-E (ウラ四エ)
2 "seemingly" CVs, 10 plus others cus. E
GRID – U-RA-1-A (ウラ一ア)
2 "seemingly" CVs, 10 plus other

CONTACT IJN
aircraft # 1
GRID: TSU-SHI-1-A
TIME: 0855(ツシ一ア)
3 - USN CV aircraft

TASK
GROUP
58.1

0535

TASK
GROUP
58.4

CONTACT IJN
aircraft #5
GRID: KI-TSU-4 TE
TIME: 0840(キツ四テ)
1 – USN - CV aircraft

TASK
GROUPS
58.2 & 3

SAIPAN →

1330

1200
RENDEZVOUS
TASK
FORCE
58

2030

2400

CONTACT IJN-15-I
GRID CHI-SO-4-TE
TIME: 1525(チソ四テ)
UNKNOWN # CVs

GUAM ◄

OUTER LIMIT
IJN 1200
AIR SEARCHES

OUTER LIMIT
IJN 0600 AIR SEARCHES.

SOUTHERN
OUTER LIMIT
USN 0535 AIR SEARCHES

19°
18°
17°
16°
15°
14°
13°
12°
11°

140°   141°   142°   143°   144°

it was just a matter of time before ship sightings would occur. Between 1525 and 1640 the Japanese received the following reports of American surface forces:

1 1525 Grid CHI–SO–4–TE. Force with unknown number of carriers (15–I★)
2 1600 Grid CHI–RA–0–WO. Force with carriers and several other ships, course west (13–I)
3 1604 Grid CHI–I–4–KE. Task Force including carriers (17–I)
4 1640 Three American groups as follows:
    a Grid U–I–2–CHI. 2 Regular carriers *Saratoga* class, 10–15 destroyers
    b Grid U–RA–4–E. 2 Seemingly carriers, 10 plus other ships, course east
    c Grid U–RA–1–A. 2 Seemingly carriers, 10 plus other ships

The aircraft reporting 4 above was No. 17 and with her sighting report the following additional information was received: Enemy course west, upper cloud layer 9000 metres, cloud cover 7, lower cloud layer 1000 metres, wind velocity 5 metres per second from 100°. In addition to these contacts which were all accurate, Admiral Ozawa received an inaccurate report from Admiral Toyoda placing an American carrier group about 350 miles NNE from the Japanese FMF. This was based on a supposed sighting by a 5 BAF aircraft. Interestingly the latter contact was close to the approximate position Clark's force would have been had he taken the independent course he desired. In any case, because of the range and sector covered by the second Japanese air search it is unlikely any American force operating north of FMF would have been long undetected. Two aircraft failed to return from this important mission, a D4Y (Judy) and a E13A (Jake).

After rendezvous at 1200 and assumption of battle disposition TF 58 sent out afternoon searches to 325 miles covering sector 180° 335° (8 VT LEX; 2 VT ENT 225–275. The time of launch was 1330, when *Lexington* was in 15° 00′ N; 142° 35′ E. They missed the Japanese fleet by about 60 miles, though one of *Hornet's* searchers destroyed a Jake at 1530, bearing 312° 250 miles from TG 58.1 and search aircraft from TG 58.3 reported shooting down a Judy and a

---

★ The Japanese serialized their contacts by the aircraft number followed by the designation of the stage of the search. In this aircraft 15 of I stage has a contact, thus contact '15-I'.

Jake. Closer to the American Task Force, *Cowpens'* combat air patrol destroyed an enemy aircraft at 1315. This intruder had been detected 29 minutes earlier bearing 240° 34 miles from *Cowpens*. At 1354 AA cruiser *Reno* transferred from TG 58.4 to TG 58.3 to bolster the latter group's anti-aircraft defences.

Admiral Mitscher's staff studied the *Cavalla* report and calculated that if the Japanese kept coming and Task Force 58 closed on their projected track afternoon searches would find the enemy at about 1530 at 300 miles range, making a night surface battle a possibility. Mitscher signalled Admiral Lee, the American battleship commander:

'Do you desire night engagement. It may be we can make air contact late this afternoon and attack tonight. Otherwise we should retire to the eastward for tonight. I am requesting Task Groups 58.1 and 58.4 to join today.'

to which message Admiral Lee replied:

'Do not repeat not believe we should seek night engagement. Possible advantages of radar more than offset by difficulties of communications and lack of training in fleet tactics at night. Would press pursuit of damaged or fleeing enemy, however, at any time.'

Though the new battleships were technically excellent there was concern about their tactical effectiveness. During the months of fast carrier operations they had few opportunities to conduct tactical exercises of the type necessary to improve their skills for surface battle, particularly in night fighting, a speciality of the Japanese Navy. Admiral Lee's reluctance does not indicate timidity on his part, in fact his previous record should dispel any suspicions. The problem was that carrier operations had reached such a degree of excellence by this stage of the war that any surface action other than night battle was highly unlikely. This meant the new battleships were now principally a mop-up team for destruction of any cripples created by the carrier aircraft. In any case Spruance threw cold water on any aggressive move far west on the night of June 18–19 when he advised Lee and Mitscher:

'TF 58 must cover Saipan and our forces engaged in that operation. I still feel that main enemy attack will come from the westward but it might be diverted to come in from the south-westward. Diversionary attack may come in from either flank or reinforcements might come from the Empire. Consider that we can best cover Saipan by advancement to the westward during daylight and retiring to the eastward at night so as to reduce possibility of enemy passing us during darkness. Distance which you can make to the westward during day will naturally be restricted by your air operations and by necessity to conserve fuel. We should, however, remain in air supporting positions of Saipan until information of enemy requires other action. Your despatch, consider seeking night action undesirable initially in view of our superior strength in all types but earliest possible strike on enemy carriers is necessary.'

This reversed Mitscher's plan issued on the 17th and approved by Spruance at that time, which called for westward movement at night when air operations were at a minimum and eastwardly in the day when general eastward steaming was dictated in any case by wind conditions. This meant that the fast carriers would remain close aboard the islands until contact was made.

At 1540 Commander Japanese First Mobile Force changed course of his force to 200° to keep the proper attack interval (400 miles) between his force and the Americans, taking full advantage of the range superiority of his aircraft and, perhaps, answering the question of whether a night battle could have been forced on the Japanese the night of June 18-19. Admiral Ozawa was apparently intent on an air battle. The false contact mentioned previously gives one something rarely presented to reviewers of historical events. What would Admiral Ozawa have done had Clark and Harrill, or Clark acting alone, taken the course suggested by Clark on the 17th? To Ozawa it appeared that the Americans had done what Clark proposed and he issued Commander Mobile Force Dispatch Operation Order No. 16 (DTG 181610) which recapitulated the tactical situation as it appeared to him and then stated, 'Mobile Force will retire temporarily, after which it will proceed north and tomorrow morning contact and destroy the enemy to the north, after which it will attack and destroy the enemy to the northeast'.

In the early morning of June 18 nine G4M (Betty) had been sent out of Yap on morning reconnaissance. They found the CVE groups southeast of Saipan. Yap now sent six P1Y (Frances VT) escorted by eleven A6M (Zeke). Palau launched 38 A6M and one D4Y (Judy) against the same target. Both groups failed to find the carriers, fast or escort, but ran upon TG 50.17, the Oiler Group, at 1645 which group was in the process of refuelling four destroyers and destroyer escorts. The aircraft hit three oilers, *Saranac* (AO–74), *Neshanic* (AO–71) and *Saugatuck* (AO–75). The latter two ships had to go to Eniwetok for repairs.

Noting the reconnaissance reports outlined above, Commander 3 SF ordered a deckload strike of 67 aircraft (essentially the raid he would launch the next day) from his ships to attack contact '15–I'. Admiral Obayashi received Ozawa's operation order No. 16 shortly after the first of his aircraft were airborne and upon its receipt felt that it required recall of the raid. Only the contingent from *Chiyoda* was airborne, 3 B6N (Jill), 15 A6M (Zeke VFB) and 4 A6M (Zeke VF), and one of these, a VFB, was lost in recovery. Should this raid have been recalled? On the one hand it would dilute the next day's strikes and, in fact, would leave the vanguard with but one A6M, 1 B6N and 17 B5N (Kate) reducing that group to a scouting force. Because of the range involved, the late hour and Admiral Ozawa's instructions the attackers who survived would have to transfer to Guam and the status of the airfields on that island was unknown. The general lack of success by Base Air Force in its dusk and night attacks (a type attack for which they had trained and for which the carrier pilots had not) certainly indicates that the raid would not have been successful, but its chances should not be dismissed out of hand. The Japanese could reasonably assume the raid would come from an unexpected quarter, when the Americans thought the Japanese carriers were well outside strike range and one or two hits on the American carriers would somewhat offset the failure of 5 BAF. The failure of the all out attack the next day makes support of the abortive raid tempting but for the fact that the Japanese pilots were trained (somewhat) for an all-out daylight attack certainly weighs against its success. Whether Ozawa was correct or not is impossible to know for certain, but Admiral Obayashi's independent action was in keeping with one of the important lessons of 1942. Bearing in mind that in 1942 the quality of aviators on each side as well as the numbers were nearly even that lesson was that the side that strikes first will have the best chance of winning in an otherwise even match. The Japanese 'Impressions and Battle Lessons (Air) in the "A" Operations' contains the following comment on the abortive raid:

'On the 18th, the 3rd flying squadron was determined to attack the enemy as soon as sighted and prepared to return to the carrier, if it was not later than 1400, and to land on Guam, if it was after 1500. But by an order from the operational unit the attack was cancelled. Although the outcome of the attack could not be predicted, a surprise was planned before sunset. If it had been carried out, it could certainly have been a surprise attack, as compared with the attack carried out next morning.

'Under these conditions it would be better to be prepared for an attack immediately after discovery of the enemy. And in case there is a risk of our operation being already known on the day of the attack, it is admittedly necessary to launch a night flanking movement on a large scale in order to administer the first blow on the enemy. If the 3rd flying squadron under the circumstance had reported its plan of attack to the flag commander of the fleet, *there would not have been any blunder*. And in receiving the order of cancelling, if it had any confidence in itself at all, it should have proposed its opinion.'

As if in anticipation of Admiral Obayashi's move Admiral Mitscher advised Task Force 58 (DTG 180449) to recover all aircraft before dusk and then set course into the setting sun to insure that Japanese torpedo aircraft would come from the lightest part of the horizon if the Japanese carriers had closed sufficiently to launch a dusk strike.

Admiral Ozawa's force was now proceeding SSW (200°) with 3 ACS trailing astern after recovering aircraft, when Commander Mobile Force received information from Admiral Toyoda that the target to the north was false. Based on this new data he issued CMF Dispatch Operation Order No. 19 (DTG 181817) which stated that the enemy west of the Marianas was the target for the next day's attack. At 1900 FMF changed course to 140° and speed to 16 knots.

At 2010 USS *Finback* (SS–230) at 14° 19′ N, 137° 05′ E sighted what appeared to be searchlights on the horizon. The lights were likely from light carrier *Chiyoda* recovering aircraft from Obayashi's cancelled raid. *Finback* also reported many enemy aircraft operating in the vicinity of her station during the day. The Japanese vanguard (C Force) was about 70 miles from *Finback*'s reported position, but 3 ACS was somewhat east of Kurita's surface forces.

At 2020 Ozawa broke radio silence to advise 5 BAF of his movements and intentions for the next day. He felt that the risk of discovery was outweighed by the advantage to be gained by a coordinated effort. The failure of 5 BAF to render any assistance the next day should not alter the essential correctness of this decision. The effectiveness of his numerically inferior force would be enhanced if its attacks were reinforced by shore based aircraft. He took the risk and nearly paid the price. US Navy high frequency direction finding (HF/DF) stations received the transmission and identified its source as 'Commander First Mobile Force' estimating the accuracy of the fix as 100 miles. Nimitz passed this valuable information on to Spruance, who received it at 2200. In fact, it gave Spruance a very good fix on Ozawa, placing him at 13° N, 136° E, when his ships were only 40 miles from that position.

At 2030 TF 58 changed course to 080° in keeping with Admiral Spruance's plan to stay close to the islands.

First Mobile Force split at 2100 to assume attack disposition. As mentioned above Spruance received the HF/DF fix and its source at 2200. Mitscher did not receive this information until 2245.

About 2230 Admiral Spruance's staff intercepted a message from Admiral Lockwood (Commander Submarines Pacific) to uss *Stingray* (ss–186) concerning the fact that one of her messages had been badly garbled due to Japanese jamming. Based on their knowledge of *Stingray*'s patrol station they estimated her location as 12° 12′ N, 139° E. Actually she was about 35 miles south by west of that position and about 175 miles ESE of the HF/DF fix. Spruance assumed that *Stingray* had found the Japanese main body, that her radio transmissions were being jammed by the Japanese (something at which the Japanese were quite efficient). Further, he assumed that the radio transmission in the HF/DF fix was a ruse. It seemed to confirm Spruance's desire to steam east during the night. At 2325 Mitscher, after reviewing the HF/DF intelligence which indicated that the Japanese were no longer closing and that TF 58's present course and speed would keep the present interval between the fleets, allowing the Japanese to attack outside US strike range, suggested that TF 58 change course to the west at about 0130 to be in position to launch aircraft as soon as possible the next day. He reasoned, 'that the indicated probable course and speed of the enemy fleet, if combined with a reversal of course to the west on our part, would result in our force attaining the ideal striking distance of 200 to 150 miles at 0500'. His staff felt that the old battleships and escort carriers should be able to handle any flanking Japanese groups reasoning:

'Even if the Japanese were successful in sending a portion of their fleet undetected to a position northeast of Ulithi it was believed that this was not a serious consideration so long as the major portion of the Japanese fleet could be engaged to the westward. The United States had a large force of old battleships, escort carriers, cruisers, and destroyers which could successfully engage any portion of the Japanese fleet, other than their new battleships, in a surface action. In an air action the Japanese would have inflicted some casualties, but the number of fighters in the CVE's would have made this attempt by the Japanese extremely expensive to them. In addition, such a small diversionary force after it once attacked could no longer remain undetected. It could be defeated or beaten off by our forces concentrated primarily for the defence of the amphibious operation, or it would be outflanked by our Fast Carrier Task Force in a sudden reverse to the south if our carrier force was not then engaged with the main Japanese fleet. The worst that could probably happen would have been some losses on our side before the southern diversionary Japanese carrier force could be destroyed. The decision was then reached that even if the Japanese chose to make such a suicidal attempt, our forces could still attack the main Japanese fleet if it approached directly from the west or southwest. It was believed that this decision was in accord with the desires of the Commander in Chief to fight a decisive battle. It appeared that there was nothing the Japanese could do with their fleet to affect seriously the occupation of the Marianas so long as the Fast Carrier Task Forces could engage the major portion of the Japanese fleet. There appeared no reason for not steaming directly for the Japanese fleet as long as our Fast Carrier Task Forces were intact. Even the slight possibility of damage to our landing forces could be avoided if the Fast Carrier Task Forces did not go more than 300 miles from the Marianas without some definite indication as to the location of the main Japanese force, for we could attack a diversionary force as easily from a position 300 miles west (down wind) of the Marianas as we could from the near vicinity of Saipan.'

After discussing Mitscher's proposal with his staff for about an hour Spruance decided that no change in previous plans was appropriate.

As the first day of fighting approaches a short recapitulation of the two fleets is in order. Note particularly the small number of destroyers in First Mobile Force.

US Navy
TASK FORCE 58

A TG 58.1
  CV *Hornet, Yorktown,*
  Belleau Wood, Bataan
  CA *Boston, Baltimore,*
  Canberra
  CL *Oakland*
  DD 14
  (135 VF, 77 VB, 53 VT–265 a/c)

B TG 58.2
  CV *Bunker Hill, Wasp,*
  Monterey, Cabot
  CL *Santa Fe, Mobile, Biloxi,*
  San Juan
  DD 12
  (124 VF, 65 VB, 53 VT–242 a/c)

C TG 58.3
  CV *Enterprise, Lexington,*
  San Jacinto, Princeton
  CA *Indianapolis*
  CL *Reno, Montpelier,*
  Cleveland

  DD 13
  (123 VF, 55 VB, 49 VT–227 a/c)

D TG 58.4
  CV *Essex, Langley, Cowpens*
  CL *Vincennes, Houston, Miami,*
  San Diego
  DD 14
  (88 VF, 36 VB, 38 VT–162 a/c)

E TG 58.7
  BB *Iowa, New Jersey,*
  Washington, North
  Carolina, South Dakota,
  Indiana, Alabama

Imperial Japanese Navy
FIRST MOBILE FORCE

A A Force
  CV *Taiho, Shokaku, Zuikaku*
  CA *Myoko, Haguro*
  CL *Yahagi*
  DD 7
  (79 VF, 77 VB, 51 VT–207 a/c)

B B Force
  CV *Junyo, Hiyo, Ryuho*
  BB *Nagato*
  CA *Mogami*
  DD 8
  (81 VF, 36 VB, 18 VT–135 a/c)

C C Force
  CV *Chitose, Chiyoda, Zuiho*
  BB *Yamato, Musashi, Kongo,*
  Haruna
  CA *Tone, Chikuma, Suzuya,*
  Kumano, Atago, Chokai,
  Maya, Takao
  CL *Noshiro*
  DD 8
  (62 VF, 26 VT–88 a/c)

CA *Minneapolis, New Orleans,*
   San Francisco, Wichita

DD 13

(For a complete tactical organization of both forces see Appendix 1.)

'The Great Marianas Turkey Shoot,' June 19, 1944

'It reads in chapter 49 in the Combat Sutra that "Tactics is like sandals. Those who are strong should wear them. A cripple should not dare to wear them." The plan in operation No *A* is minutely worked out and the strategy of the operational unit has been checked in great detail. But the training for combat duty in each detachment is not complete. Therefore, it looks, as said in the Combat Sutra, as if well-made sandals were allowed to be worn by a cripple.'
Impressions and Battle Lessons (Air) in the 'A' Operations.

The Japanese take up attack disposition: Spruance's decision
At 0038 Spruance advised Mitscher of his decision regarding the proposed course change:

'Change proposed does not appear advisable. Believe indications given by *Stingray* more accurate than that determined by direction-finder. If that is so continuation as at present seems preferable. End run* by other carrier groups remains possibility and must not be overlooked.'

Mitscher's staff could not believe Spruance's decision. They had not intercepted the *Stingray* dispatches. In fact, the submarine had had a fire in her superstructure and her radio difficulties had nothing to do with Japanese Fleet movements. It is strange that Admiral Spruance placed greater reliance on a vague inquiry than he did upon a substantive piece of intelligence, i.e. the HF/DF fix, particularly since the former was 'someone else's mail'. American intelligence had discovered that Japanese carrier doctrine favoured pincer type dispositions and use of decoys, and Admiral Spruance was determined that he would not be lured out of position. Of course, one of the real problems in trying to anticipate what an opponent might be doing is the natural inclination toward placing undue importance on events which indicate that one's theory of enemy intentions is in fact the course of action they have taken. In the analysis of the battle Admiral Spruance enumerated his reasons for not going west that night as:

---

* End Run – American football term meaning flank attack.

A The position of the force located by direction-finder bearings was not definite, being within 100 miles.
B The originator of the enemy radio transmission was not known positively.
C The size and composition of the enemy force concerned was not known.
D It was of highest importance that our troops and transport forces on and in the vicinity of Saipan be protected and a circling movement by enemy fast forces be guarded against.
E There was the possibility that the enemy radio transmission was a deliberate attempt to draw our covering forces from the vicinity of Saipan.
F The fact that a *Stingray* transmission at 2346K in the vicinity of Latitude 12–20 N, Longitude 139–00 E had been jammed by the enemy indicated that *Stingray* might have made contact in that vicinity. *Stingray*'s position was 435 miles, 246° from Saipan.

At 0100 a Japanese aircraft dropped flares near TG 58.1 which was near Lat. 14° 40′ N, Long. 142° 30′ E. Destroyer *Cowell* fired at the intruder which promptly retired. No attack developed and it is assumed that the aircraft came from Guam. *Burns* depth charged the flares in an unsuccessful attempt to extinguish them.

A PBM flying-boat from Garapan (Saipan), part of a four aircraft 600 mile search launched at 2300, covering sectors 245°–265° and 275°–295° picked up 40 ships in two groups about 75 miles northeast of the HF/DF fix at 0115. Due to atmospheric conditions the report of this important find was not received and no one in command position knew about it until the aircraft returned to base at 0845. It has also been suggested that the radio operator on the PBM might have failed to extend the trailing wire antenna used for such transmissions. Whether Admiral Spruance would have allowed the carriers to move west based on this contact is pure speculation, but his reaction to other indications of a concentrated Japanese force made it doubtful that he would have changed his basic tactics on this one additional indication, though the number of ships detected by the PBM closely approximated the Japanese FMF's actual size. Spruance's action report indicates this additional information would not have altered his decision:

'The force sighted by plane 9-V-211 may have been that sighted by *Cavalla* at 2155K, June 17, that sighted by *Finback* at 2110K,

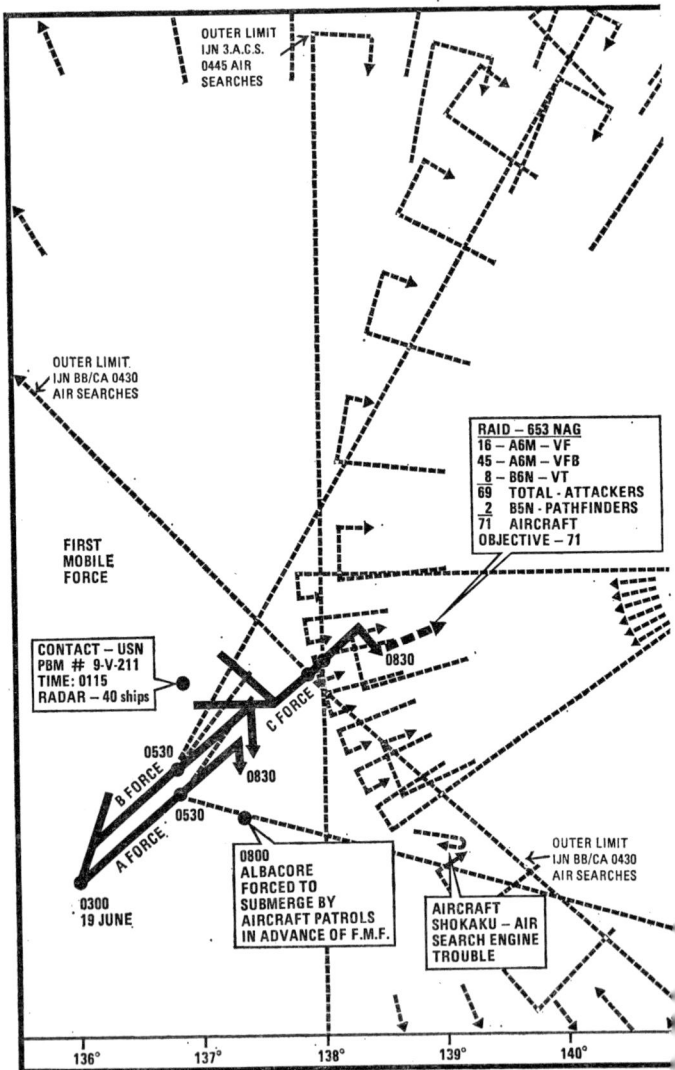

OUTER LIMIT
IJN 3.A.C.S.
0445 AIR
SEARCHES

OUTER LIMIT
IJN BB/CA 0430
AIR SEARCHES

RAID – 653 NAG
16 – A6M – VF
45 – A6M – VFB
8 – B6N – VT
69 TOTAL - ATTACKERS
2 B5N – PATHFINDERS
71 AIRCRAFT
OBJECTIVE – 71

FIRST
MOBILE
FORCE

CONTACT – USN
PBM # 9-V-211
TIME: 0115
RADAR – 40 ships

0830

C FORCE

0530

B FORCE

0830

0530

A FORCE

0300
19 JUNE

0800
ALBACORE
FORCED TO
SUBMERGE BY
AIRCRAFT PATROLS
IN ADVANCE OF F.M.F.

OUTER LIMIT
IJN BB/CA 0430
AIR SEARCHES

AIRCRAFT
SHOKAKU – AIR
SEARCH ENGINE
TROUBLE

136°   137°   138°   139°   140°

96

DIAGRAM 5
MOVEMENT of FORCES 0000 – 0830 19 JUNE 1944
SHOWING AIR SEARCHES AS FOLLOWS:

USN
0200 AIRCRAFT 1V12 - 7V12
SECTOR 240° - 270°
325 MILES
0600 AIRCRAFT - 1V24 - 21V24
SECTOR 185° - 345°
325 MILES

IJN
0430 PLAN 5D - SECTORS 12-19,
16 E13A (MEDIAN SECTOR) #1
050° (SECTOR 315° - 135°)
350 MILES
0445 PLAN 5D - SECTORS - 12-15,
13 B5N, 1E13A; SECTOR #1 090°
(SECTOR 000° - 180° - 300 MILES)
0530 PLAN 8C - SECTORS 12-15 LESS 8
11 D4Y - 2E13A; SECTOR #1 - 050°
(SECTOR 020° - 105° 560 MILES)

CONTACT - IJN - 7-1
GRID: NA - SO - 4-TE
TIME: 0730 (ナ) □ テ
2-CV, 4BB, 10 OTHERS
COURSE-WEST

CONFIRMED 0734
BY A/C # 9-1 AS
4 BB - 10 OTHERS
A/C 7-1 ADDED
4 MORE CVs

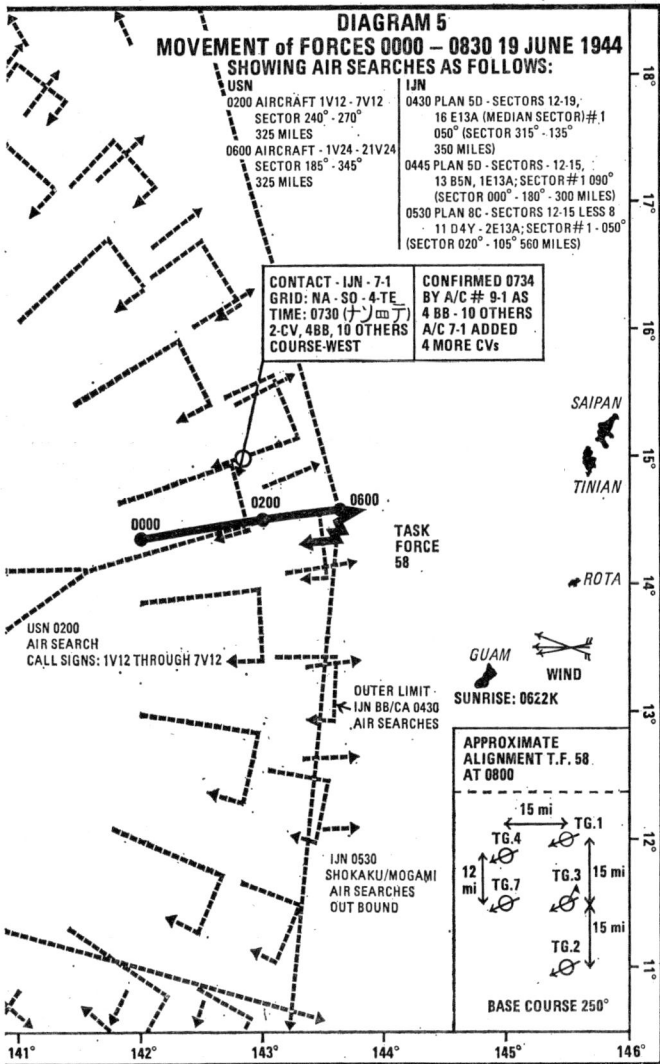

SAIPAN

TINIAN

0000   0200   0600

TASK
FORCE
58

→ *ROTA*

USN 0200
AIR SEARCH
CALL SIGNS: 1V12 THROUGH 7V12

GUAM

WIND

OUTER LIMIT
← IJN BB/CA 0430
AIR SEARCHES

SUNRISE: 0622K

IJN 0530/
SHOKAKU/MOGAMI
AIR SEARCHES
OUT BOUND

APPROXIMATE
ALIGNMENT T.F. 58
AT 0800

├── 15 mi ──┤
TG.4   TG.1

12
mi   TG.7   TG.3   15 mi

TG.2

BASE COURSE 250°

June 18, that located by direction-finder by CinCPac at 2023K, June 18, or that which may have been sighted by *Stingray* at 2300K, June 18. It may have been a concentration of all the groups which had been operating west of our search areas on June 17 and 18. It may have been a concentration of one or more groups, or it may have been a single group. It did not preclude the possibility of a flanking movement to either the north or south as well as a movement from the westward.'

In fact the force sighted was Kurita's vanguard force. Nimitz indicates he felt this sighting should have been sufficient to alter Spruance's tactics (had it been received during the night), hinting a possible dissatisfaction (though never expressed) with Commander Fifth Fleet's movements the night of June 19 when he signalled Spruance:

'We are following with the closest interest your operations around the Marianas and we share with you a feeling which I know you must have – that of frustration in our failure to bring our carrier superiority to bear on the Japanese fleet during the last days. We all understand, of course, that the Japanese had better information of our whereabouts through their shore based long-range search than we had of their locations. It is exasperating to have one of the early reports of the first long-range search conducted from Saipan be delayed eight hours in reaching. Whether or not the situation would have been different had this delay not occurred is, of course, problematical. . . .'

Finback's report of the lights on the horizon at 2010 was received at 0150. The fact that it was in the general area of the HF/DF fix led Spruance to believe it was another ruse. After all, Spruance reasoned, why would a force trying to conceal its movements turn on its lights and transmit long range radio signals?

Task Group 58.3 had reached 14° 30′ N, 143° E at 0200 when USS *Enterprise* (CV–6) launched 14 radar equipped TBFs (Avenger). The aircraft left the carrier and flew on course 255° for 100 miles then split to cover 5° sectors to a range of 225 miles covering sector 240°–270°. They missed Admiral Kurita's C Force by about 50 miles, sighting a friendly submarine, probably *Finback* or *Bang*.

By 0300 the ships of the Japanese First Mobile Force had reached the positions designated for their attack disposition and set attack course. C Force formed a vanguard 100 miles in advance of the main body, which was composed of A Force and B Force. A Force was directly astern of C Force, while B Force was 15 kilometres north of A Force. The disposition course and axis was 050°. Originally B Force was to be ahead of A Force, but, apparently, because of Clark and Harrill's raids against the Bonins, Ozawa covered his big carriers on his northern flank as well as ahead. The ships of C Force were in three circular formations with a carrier at the centre of each formation and the battleships, cruisers and destroyers in a circle around the carriers. That force was formed in a line abreast with 10 kilometre intervals between groups at a right angle to the disposition axis. The six carriers of the main body were in two circular formations screened by battleship *Nagato*, cruisers and destroyers. The bulk of the battleships and cruisers were in the vanguard force. After Midway the Japanese determined that their carriers would get the first contact in future battles. This disposition was designed to insure this by placing the battleships and cruisers ahead of the main body where they could use their scout seaplanes to advantage. Third S.F. provided striking power for the vanguard. The main body was placed astern of the vanguard a distance equal to the difference in strike range of Japanese aircraft (300 miles) and American aircraft (200 miles). Thus in theory the Japanese could stand off and strike the Americans while the vanguard acted as a magnet for any American attacks and at the same time act as a shield. The reader who is familiar with World War I naval tactics might notice an interesting similarity between the Japanese disposition and those used by the British and Germans at Jutland where the battle-cruiser forces formed scouting vanguards 50–75 miles in advance of the battleship main bodies. Much has been written about how much Jutland influenced naval thinking in the US and Royal Navies but the Imperial Japanese Navy was obsessed by that battle as well. The Japanese War History Office has assured the writer that the lessons of Midway were the determining factors in the Japanese disposition and therefore it appears that any Jutland influence was coincidental. The disposition axis was based on the contacts reported the previous day and was actually offset somewhat to the north of Task Force 58's actual position. If Mitscher had come west during the night he probably would have found Kurita almost due west, while Ozawa's main body would have been at about 255° and only 60 miles west of Kurita. At the time Ozawa changed course (0300) *Taiho* was at 12° 20′ N, 136° 25′ E. He also ordered speed increased to 20 knots.

The Morning Watch (0400–0800), The Morning Air Searches and Preliminary Skirmishes

After First Mobile Force had been on attack course for an hour and a half the cruisers and battleships of C Force now at about 13° 15′ N, 138° 05′ E (Grid NO–SA–OO–YU) commenced launching the first stage of the Japanese reconnaissance effort. It was composed of sixteen E13A (Jake) scout seaplanes which were to search 315°–135° to 350 miles. They would reach the end of their outward leg at 0700, spaced about sixty miles apart, turn right about 90°, fly about 30 miles and then turn right again to return to their ships. This would give nearly complete coverage in front of the force and would have very probably discovered Clark's movements had he taken the independent action he desired. Launching was complete by 0445. Ten of these aircraft failed to return. The second phase, composed of 13 B5N (Kate), launched by Admiral Obayashi's carriers together with an E13A (Jake) from cruiser *Chikuma*, were sent out between 0515 and 0520. Their point of departure was the same as that of the first stage. This group was to search sector 000°–180° to a range of 300 miles. It achieved no important results, sighting some destroyers – probably TG 58.7 pickets, Seven were destroyed when they ran afoul of TF 58's dawn searches, primarily *Langley* aircraft. Because of the allocation of aircraft to air searches and air strikes, only combat air patrols were flown over FMF and no aircraft were available for anti-submarine patrols. This cutting of corners, contrary to Japanese doctrine, was to be disastrous.

Cabot detected 2–3 aircraft at 0515, followed at 0520 by another snooper, all of which escaped. Ten minutes later, when the American flagship was at 14° 40′ N, 143° 40′ E, a course change to 090° was ordered when dawn air searches were launched to cover sector 185°–345° (*Lexington*: 9 VT, 5 VF–225°–275°, *Essex* 3 two plane teams). They failed to find any Japanese ships, however the *Essex* contingent reported shooting down 1 Jake, 2 Kates and 1 Jill. Admiral Spruance also asked Admiral Hill to increase his long range shore based patrol aircraft searches and to extend their ranges to 700 miles. Hill received this request at 1200, June 19. At the time of the course change (0530) radars detected 'bogeys' in the direction of Guam. A section of CAP from *Monterey* (CVL–26) was sent to investigate, finding two D4Y (Judy) near that island, shooting one down.

At 0530 aircraft carrier *Shokaku* launched eleven D4Y (Judy), accompanied by two E13A (Jake) from cruiser *Mogami* which were

DIAGRAM 6

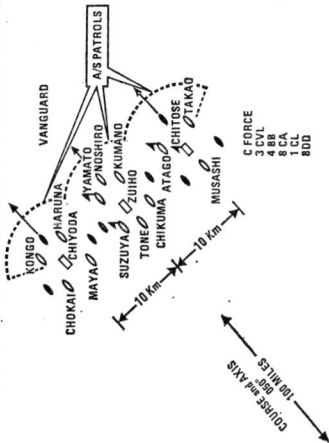

FIRST MOBILE FORCE 19 JUNE 1944

"NUMBER ONE BATTLE DISPOSITION (MODIFIED)"
ZIG-ZAG- FIVE MINUTE INTERVAL.
A/S PATROL NOT FLOWN (NORMALLY
EACH FORCE WOULD LAUNCH 2
B5N/B6N TO COVER 60° ON EACH
SIDE OF BASE COURSE TO 6 KM.)
FOR AIR OPERATIONS:
    CV/BB/CA – 7000 M. CIRCLE
    CL/DD (EXCEPT PLANE GUARD) – 10000 M.
FOR AIR DEFENSE:
    CV/BB/CA – 1500 M. CIRCLE
    CL/DD – 2000 M. CIRCLE
LEGEND:

AIRCRAFT CARRIER	
BATTLESHIP or CRUISER	
DESTROYER	
FLAGSHIP	

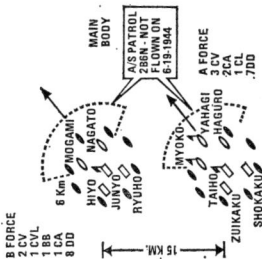

VANGUARD
A/S PATROLS

KONGO
HARUNA
CHIYODA
MAYA
CHOKAI
YAMATO
NOSHIRO
KUMANO
SUZUYA
TONE
ZUIHO
CHIKUMA ATAGO
CHITOSE
TAKAO
MUSASHI

C FORCE
3 CVL
4 BB
8 CA
1 CL
8 DD

COURSE and AXIS
100 MILES

←10 Km.→ ←10 Km.→ ←10 Km.→

B FORCE
2 CV
1 CVL
1 BB
1 CA
8 DD

HIYO
JUNYO
MOGAMI
NAGATO
RYUHO

MAIN
BODY
A/S PATROL
2 B6N - NOT
FLOWN ON
6-19-1944

TAIHO
ZUIKAKU
SHOKAKU

MYOKO
YAHAGI
HAGURO

A FORCE
3 CV
2 CA
1 CL
7 DD

←15 KM.→

to fly to 560 miles covering sector 020°–105°. One hour before sunrise (0622) the Japanese had forty-three scout aircraft airborne, searching for the US Fleet. Shortly after it was launched one of the third wave aircraft turned back due to engine trouble. Her sector was one of the southernmost to be covered and contained no American ships.

Admiral Kakuta ordered the remaining operational aircraft on Truk to proceed to Guam. The former base was able to send 15 A6M (Zeke) and four bombers (type unknown) which left just before 56 USAAF B-24s (Liberator bombers) hit that island. This transfer would bring air strength up to about fifty aircraft of all types, far short of '*A-Go*' plans.

As air activity over Guam increased Spruance suggested that if the Japanese were not found by the dawn searches perhaps a strike against Guam and Rota would be in order. He assumed that the aircraft over Guam had possibly shuttled in from the Japanese carriers during the night. Mitscher begged off,

'Cannot neutralize Rota and Guam due to lack of bombs. Believe best we can do is to watch situation with fighters until they are tired of sending them in. We will have to do something when they start sending them in from the north thru' Pagan.'

The real reason was probably the desire to hit the Japanese carriers with as little diversion as possible and in fact Admiral Montgomery signalled Mitscher, information addressee Admiral Spruance (likely his intended recipient were it not for the chain of command):

'I consider that maximum effort of this force should be directed toward enemy force at sea; minor strikes should not be diverted to support the Guam–Saipan area. If necessary to continue divided effort recommend detachment of sufficient force for this purpose.'

In fact the attacks on Guam were very important in the battle, but the aviators were anxious for a fight with the Japanese carriers.

A group of five or six A6M (Zeke) fighter-bombers, probably from Guam approached picket destroyers *Stockham* (DD–683) and *Yarnall* (DD–541) and one attacked the former dropping a 250 KG bomb which missed. *Yarnall* shot the intruder down at 0550, while CAP destroyed another enemy aircraft at 0554 bearing 205° 37 miles from the force. At 0600 destroyers from TG 58.7 shot down a D3A (Val) possibly from Guam and CAP dispatched a Japanese scout

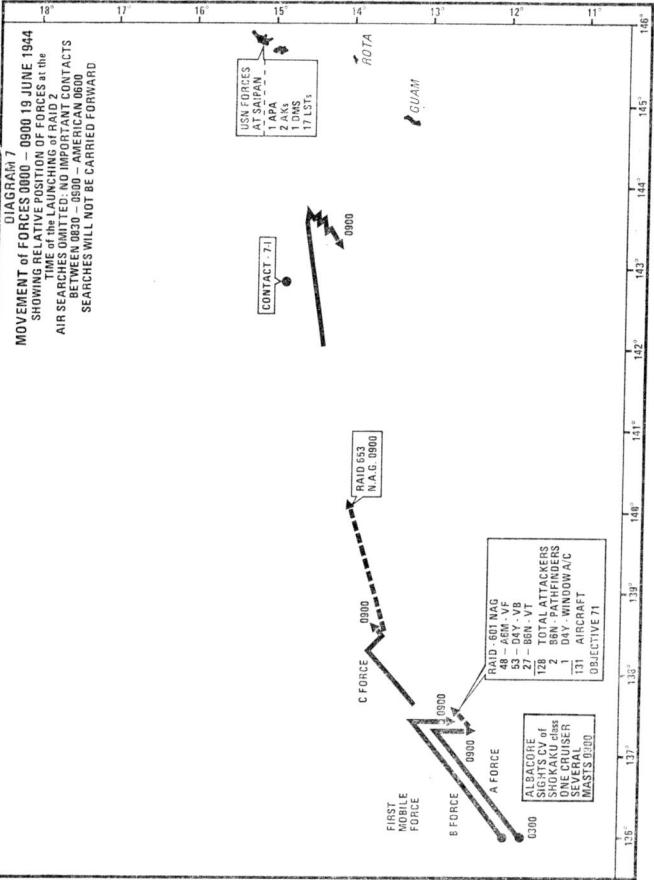

DIAGRAM 7

MOVEMENT of FORCES 0000 — 0900 19 JUNE 1944
SHOWING RELATIVE POSITION OF FORCES at the
TIME of the LAUNCHING of RAID 2
AIR SEARCHES OMITTED: NO IMPORTANT CONTACTS
BETWEEN 0830 — 0900 — AMERICAN 0600
SEARCHES WILL NOT BE CARRIED FORWARD

USN FORCES
AT SAIPAN
1 APA
2 AKs
1 DMS
17 LSTs

ROTA

GUAM

CONTACT : 7-1

RAID 653
N.A.G. 0900

0900

C FORCE 0900

RAID - 601 NAG
48 — AEM - VF
53 — DAY - VB
27 — BEN - VT
128 TOTAL ATTACKERS
2 B6N PATHFINDERS
1 D4Y - WINDOW A/C
131 AIRCRAFT
OBJECTIVE 7-1

0900

A FORCE 0900

FIRST
MOBILE
FORCE

B FORCE

0300

ALBACORE
SIGHTS CV of
SHOKAKU class
ONE CRUISER
SEVERAL
MASTS 0900

plane about 35 miles SSW from TF 58. The American force changed course at 0619 to the southwest to make up some of the distance lost in flight operations. Air activity over Guam was such that a division of CAP from *Belleau Wood* (CVL-24) was sent to investigate at 0630. When they arrived many aircraft were operating around the Guam airfields. The *Belleau Wood* fighters promptly reported this activity. The report was intercepted by CTG 58.2 who passed it on to CTF 58 at 0716, 'We intercepted report from *Belleau Wood* 4 on VHF-1 that six planes were taking off from Guam. Request help.' Task Force 58 changed course to the southeast to launch aircraft. The *Belleau Wood* division was reinforced by aircraft from *Cabot* (CVL-28), which were on a vector to intercept a target in the vicinity of Guam at the time they were ordered to join *Belleau Wood*'s division; *Yorktown* (CV-10), *Hornet* (CV-12) (8-12 aircraft from each ship) with another division from *Belleau Wood* joining, but too late since the Japanese aircraft had landed and were now concealed.

The standard disposition of Task Force 58 for the battle had the three largest carrier groups in a north-south line with TG 58.1 on the northern flank, TG 58.3 in the centre and TG 58.2 to the south, spaced twelve miles apart. A carrier was at the centre of each group and the other carriers were on a 2000 yard circle and the cruisers and destroyers (except plane guard destroyers) on a 4000 yard circle. Task Group 58.7 was fifteen miles west of TG 58.3 in a similar formation with battleship *Indiana* in the centre as guide and the remaining battleships, cruisers and destroyers on a 6000 yard circle. Task Group 58.4 operated north of TG 58.7 and west of TG 58.1 and acted as battle line carrier group with orders to 'furnish CAP, ASP, and other air operations desired by him (CTG 58.7) . . .' In fact, each carrier group operated independent of the other groups when conducting flight operations and the disposition was rarely in alignment. Generally when operating aircraft a group would turn into the wind simultaneously however TG 58.1 employed a different method which was designed to reduce fuel consumption, particularly in the destroyers. The carrier(s) operating aircraft would proceed to the downwind side of the formation, building up flight operations speed, then turn into the wind and only when necessary would the remainder of the formation change course. This reduced the number of times the entire formation had to increase speed considerably and also reduced the amount of distance lost to the west.

Number seven aircraft of the first phase searches (an E13A) made the first contact of this day with the US fleet at Grid NA–SO–4TE (264°, 160 miles from Saipan), reporting two large aircraft carriers, one with CAP aloft, four battleships and ten other ships on course west, designated contact '7–I'. The time was 0730. Aircraft number 9 confirmed this sighting four minutes later, as four battleships and ten other ships (No. 9 did not report carriers and its sighting might have been TG 58.7). These reports were the northern groups, probably Harrill's TG 58.4 and Lee's TG 58.7. The pilot of No. 7 aircraft soon added four more large carriers (probably TG 58.1) and reported that the weather in the vicinity of the US fleet was, '. . . clear. Cloud cover 8, lower cloud cover level at 300 metres, visibility 10 nautical miles.' The initiative was completely in the hands of the Japanese and they now prepared to launch an all out attack on the US Fleet.

'The Turkey-Shoot' begins

Except for the wind, the weather could not have been better for Task Force 58. Ceiling and visibility were unlimited and more important the atmospheric conditions were such that contrails formed at the aircraft wingtips at very low altitudes. This coupled with the almost complete lack of clouds allowed American CAPs to see the incoming Japanese aircraft at unusually long ranges.★ Wind was 9–12 knots from the east forcing the US force to steam away from the Japanese when operating aircraft. Temperatures were in the mid-80s. At 0800 TF 58 was on course west, speed 24 knots.

USS *Albacore* (SS–218) was forced under by a Japanese aircraft patrolling ahead of FMF at 0800.

Shortly after 0800 TF 58 changed course into the wind in response to a large group of bogeys which appeared on radar over Guam, then bearing SW 81 miles. By 0807 three Task Groups (58.1, 58.2 and 58.3) had 36 fighters (12 each) airborne and headed toward that large bogey (TG 58.4 did not send aircraft against this raid). At this time Mitscher received the PBM report of the night before and ordered TG 58.4 to cancel its portion of the Guam sweep until that contact had been analysed. *Essex* action report contains the following entry: '0820 Several bogeys 170° 75 miles on course 080°, evidently headed for Guam. Faded from our radars at 0829. Dispositions to south of us may have attempted interception, but no

---

★ Tally-ho of Raid 1 (NAG 653) was at 35 miles.

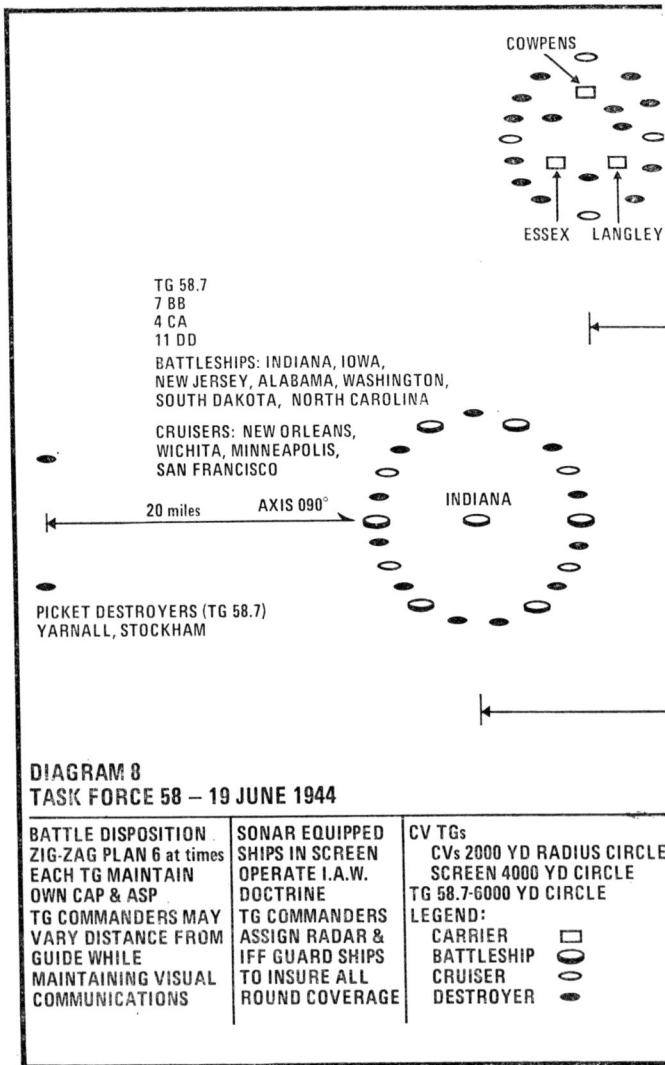

COWPENS

ESSEX LANGLEY

TG 58.7
7 BB
4 CA
11 DD
BATTLESHIPS: INDIANA, IOWA,
NEW JERSEY, ALABAMA, WASHINGTON,
SOUTH DAKOTA, NORTH CAROLINA

CRUISERS: NEW ORLEANS,
WICHITA, MINNEAPOLIS,
SAN FRANCISCO

20 miles   AXIS 090°   INDIANA

PICKET DESTROYERS (TG 58.7)
YARNALL, STOCKHAM

DIAGRAM 8
TASK FORCE 58 — 19 JUNE 1944

BATTLE DISPOSITION ZIG-ZAG PLAN 6 at times EACH TG MAINTAIN OWN CAP & ASP TG COMMANDERS MAY VARY DISTANCE FROM GUIDE WHILE MAINTAINING VISUAL COMMUNICATIONS	SONAR EQUIPPED SHIPS IN SCREEN OPERATE I.A.W. DOCTRINE TG COMMANDERS ASSIGN RADAR & IFF GUARD SHIPS TO INSURE ALL ROUND COVERAGE	CV TGs CVs 2000 YD RADIUS CIRCLE SCREEN 4000 YD CIRCLE TG 58.7-6000 YD CIRCLE LEGEND: CARRIER □ BATTLESHIP ⬯ CRUISER ⬯ DESTROYER ⬭

TG 58.4
1 CV
2 CVL
3 CL, 1 CLAA
14 DD

CRUISERS: SANDIEGO,
VINCENNES, HOUSTON,
MIAMI

BATAAN   BELLEAU WOOD

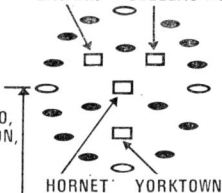

TG 58.1
2 CV
2 CVL
3 CA
1 CLAA
14 DD

CRUISERS: OAKLAND, BOSTON,
BALTIMORE, CANBERRA

HORNET   YORKTOWN

12 miles

— 12 miles —

ENTERPRISE   PRINCETON

TG 58.3
2 CV
2 CVL
1 CA
2 CL, 1 CLAA
13 DD

CRUISERS: RENO, MONTPELIER,
INDIANAPOLIS,
CLEVELAND, BIRMINGHAM

SANJACINTO   LEXINGTON

- 15 miles —

12 miles

WASP   MONTEREY

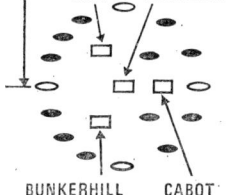

TG 58.2
2 CV
2 CVL
3 CL, 1 CLAA
12 DD

CRUISERS: SAN JUAN, MOBILE,
BILOXI, SANTA FE

BUNKERHILL   CABOT

evidence.' About 30–35 enemy aircraft were encountered in the air and a like number destroyed, either in the air or on the ground. The air activity over Guam and the presence of the Japanese fleet to the west caused Admiral Mitscher to comment, 'We were probably due for a working over by both land based and carrier based aircraft and it was desirable for us to destroy as many land based aircraft as possible before the carrier planes came in,' somewhat reversing an attitude mentioned earlier.

At 0807, after receiving the '7–I' contact, Ozawa turned A and B Forces due south to keep the range between forces at about 380 miles to his main body, while C Force turned southwest to close slightly and launch aircraft. Anxious for a fight, Admiral Obayashi had aircraft airborne from his three light carriers, *Chitose*, *Chiyoda* and *Zuiho*, as quickly as possible. First *Chitose* launched two B5N (Kate) as pathfinders at 0800. These were followed shortly by 653 Group's First Special Attack Unit (*Tokubetsu Kogeki Tai*) of 45 A6M (Zeke) fighter-bombers each with a 250 KG bomb (551 lb), 16 A6M (Zeke) fighters as escorts and eight B6N (Jill) with 1761 lb 18-inch torpedoes.* The aircraft were evenly divided among the three carriers. Their objective was the American force designated '7–I'. Third ACS had shot its bolt by 0830 and at 0900 Obayashi turned northwest away from the American force to keep his force outside US strike capabilities. One of the search aircraft (a B5N) of 3 SF found an American battleship group (Lee's TG 58.7) at Grid RE–I–3–TSU at 0820, but failed to report its finding until it returned to its ship. Because of the great range, the Japanese air attack leaders were instructed to determine the fuel status of their aircraft after their attacks. If they had sufficient fuel to return to their ships then they should do so. If not, they should land on Guam, rearm and refuel, hitting the Americans on the return flight.

By 0824 the 36 F6Fs which had been sent by TGs 58.1, 58.2 and 58.3 (12 from each group) reached Guam and in a fight that lasted over an hour shot down about thirty A6M (Zeke) and five bombers of various types. Most of these aircraft were from the Truk group mentioned earlier. In spite of this working over Guam continued sporadic operations throughout the day.

When the Americans were found, the attack leaders of *Taiho*'s

---

* Not the famous '*Long Lance*' which was a shipboard weapon and weighed 6107 lbs, 1664 lbs more than an unloaded Jill. Sources which refer to Japanese aerial torpedoes as 'Long Lance' are incorrect.

group, led by Lt Takashi Ebata, came to Admiral Ozawa's operations room and declared that the disgrace of Midway would be avenged. Similar meetings took place on *Junyo* and *Chitose*, flagships of Admirals Joshima and Obayashi. The leaders were instructed to concentrate on the American carriers. After the first mentioned meeting First S.F. now at $12°39'$ N, $136°58'$ E, launched a very large raid composed of 27 torpedo equipped B6N (Jill); 53 D4Y (Judy), each armed with a 500 KG (1102 lb) bomb; escorted by 48 A6M (Zeke) fighters. The time of the launch was 0856 and the course to objective was given as $064°$. This raid was preceded by two B6N pathfinders and its target was designated as '7–I'. In addition to the pathfinders and main raiders, *Taiho* launched a D4Y (Judy) equipped with fifteen packages of 'Window'.* This aircraft's mission was to proceed to a point northeast of TF 58 in an attempt to draw off some of the American CAP. As will be seen, this little diversion worked well, but had little effect on the outcome of the battle. One wonders why the Japanese did not use more 'Window' in their attacks. Eight of the aircraft of this raid had various mechanical difficulties and returned to their ships.

About an hour after being forced to submerge by Japanese patrol aircraft, USS *Albacore* sighted a large Japanese aircraft carrier (either *Shokaku* or *Zuikaku*), a cruiser and several masts at 13,000 yards with 70° angle on the bow. Commander Blanchard turned his boat to close to attack range. While approaching this target he saw a second carrier, a cruiser and several destroyers in much better position for attack, only 10° angle on the bow. Commander Blanchard changed course for a 70° starboard track. By 0901 the range had closed to 9000 yards, track distance 2300 yards with an angle on the bow of 15° when a destroyer crossed through his line of sight masking the target. Blanchard changed course to north to clear the destroyer and at 0904 when he put his periscope up for another check the range had closed to 5300 yards with a track distance of 1959 yards. The carrier's speed was estimated at 27 knots and she was launching aircraft. At 0906 Blanchard made one last check, then at 0908, when he raised the 'scope for the firing run the torpedo data computer malfunctioned. Blanchard quickly brought his 'scope down, checked the computer and found the malfunction could not be rectified and decided to fire 'by the seat

---

* 'Window' – Strips of aluminium foil dropped from an aircraft to interfere with radar reception.

of his pants'. Setting his six torpedoes for an extra wide spread Blanchard fired, based on hand calculated TDC computations, at 0909.32. He dove deep and heard one torpedo hit. Blanchard reported probable damage.

Warrant Officer Sakio Komatsu in an A6M had just completed his take off from Admiral Ozawa's flagship *Taiho*, when he sighted one of *Albacore*'s torpedoes. He crashed his aircraft destroying one of the torpedoes. Only one of *Albacore*'s 'fish' hit. The damage seemed insignificant.

Eleven F6Fs (Hellcats) from uss *Essex* (cv–9) led by Lt Cdr C. W. Brewer were flying CAP over TG 58.4 at 0910. At 0927 three of them were vectored onto a bogey, which they tally-hoed at 0950. It was a TBF (Avenger) with an inoperative IFF. Admiral Lee asked Admiral Reeves the course and speed of his force at 0925 and at 0930 Reeves responded, 'Mike Baker Corpen 250, Tackline Speed 18, Swing it 6'.* One minute later Admiral Clark advised his group that he had a bogey bearing 014°/40 miles. At 0935 a four plane division from uss *Bataan* (cvl–29) was ordered to investigate the contact which was now at 000°/36 miles from Clark's group. When they tally-hoed at 0938 (at 355°/33 miles) from the force a lone A6M was found, low on the water, and was promptly shot down, at 0940, and the division returned to its CAP station missing a target, when sent on another vector.

One of *Hornet*'s search aircraft encountered a Zeke at 14° 27′ N, 143° 20′ E and shot it down at 0935.

Plane 15 of the *Shokaku/Mogami* air searches was on its return leg at 0945 when it found three American carriers accompanied by five battleships and ten other ships at grid *KO-KI-3-U*, which worked out about 70 miles southwest of Guam. This was probably Montgomery's TG 58.2, but due to compass error was reported considerably south of its actual position. This contact was designated '*15-Ri*'.

The large raid from NAG 601 passed over the vanguard at 1000. Through mistaken identification the ships of Kurita's C Force opened fire shooting down two of the raiders and damaging eight more to such a degree that they were forced to turn back. The remainder now turned towards contact '*7-I*'. This little incident points up one of the problems of large scale operations; insuring that one's own forces do not get into a fight through mistaken identification.

---

* 'MB Corpen 250/speed 18 swing it 6'= My Base Course 250°, Speed 18, Zigzag Plan 6.

Why the Japanese allowed this raid to fly over the vanguard is a mystery though it seems that the offset approach was designed to focus American attention on the bearing of C force and away from the main body.

At 1000 one American carrier, one light carrier, one battleship and five destroyers were found at Grid *NA-SHI-2-SHI*, fifty miles north of '*7-I*', by aircraft No. 3 of the third phase reconnaissance and designated '*3-Ri*'. Second ACS was just starting to launch its attack on '*7-I*' when the '*3-Ri*' contact was received and this raid, composed of 15 A6M (Zeke) fighters, 25 A6M fighter-bombers and 7 B6N (Jill) torpedo planes, was diverted to the newly discovered target. This target was very likely TG 58.4 or TG 58.1, but due to compass error, was plotted considerably to the north of the actual location of those forces. The change of target was transmitted to the pilots of NAG 652 at 1030.

While the aircraft of NAG 601 were being shot down by their own ships and those of NAG 652 were taking off, the planes of Group 653 were beginning to appear on the radars of TG 58.7, uss *Alabama* reporting a bogey at 265°/125 miles/angels 24.[*] This contact was promptly confirmed by uss *Iowa*. The time was 1000. At 1004 all ships which had not previously done so sounded 'General Quarters'. Admiral Mitscher transmitted the brevity code signal '*Hey Rube*'[**] to his fighters at this time. The 'prepare to launch all fighter aircraft' was given at 1010 by CTF 58. Admiral Reeves group now reported 'Large bogey 265°/105 miles, course 085°'. Mitscher also ordered all bombers and torpedo-planes to take off and rendezvous east of the Task Force to keep flight decks clear of anything but fighters. At this time the carriers had been spotted for deckload strikes for the eventuality of early discovery of the Japanese fleet about as follows: cvs 16 VF, 12 VB, 9 VT and 12 VF, 4 VT on the cvls, the fighters being used in CAP. All attack aircraft on hangar decks were degassed and disarmed to reduce fire hazard. Admiral Mitscher ordered all Task Groups to 'Stay on course into wind. Set fire control radar silence (conditions) and assume air defense formation'. *Izard* relayed a request by CTG 58.2 to Mitscher asking permission to launch additional fighters. CTF 58 promptly authorized this in a blanket order to all carriers to launch additional fighters. By this time,

---

[*] Angels – CIC code for Altitudetimes 1000 feet – Angels 24=24000'.
[**] *Hey Rube* – CIC code for all fighters return to mother ship.

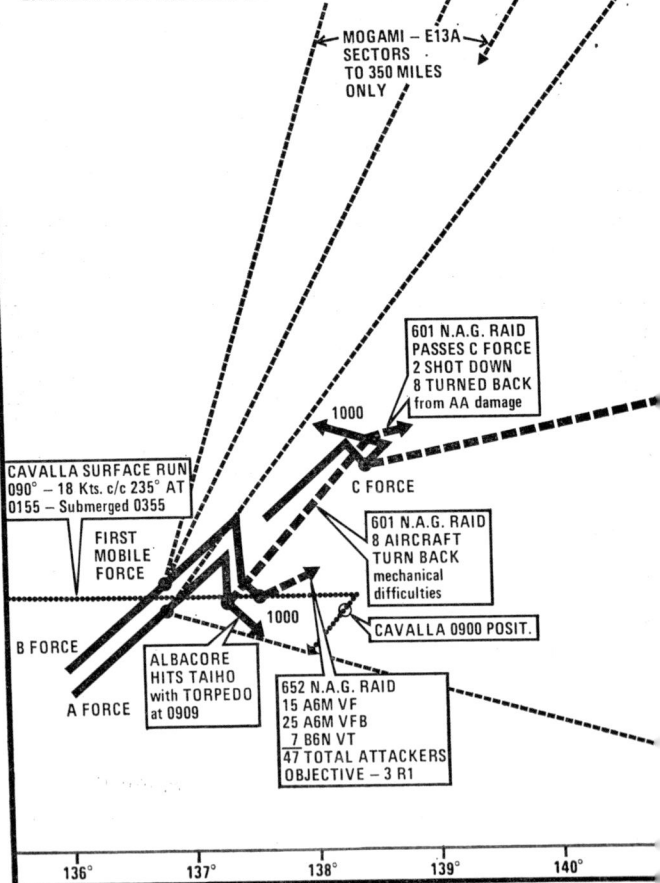

DIAGRAM 9
MOVEMENT of FORCES 0400 – 1000 19 JUNE '44
SHOWING RELATIVE POSITION of FORCES at
the TIME of the LAUNCHING of RAID – 3
SHOKAKU/MOGAMI AIR SEARCHES SHOWN
BECAUSE of 3RI and 15RI CONTACTS
BALANCE of IJN and USN AIR SEARCHES OMITTED

← MOGAMI – E13A →
SECTORS
TO 350 MILES
ONLY

601 N.A.G. RAID
PASSES C FORCE
2 SHOT DOWN
8 TURNED BACK
from AA damage

1000

CAVALLA SURFACE RUN
090° – 18 Kts. c/c 235° AT
0155 – Submerged 0355

FIRST
MOBILE
FORCE

C FORCE

601 N.A.G. RAID
8 AIRCRAFT
TURN BACK
mechanical
difficulties

B FORCE

1000

CAVALLA 0900 POSIT.

A FORCE

ALBACORE
HITS TAIHO
with TORPEDO
at 0909

652 N.A.G. RAID
15 A6M VF
25 A6M VFB
7 B6N VT
47 TOTAL ATTACKERS
OBJECTIVE – 3 R1

136°   137°   138°   139°   140°

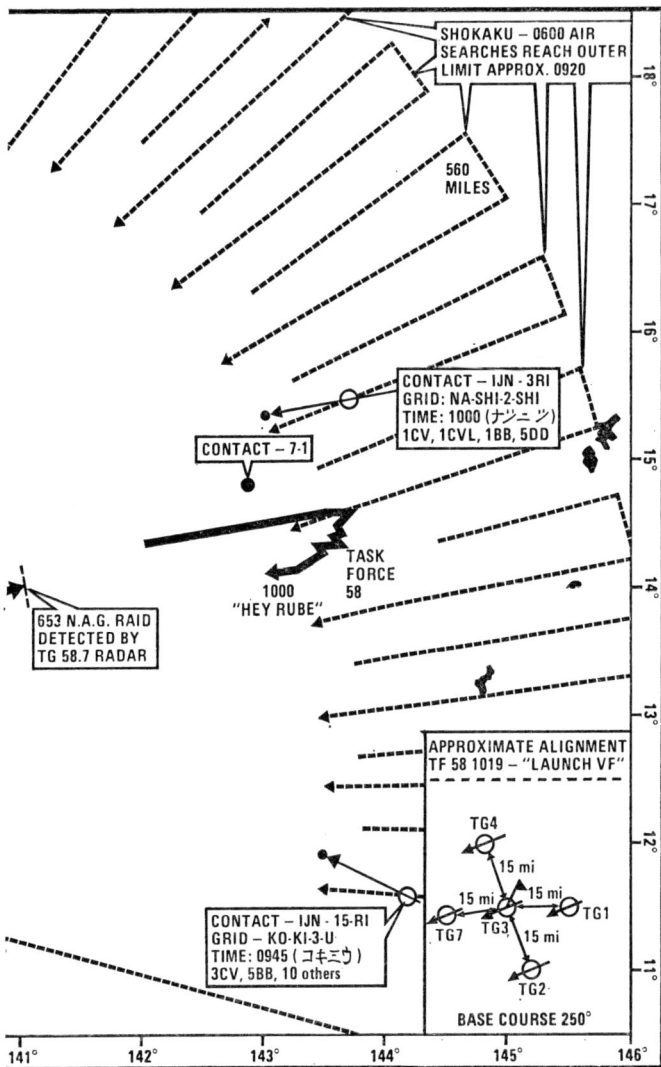

SHOKAKU – 0600 AIR
SEARCHES REACH OUTER
LIMIT APPROX. 0920

18°

560
MILES

17°

16°

CONTACT – IJN · 3RI
GRID: NA·SHI·2·SHI
TIME: 1000 (ナジ·ニ·ジ)
1CV, 1CVL, 1BB, 5DD

15°

CONTACT – 7·1

TASK
FORCE
58
1000
"HEY RUBE"

14°

653 N.A.G. RAID
DETECTED BY
TG 58.7 RADAR

13°

APPROXIMATE ALIGNMENT
TF 58 1019 – "LAUNCH VF"

12°

TG4

15 mi

15 mi   15 mi
TG7   TG3   TG1
15 mi
TG3

CONTACT – IJN · 15·RI
GRID – KO·KI·3·U
TIME: 0945 (コキ三ウ)
3CV, 5BB, 10 others

11°

TG2

BASE COURSE 250°

141°   142°   143°   144°   145°   146°

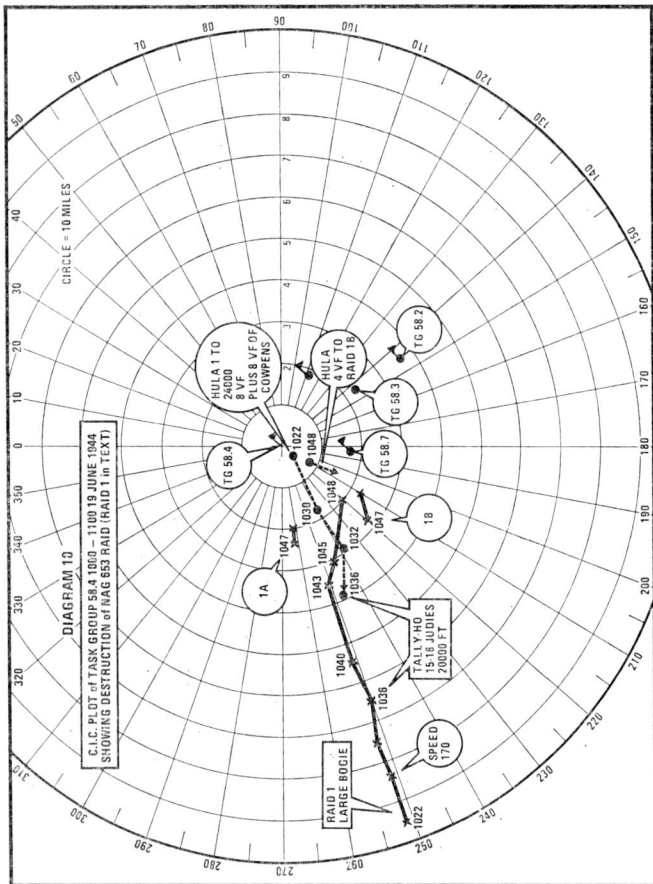

DIAGRAM 10

C.I.C. PLOT of TASK GROUP 58.4 1000 – 1100 19 JUNE 1944
SHOWING DESTRUCTION of NAG 653 RAID (RAID 1 in TEXT)

CIRCLE = 10 MILES

HULA 1 TO
24000
8 VF
PLUS 8 VF OF
COWPENS

HULA
4 VF TO
RAID 1B

TG 58.2

TG 58.3

TG 58.4

TG 58.7

1022
1049

1048

1030

1047

1045

1032

1043

1036

1B

1A

1040

1036

TALLY-HO
15-16 JUDIES
20000 FT

SPEED
170

RAID 1
LARGE BOGIE

1022

114

because of the scale of air operations that morning, the alignment of the disposition of TF 58 had changed considerably.

The Japanese attack commander now made a serious tactical blunder which allowed the Americans to clear their decks as ordered above. He ordered his aircraft to orbit for final instructions and to insure proper formations etc. Whether this decision was crucial will never be known, suffice it to say that the only chance the Japanese had for success was for them to strike quickly without regard for losses. This would not have happened in 1942 and is indicative of the drop in the quality of Japanese leadership in the air.

By 1013 NAG 653's raid had closed to 118 miles and was bearing 250° from uss *Essex* (cv–9). Combat Air Patrol was ordered to 24,000 feet to standby and at 1022 eight *Cowpens* (cvl–25) F6Fs (Hellcats) were ordered on a vector (first vector of the day against Japanese carrier based aircraft) to intercept the raid now tracking on radar at 254°/93 miles/angels 22. These aircraft were followed by eight *Essex* fighters at 1024. The raid was now tracking at 268°/93 miles/angels 22 by TG 58.3. The two groups which were vectored were promptly replaced in standing cap by fresh fighters from the carriers, setting the pattern for the day; fighters sent on a vector against a raid promptly replaced on station. In TG 58.2 the same target was tracked at 1010 by *Cabot* bearing 270°/133 miles. *Monterey* followed at 1013 with a bogey at 275°/125 miles. *Bunker Hill* was ordered to provide high cover over TG 58.2 at 18,000 feet while a division of *Monterey* fighters were placed at low altitude along the attack bearing. Each carrier in TG 58.2 handled its own fighter direction. Task Group 58.3 was tracking the incoming raiders; 265°/72 miles at 1029; 1034, 265°/63 miles; 1039, 270°/48 miles, many friendly aircraft attacking.

At 1035 Lt Cdr C. W. Brewster of vf–15 (uss *Essex*) signalled TF 58, 'Tally-ho, Raid one bears on 255°. Distance from disposition 55 miles. Estimate 24 Rats, 16 Hawks, no Fish at 18,000'* (Actual composition 16 vf, 45 vfb, 8 vt). The Japanese formation was stacked with fighters on each flank and high cover above and behind at about 20,000 feet. Brewer heading the first division of *Essex* 'Hellcats' and Lt (jg) C. R. Carr commanding the second division bracketed the Japanese formation. Brewer claimed three Judys (actually Zeke vfb which looked somewhat like Judy though the latter was an in-line

---

* Rat – Fighter (enemy); Hawk – dive bomber (enemy); Fish – Torpedo plane (enemy).

engine aircraft while Zeke was a radial engined machine) and a Zeke while Carr claimed four Judys and a Zeke. During this short action Carr counted seventeen oil slicks and splashes and the *Essex* divisions were credited with 21 kills (11 VFB and 10 VF). The *Essex* fighters were joined by the eight *Cowpens* aircraft and three divisions from *Bunker Hill* (CV–17), and probably one division each from *Princeton* (CVL–17), *Lexington* (CV–16), *Cabot* (CVL–28) and *Monterey* (CVL–26). The latter two claimed two Judys, one Jill and 23 Zekes. Three F6Fs on ASW patrol from *Bataan* (CVL–29) also joined in this interception bringing the total to about fifty F6Fs against the 69 attackers. About forty of the Japanese attackers broke through this initial onslaught and at 1047 TG 58.4 radars picked up two groups, both evaluated as 'few bandits' at 260°/20 miles and 220°/18 miles from TG 58.4, designated Raid 1A and 1B respectively (by TG 58.4). At 1048 a division of *Essex* F6Fs (Hellcats) were vectored onto each of these contacts. After this interception radars showed few scattered single bogeys from 210°–250°, 15–30 miles as some of the raiders continued on through the gauntlet and found picket destroyers *Yarnall* (DD–541) and *Stockham* (DD–683). A few attacked the destroyers, but some pressed on toward TG 58.7, where they and the F6Fs chasing them (a division of *Bataan* fighters had now joined in the melee) were met by intense anti-aircraft fire. At 1049 a Zeke VFB hit USS *South Dakota* (BB–57) with a 250 kg bomb killing 23 men and wounding 23. The hit did not effect the battleship's fighting efficiency. *South Dakota* claimed the aircraft, but *Alabama* crewmen said it escaped. Near misses were obtained on *Minneapolis* (CA–36) and *Wichita* (CA–45), but neither ship suffered any damage. As the air battle approached the ships CTG 58.3 signalled, 'Try to avoid shooting down own planes. They are our best protection'. followed at 1054 with, 'Small group flying low 225°/15 miles closing'. By 1100 TF 58 radars were clear of bogeys and Raid 1 was over. Eight A6M, 13 A6M VFB and six B6N returned to their ships. All carrier groups were ordered to, 'Land, service, rearm and launch Guam fighters as soon as possible', to insure that CAP was sufficient to repel any incoming raiders, in accordance with Admiral Mitscher's appraisal of the tactical situation, 'Expect repeated attacks. Keep planes available to repel these attacks. Land planes as necessary.'

The Japanese air attack coordinator, noting the devastating fire of the battle line advised the later raids to take courses to avoid this group. This transmission was intercepted by TF 58 radio intelligence per-

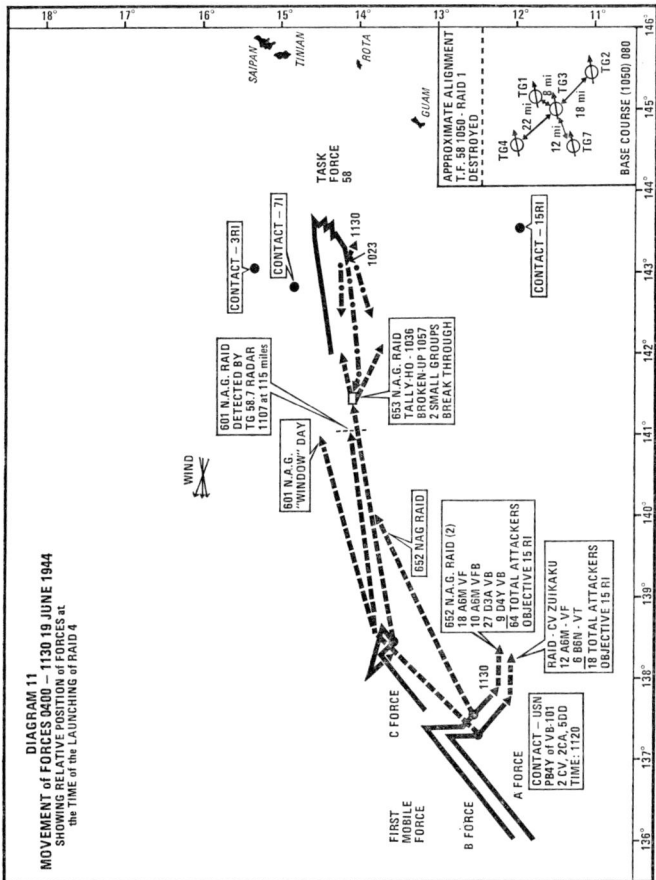

DIAGRAM 11
MOVEMENT of FORCES 0400 – 1130 19 JUNE 1944
SHOWING RELATIVE POSITION of FORCES at
the TIME of the LAUNCHING of RAID 4

WIND

FIRST MOBILE FORCE

B FORCE

A FORCE

C FORCE

1130

1130

CONTACT – USN
PB4Y of VB-101
2 CV, 2CA, 5DD
TIME: 1120

RAID. CV ZUIKAKU
12 A6M - VF
6 B6N - VT
18 TOTAL ATTACKERS
OBJECTIVE 15 RI

652 N.A.G. RAID (2)
18 A6M VF
10 A6M VFB
27 D3A VB
9 D4Y VB
64 TOTAL ATTACKERS
OBJECTIVE 15 RI

652 NAG RAID

601 N.A.G.
"WINDOW" DAY

601 N.A.G. RAID
DETECTED BY
TG 58.7 RADAR
1107 at 115 miles

653 N.A.G. RAID
TALLY HO. 1036
BROKEN-UP 1057
2 SMALL GROUPS
BREAK THROUGH

1023

1130

CONTACT – 3 RI

CONTACT – 7 RI

CONTACT – 15 RI

TASK FORCE 58

SAIPAN

TINIAN

ROTA

GUAM

APPROXIMATE ALIGNMENT
T.F. 58 1050 - RAID 1
DESTROYED

TG1
TG3
TG2
TG5
TG6
TG7
TG4

22 mi
9 mi
12 mi
18 mi

BASE COURSE (1050) 080

117

sonnel and was assumed to be the reason for the offset approach of Raids 3 and 4.

While Raid 1 was underway TG 58.1 radars detected a bogey north of that force at about 60 miles at 1042, closing. At 1047 the bogey began to open and a division of *San Jacinto* (CVL–30) fighters (call-sign 'Longhorn 1' on TG 58.1 CIC plot) attempted interception, but the contact 'turned away' and faded from TG 58.1 radars at 1052. Perhaps this was one of the B5N (Kate) pathfinders launched with Raid 1.

At 1030 Vanguard Force (C Force) changed course to southeast to roughly parallel A and B Forces' course. The only contact which had not received attention by now was '*15 Ri*', the mistaken report of an American Task Group (probably Montgomery's) 70 miles southwest of Guam. *Zuikaku* and the three ships of 2 S.F. (*Junyo*, *Hiyo*, *Ryuho*) mustered a raid of nine D4Y (Judy), 27 D3A (Val), 6 B6N (Jill), 10 A6M VFB escorted by 30 A6M (Zeke) fighters. The entire raid was airborne by 1130.

Admiral Reeves felt the orbiting bombers and torpedo planes could be put to better use and at 1103 signalled Mitscher, 'My 190005 (1005K) Desire issue following instructions my airborne deckloads before fuel depletion; *Enterprise* VT search 10° sectors to 250 miles median line 260° true. Attack groups follow along median thirty miles behind. Search plane retire on contact concentrate and attack in coordination other planes.' This search-attack method was standard American doctrine in 1944 and would be used with success at Leyte Gulf, but this day the range would be too great. Mitscher responded, 'Approved, approved, wish we could go with you,', however the heavy radio traffic prevented dispatch of the necessary orders and the raid never materialized. Seven minutes later CTF 58 ordered strike groups to hit Guam if fighter cover was available.

A Manus based PB4Y of VB–101 found *Shokaku*, *Zuikaku*, 2 cruisers and 5 destroyers at 12° 03′ N, 137° 30′ E at 1120.

At 1107 the large raid from 1 S.F. appeared on TF 58 radars at 115 miles bearing 260° from TG 58.1, estimated as 50 bogeys. By 1109 the raid was plotted at 250°/112 miles apparently in orbit (repeating the error of Raid 1). At 1117 TG 58.4 opened fire on an aircraft to the south which turned away. Whether this was one of Raid 2's pathfinders or a friendly is not known. One minute later TG 58.3 had two small bogeys at 290°/20 miles and 165°/15 miles. They merged at 1120 when bearing 295°/15 miles. The source of these contacts is likewise unknown. By 1123 Raid 2 had closed to 250°/108 miles from TG 58.4 (reported at the same time by *Montpelier* (CL–57) at 252°/89 miles) and three minutes later that group vectored twelve *Essex* fighters at 24,000 feet. Task Group 58.3 plotted the raiders at 265°/100 miles at 1126. The radar plot in TG 58.1 flagship showed Raid 2 at 245°/88 miles at angels 20, composed of 20 aircraft at 1130 (at 1132 TG 58.3 held contact at 255°/80 miles) and at 1133 the raid appeared to split on the radars of TG 58.1, the main group merging with the US fighters at 1136. When Raid 2 had reached a position 248°/60 miles from TG 58.4 the three divisions of *Essex* fighters tally-hoed (time 1139) reporting the enemy formation as 30–40 aircraft, mostly 'hawks' at 18,000 feet, bearing 260°/60 miles on TG 58.3 radars and 280°/65 miles from TG 58.2. As soon as the size of the raid was determined fourteen F6Fs from *Cowpens* were vectored out at 1142 to assist the *Essex* fighters which were now tearing up the Japanese formation. *Wasp*, *Cabot* and *Monterey* divisions joined in claiming 21 aircraft destroyed. Early in the action, Commander McCampbell, leader of the *Essex* group advised TF 58 that the Japanese flight leader and his wingman had been shot down in the first minutes of the interception and because of the numbers the Japanese lost in the initial fight he doubted that any would break through, however the merged plot continued to close the force on Task Force radars. About three small groups totalling about twenty aircraft did break past the first line of interceptors. The first group was picked up on radar at 1151 bearing 230°/30 miles at low altitude, evaluated as torpedo planes, and two minutes later two groups (designated 2A and 2B by TG 58.4), at 245°/23 miles and 221°/30 miles respectively. TG 58.3 showed these contacts at 250°/20 miles and 285°/19 miles. A division of *Essex* fighters was vectored onto each of these small raids at 1154. Admiral Reeves ominously signalled, 'Torpedo planes approaching astern, torpedo planes approaching astern.' The group which TG 58.1 had tracked as a split at 1133 was tally-hoed at 1159 and reported as 10 aircraft. These groups were also hit by 16 F6Fs from *Yorktown* (CV–10) as they approached TG 58.7. Two Jills made for *South Dakota* and were taken under fire by *Alabama* and driven off. *Indiana* (BB–58) was crashed at the waterline by one of the Jills. Fortunately the torpedo's warhead didn't explode and the battleship suffered minor structural damage only. Two Judys went after *Alabama* and a Jill headed for *Iowa* but neither ship was hit. About six Judys continued past the battle line and at 1200

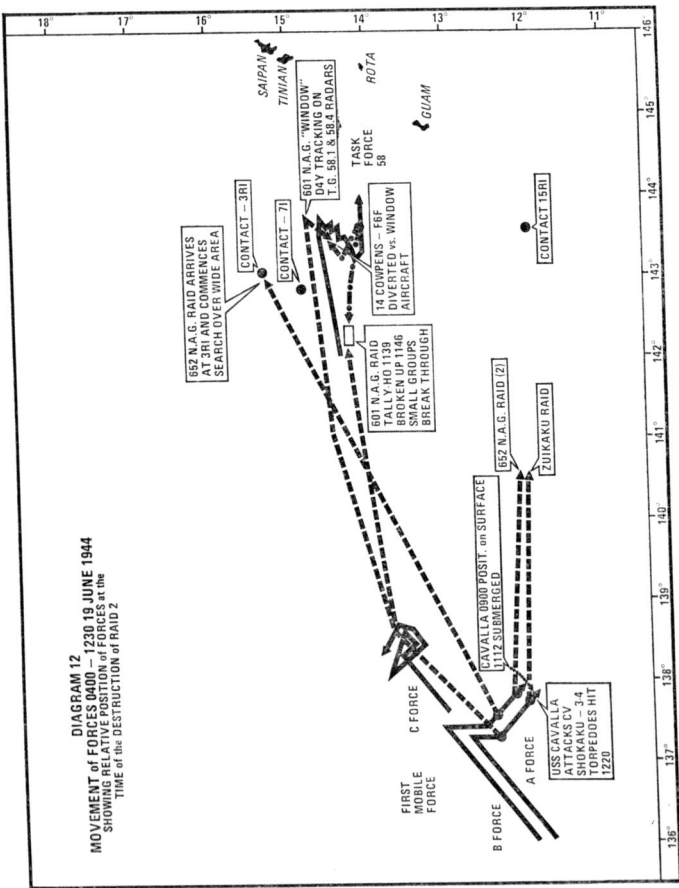

DIAGRAM 12
MOVEMENT of FORCES 0400 — 1230 19 JUNE 1944
SHOWING RELATIVE POSITION of FORCES at the
TIME of the DESTRUCTION of RAID 2

SAIPAN
TINIAN
ROTA
GUAM

601 N.A.G. "WINDOW"
DAY TRACKING ON
T.G. 58.1 & 58.4 RADARS

TASK
FORCE
58

CONTACT — 3RI
CONTACT — 7I

14 COWPENS — F6F
DIVERTED vs. WINDOW
AIRCRAFT

CONTACT 15RI

652 N.A.G. RAID ARRIVES
AT 3RI AND COMMENCES
SEARCH OVER WIDE AREA

601 N.A.G. RAID
TALLY HO 1139
BROKEN UP 1146
SMALL GROUPS
BREAK THROUGH

652 N.A.G. RAID (2)

ZUIKAKU RAID

CAVALLA 0900 POSIT. on SURFACE
112 SUBMERGED

FIRST
MOBILE
FORCE

C FORCE

A FORCE

B FORCE

USS CAVALLA
ATTACKS CV
SHOKAKU — 3,4
TORPEDOES HIT
1220

forward AA control on *Wasp* (CV–18) reported two bogeys at 20,000 yards on the starboard bow. Sector control on that ship was advised that the aircraft were not friendly and they were tracked until they passed behind the superstructure and into the ship's aft AA control group. They were now evaluated as friendly, when suddenly one made for the *Wasp* dropping its 500 kg bomb before it was destroyed. The bomb, a phosphorus type, exploded above the flight deck killing one man and wounding twelve, but otherwise not seriously damaging the ship, though the phosphorus pieces were a dangerous nuisance. Another bomb hit about 200 feet off the port beam of *Wasp*, causing no damage. Two of the Judys went for *Bunker Hill* and both got very near misses, killing three and wounding 73, damaging the side aircraft elevator, starting several small fires, blowing an F6F overboard and knocking out the hangar deck aviation gasoline system for several days. Only two of these attackers survived, one heading for Guam while the other landed on Rota. Two parachutes were seen and another aviator was seen thrown from his aircraft as it struck the water. There is no indication that any of these aviators were picked up. The remaining torpedo planes, numbering about six went after TG 58.3 losing four of their number to anti-aircraft fire and causing that group some exciting moments as the following extract from TF 58 signal log indicates:

Time	From	To	Message
1154	CTG 58.3	TG 58.3	Torpedo planes 270–11 closing, out.
1156	CTG 58.3	TG 58.3	Small group torpedo planes 240–19 closing also group 230–20 closing out.
1157	CTG 58.3	TG 58.3	Large bogey 257° 55 closing out Emergency 4 Turn★ Emergency Turn 5 Comdesron 50 Acknowledge.★★
1158	CTG 58.3	TG 58.3	Large bogey 252–42 closing low out.
	CTF 58	CTG 58.3	The Jap air commander said that he would make his attack later out.
1159	CTG 58.3	TG 58.3	Mike Corpen 150. ComDesRon 50 Acknowledge.

★ 4-Turn – Simultaneous turn to port 40°.
★★ Turn-5 – Simultaneous turn to starboard 50°.

1200	CTG 58.3	TG 58.3	Small bogey 4–6, 225–40 closing Angels low.
	CTG 58.3	CVL–30	Do not launch any more ASP.* over.
1201	CTG 58.3	CVL–30	Did you receive my last transmission over.
	CVL–30	CTG 58.3	Affirmative, Wilco. Four gone.
1202	CTG 58.3	TG 58.3	Emergency Tackline 5 Turn. Comdesron 50 acknowledge over
	CDR 50		Wilco out.
1203	CTG 58.3	TG 58.3	Look out for torpedoes on starboard hand. Out.
1204	CTG 58.3	TG 58.3	Mike Corpen 060.** ComDesron. Acknowledge over.
	CTG 58.3	TG 58.3	Small group 2–3 planes 255–26 closing. Out.
1205	CTG 58.3	TG 58.3	Group bogeys 295–40 Angels 4, closing. Out.
1207	CTG 58.3	TG 58.3	Execute to follow, Break Turn 100. ComDesron 50 Acknowledge, Over.
1207	CTG 58.3	TG 58.3	Execute turn 100.*** *San Jacinto* acknowledge, over.

One of these torpedo planes managed to drop its weapon, which exploded in the wake of *Enterprise*. *Princeton* was the target of three Jills about noon and had to manoeuvre radically to avoid the wreckage of one of the torpedo planes. At 1158 TG 58.4 radars picked up 'few bogies' at 350°/35 miles and at 1159 a division of *Cowpens* F6Fs were diverted from Raid 2 to investigate this contact. At 1204 the bogey disappeared from TG 58.4 radars while at 298°/28 miles and the *Cowpens* division was recalled to its CAP station. This contact was very likely the 'Window' equipped Judy from *Taiho* (Refer also to TG 58.1 plot; 'Window' contact probably Raid IX on that plot). By 1208 there were a few single bogeys scattered outside twenty-five miles and three minutes later TG 58.4 reported all radars clear of enemy aircraft. All fighters were recalled for

---

* ASP – Anti-Submarine Patrol.
** Mike Corpen 060—my course is 060°.
*** Turn 100 – Execute simultaneous turn to course 100°.

refuelling. TG 58.2 kept 12 *Wasp* and 8 *Monterey* fighters in CAP. Task Group 58.3 reported 'scattered bogies' until 1246. Only sixteen A6M, 11 D4Y and four B6N (of 48 A6M, 53 D4Y, 27 B6N) survived this raid.

'The Turkey Shoot' concluded

At 1148, four hundred miles to the west of the air battles described above, USS *Cavalla* (SS-244), one of the most persistent participants in the battle, sighted an aircraft carrier of the *Shokaku* class, two cruisers and a destroyer. Lt Cdr Kossler now commenced a sub-merged approach on a 90° starboard track intending to conduct a bow tube attack. The carrier (which was *Shokaku*) was conducting flight operations. Though the destroyer (*Urakaze*) appeared to be in position to prevent the submarine attack she apparently did not see *Cavalla*'s periscope and after Kossler saw *Shokaku*'s colours, '. . . the Rising Sun, big as hell,' he fired six torpedoes at 1200 yards. As the torpedoes passed *Urakaze* the destroyer came to life and turned on *Cavalla*. The submarine went deep as at least three and perhaps four of her torpedoes hit the carrier at 1220. As *Shokaku* dropped out of formation *Urakaze* stood by while other destroyers dropped over 100 depth charges, many quite close to *Cavalla*. The submarine escaped and later surfaced and sent the following message:

'Hit *Shokaku* class carrier with three out of six torpedoes at 0215 . . . accompanied by two *Atago* class★ cruisers three destroyers possibly more . . . received 105 depth charges during three hour period . . . supersonic gear out of commission . . . hull induction flooded . . . no other serious trouble . . . sure we can handle it . . . heard four terrific explosions in direction of target two and one half hours after attack . . . believe that baby sank.'

She did.

Spruance ordered Saipan based aircraft to 'Get additional patrol planes as soon as you can handle them. Increase night search to 700 miles' at about 1200. At 1241 CIF 58 ordered, 'Launch search planes at same time as yesterday, same areas and same calls.'

At noon C Force changed course to the northwest to clear the battle area and about the same time A and B Force changed course to the east to close '15–*Ri*'.

★ Actually *Myoko* class.

RAID 3
FEW

1156
1200
1201
1202
1203
FADE
1204

14 COWPENS
VF - RECALLED
AFTER ORBIT
and SEARCH
1204

14 COWPENS
VF VECTOR
TO RAID 3
1159

2A

1155
1153
1156
1151

TALLY-HO
30-40 BANDITS

1139
1141
1146
1142 1144 1148 1150 1152
1140

2B

1130
1139

RAID 2
MANY
Sp. 170

RAID - 2
DESTROYED
EXCEPT FOR
SMALL GROUPS
SPLIT & UNCO-ORD-
INATED RAIDS
2A & 2B

310 320 330 340 350 0
300
290
280
270
260
250
240
230
220
210 200 190

124

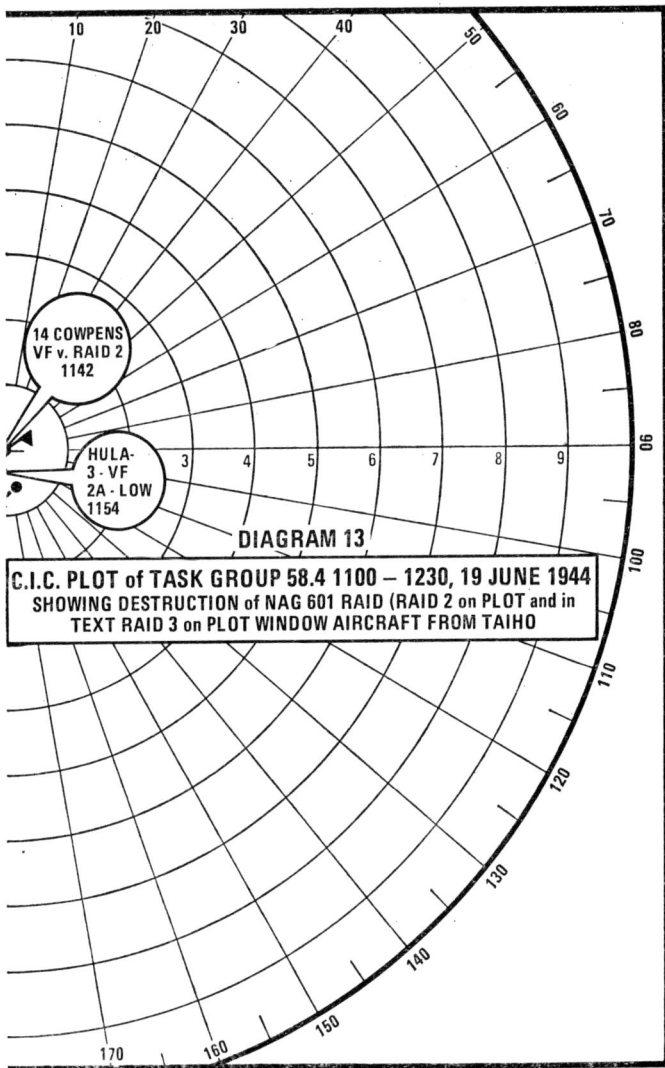

14 COWPENS
VF v. RAID 2
1142

HULA-
3 - VF
2A - LOW
1154

DIAGRAM 13

C.I.C. PLOT of TASK GROUP 58.4 1100 – 1230, 19 JUNE 1944
SHOWING DESTRUCTION of NAG 601 RAID (RAID 2 on PLOT and in
TEXT RAID 3 on PLOT WINDOW AIRCRAFT FROM TAIHO

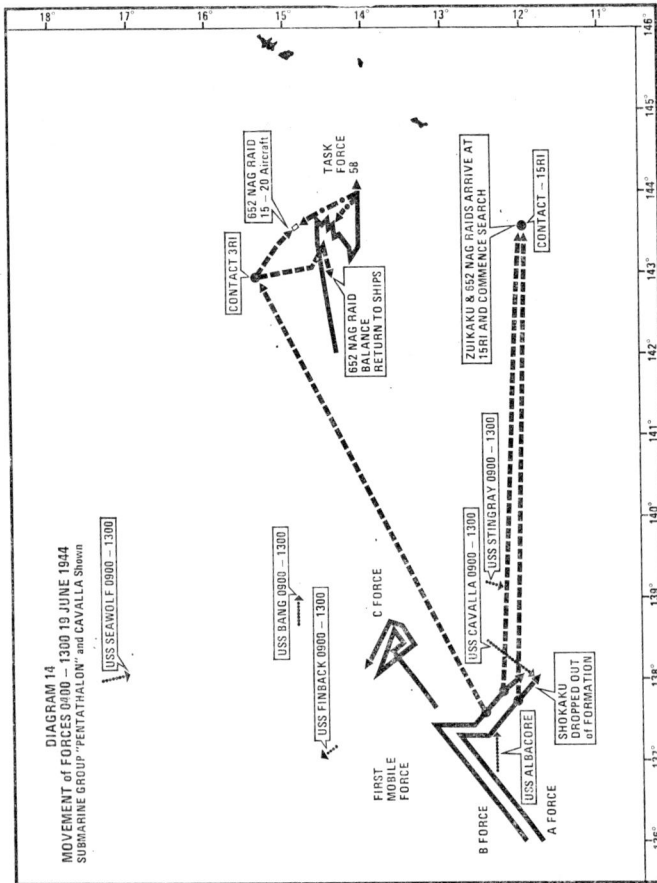

DIAGRAM 14
MOVEMENT of FORCES 0400 – 1300 19 JUNE 1944
SUBMARINE GROUP "PENTATHALON" and CAVALLA Shown

USS SEAWOLF 0900 – 1300

652 NAG RAID
15 – 20 Aircraft

TASK
FORCE
58

CONTACT 3RI

652 NAG RAID
BALANCE
RETURN TO SHIPS

ZUIKAKU & 652 NAG RAIDS ARRIVE AT
15RI AND COMMENCE SEARCH

CONTACT – 15RI

USS BANG 0900 – 1300

C FORCE

USS FINBACK 0900 – 1300

USS CAVALLA 0900 – 1300

USS STINGRAY 0900 – 1300

FIRST
MOBILE
FORCE

SHOKAKU
DROPPED OUT
of FORMATION

USS ALBACORE

B FORCE

A FORCE

126

The aircraft of Raid 3 arrived at target '3–Ri' and found nothing and began searching over a broad area. At 1225 TG 58.4 radars detected some of these aircraft at 295°/110 miles. At 1238 they had closed to 312°/100 miles and appeared to be in orbit. At 1248 Raid 3 was again in orbit, now at 325°/85 miles and TG 58.1 vectored two divisions from *Hornet* (Iron 10 and 14 on TG 58.1 CIC plot) and one from *Yorktown* (Coal 11) while 12 from *Langley* were vectored to assist if necessary. At 1301 TG 58.3 detected the raiders at 335°/60 miles. At 1304 (1306 on TG 58.4 plot) *Hornet*'s divisions tally-hoed sixteen Zekes at 16,000 feet and hit them when the raid was about 330°/50 miles from TG 58.4 (336°/55 miles from TG 58.3) claiming fifteen of the sixteen Japanese aircraft intercepted. Actually only seven aircraft of Raid 3 were lost. The *Langley* divisions were ordered to orbit since it appeared TG 58.1 aircraft could handle the enemy raid. At 1239 another group, probably from Raid 3 was detected at 275°/110 miles from TG 58.4. This portion of that raid closed to 285°/63 miles and at 1314 and after orbiting for a short period, opened to 270°/75 miles. Four *Langley* and four *Essex* fighters which had been vectored to meet this threat were ordered to orbit at 12,000 feet when it appeared the raiders would not close. At 1320 a few aircraft of Raid 3 found TG 58.4 and in the only attack by that raid dropped a bomb about 100 feet from *Essex*.

At 1300 a group of *Lexington* SBDs (Dauntless) hit Orote Field on Guam noting that there were 20–30 Japanese aircraft on the ground. The American aircraft had been armed with armour piercing bombs in anticipation of the hoped-for carrier battle and achieved no major damage. One of the Dauntlesses was shot down by AA fire, but managed to make a water landing, off the west coast of Guam, where the crew was picked up by two SOC from *Montpelier* (CL–57). The float planes could not take off with the added weight and had to ask for assistance from a destroyer. Admiral Mitscher signalled TF 58 his estimated 1330 position as 14° 30′, 143° 30′.

Like those of Raid 3, the aircraft of Raid 4 arrived at the false contact (15–Ri) they had been ordered to attack and began a wide search over the area of targets. When they found nothing they headed for Guam and Rota since the search consumed too much fuel to allow them to return to their carriers. *Monterey* picked them up at 1320 bearing 214°/134 miles, angels 20; followed by *Alabama* at 1331 with a 205°/150 mile plot. At 1403 a group, the 18 aircraft from *Zuikaku* and 15 from the other ships, were detected on the radars of TG 58.1 and evaluated as 10–12 planes. Two minutes later *Monterey* was tracking the raid at 187°/68 miles on course 030° at 24,000 feet. She attempted to vector TG 58.2 fighters but was unable to establish radio communications. Task Group 58.3 reported plots on the incoming raid between 1416 and tally-ho; 'Large bogey raid closing 175°/40 estimated 10–15 planes course 020° – changing to 000°, 1419 Bogey raid 175°/14 miles angels 15, Large bogey 185°/15 closing estimated 10–15 planes angels 15'. At 1427 TG 58.3 executed an emergency turn to starboard, returning to base course three minutes later. Many of the aircraft of Raid 4 were not 'tally-hoed' until they were within sight of TG 58.2 at 1421. Three divisions of *Monterey* CAP finally sighted them. Task Group 58.2 had picked them up on radar at 45 miles but many came under the CAP. *Wasp* reported that her aircraft dispatched three. The carriers of TG 58.2 were recovering aircraft when light cruiser *Mobile* (CL–63) opened fire at 1423 and *Wasp* and *Bunker Hill* had to manoeuvre to avoid bombs, which caused minor hull damage to *Bunker Hill*. The remainder of Raid 4 (20 A6M, 27 D3A, 2 B6N) were detected after they had jettisoned their weapons on the radars of TG 58.1 at 1443 and at 1449 twelve *Cowpens* F6Fs were vectored over Guam finding 'forty enemy planes circling Orote Field at Angels 3'. Seven *Essex* and eight *Hornet* F6Fs joined the *Cowpens* aircraft and broke into the landing circle, accounting for 30 of the 49 Japanese aircraft in the pattern. None of the aircraft which landed were in flying condition the next day. Seventy-three of the 82 aircraft of Raid 4 were lost. *Yorktown* sent a sweep over Guam which lasted until sundown, at which time *Hornet* and *Essex* divisions took over.

At 1400 Task Force 58 launched afternoon searches to 325 mile covering sector 185°–345°. The searches reported shooting down three Japanese search aircraft, but found no enemy ships. Some of the searchers ran foul of Raid 4 and had a heavy fight in the vicinity of 12° 20′ N 141° 26′ E at 1530. One section of *Bunker Hill* searchers (an SB2C (Helldiver) and F6F–3 (N) (Hellcat)) in sector 205°–215° failed to return and probably were accounted for by that raid. A fighter searching in the adjacent sector reported a radio conversation in which a US aircraft radioed that it was being, 'attacked by five Zekes'. The same fighter reported shooting down a Jill in its sector. At 1531 TF 58 executed a simultaneous turn to course 300°.

At 1430 A Force changed course to due north. The initial damage to *Shokaku* had been handled promptly, but aviation gasoline fire

Top: Japanese phosphorous bomb exploding above uss *Wasp* (cv-18) as seen from uss *Cabot* (cvl-28). Note the *South Dakota* class battleship of TG 58.7 to right of photograph. Approximately 1200, June 19, 1944. */US Navy*

Above: First near miss explodes close aboard uss *Bunker Hill* (cv-17), as seen from uss *Monterey* (cvl-26). Time approximately 1200, June 19. *Cleveland* class cL on starboard bow. */US Navy*

Below: Second near miss on uss *Bunker Hill* (cv-17) as seen from uss *Monterey*. Formation has reversed course (*Bunker Hill* now seen from starboard side). *Cleveland* class cL now on cv-17 port quarter. Note that *Bunker Hill* is painted in dazzle scheme (Measure 32). */US Navy*

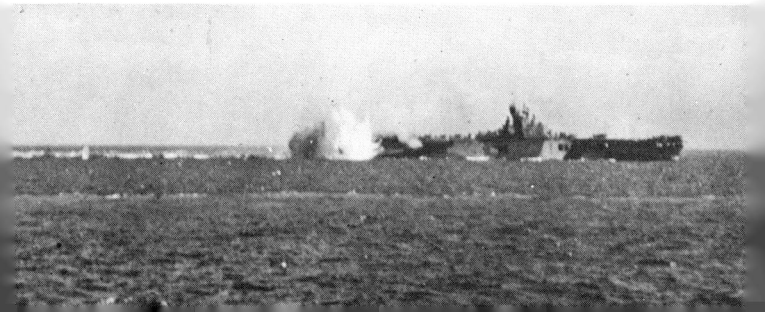

Top: The Japanese fleet manoeuvres under air attack, June 20.
/US Navy
Above: Japanese southern group (*Chiyoda*) manoeuvres in
formation early in the battle, June 20. */US Navy*

Above: Chiyoda Group continues manoeuvres as *Kongo* class battleship fires main battery (or receives hit), June 20. /*US Navy*

Below: Chiyoda group (C Force) under attack. Ship on the left is either *Chokai* or *Maya*, followed by two destroyers. Ship with bomb flash in right background is *Haruna* on fire aft from bomb hit. Almost totally obscured by cloud and smoke from own **gunfire just right of centre is carrier *Chiyoda*. /*US Navy***

Top: Chiyoda group (C Force) *Haruna* in foreground. *Chiyoda* in right background with destroyer in middle background. /US Navy

Above: Chiyoda group (C Force) *Chokai* and *Maya* in foreground. *Chiyoda* and *Haruna*, both on fire, narrowly avoid collision in right background. /US Navy

Above: Close-up of *Chiyoda* with both aircraft clearly burning aft, June 20. /*US Navy*

Below: Numerous bombs explode close aboard *Chiyoda* as she manoeuvres under attack, June 20. /*US Navy*

Bottom: Explosion on *Chiyoda*, June 20. /*US Navy*

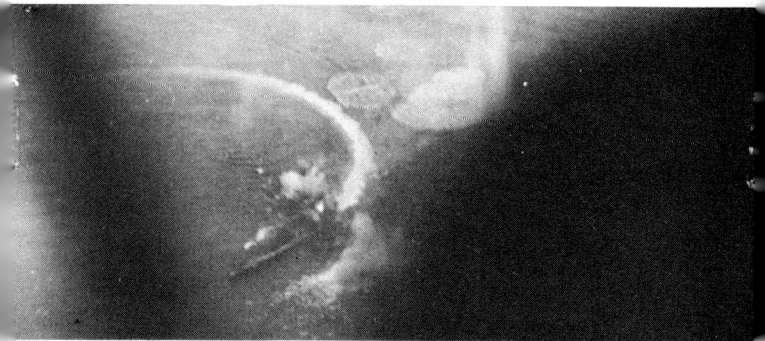

Above: Pilots and aircrew of VT-28, USS *Belleau Wood* who torpedoed and sank *Hiyo* on June 20, 1944. Back row, left to right: Lt (jg) W. R. Omark, Lt (jg) B. C. Tate, Lt (jg) W. D. Luton are the pilots; middle row, left to right: R. E. Ranes, J. R. Dobbs, P. E. Whiting, E. C. Babcock; bottom row, left to right: J. E. Prince, G. H. Platz, J. A. Brookbank. The front two rows are the aircrewmen. Inset: Lt (jg) G. P. Brown killed in the attack. His aircrewmen Babcock and Platz were picked up on June 21. /US Navy
Below: Lt (jg) Alexander Vraciu, USNR was high scorer in the 'Turkey Shoot'. Six kills, June 19, 1944. /US Navy

Above: Vice Admiral Willis A. Lee, USN, Commander Task Group 58.7, Commander Fast Battleship Force Pacific Fleet. Photo dated February, 1945 aboard USS *South Dakota* (BB-57). */US Navy*

Left: Admiral Raymond A. Spruance, USN, Commander Fifth Fleet. */US Navy*

Left: Vice Admiral Marc A. Mitscher, USN, Commander Task Force 58. /*US Navy*
Bottom left: Rear Admiral J. J. Clark, USN, Commander Task Group 58.1 (Photo taken when Admiral Clark was commanding officer USS *Yorktown*.) /*US Navy*

Top right: Rear Admiral A. E. Montgomery, USN, Commander Task Group 58.2. /*US Navy*
Right: Rear Admiral J. W. Reeves, USN, Commander Task Group 58.3. /*US Navy*

Far right: Rear Admiral W. K. Harrill, USN, Commander Task Group 58.4. /*US Navy*

Left: USS *Lexington* (CV-16), Flagship, Commander Task Force 58 (*Essex* class aircraft carrier). /*US Navy*

Bottom left: USS *Enterprise* (CV-6), Flagship, Commander Task Group 58.3 and America's most famous carrier (old *Yorktown* class). /*US Navy*

Below: USS *Belleau Wood* (CVL-24), *Independence* class. /*US Navy*

Top: USS *Washington* (BB-56). Flagship, Commander Task Group 58.7 (Battle Line) (*North Carolina* class battleship). /*US Navy*

Above: USS *Indianapolis* (CA-35), Flagship, Commander Fifth Fleet (*Portland* class heavy cruiser). /*US Navy*

Top: USS *San Juan* (CLAA-54), anti-aircraft cruiser. /US Navy

Above: USS *England* (DE-635) sank six Japanese submarines in twelve days. /US Navy

Above: Superstructure of aircraft carrier *Junyo* in 1945. */US Navy*

Right: Flight deck of *Junyo* looking aft from superstructure with arresting gear removed. Note HF/DF loop in foreground. The lattice grid on the leading edge of the tripod mast is a Type 13 radar antenna. */US Navy*

Heavy cruisers *Tone* and *Suzuya* refuelling at sea during *A-Go*, June 17, 1944. Note Type 21 Radar on *Tone* foremast.

broke out and quickly spread throughout the 25,675 ton ship as she settled by the bow. The leading edge of the flight deck soon touched the water, which entered the forward elevator. In this condition the veteran carrier lost stability, turned turtle and sank at 12° 00′ N 137° 46′ E carrying 1263 of her officers and men (complement about 2000) and nine aircraft with her. The remainder of her aircraft were either in raids, combat air patrol, air searches or local patrols. The time was 1501 when one of Admiral Nimitz's fondest dreams was realized. *Shokaku* had been one of the Imperial Navy's best ships in the war and prompted Nimitz to remark that the happiest day of his life would be the day he received the report that 'those two ships' (*Shokaku* and *Zuikaku*) were sunk!

The lone torpedo hit on *Taiho* at 0910 should have caused no real trouble to a new heavily armoured carrier, but because of inept damage control, quite the opposite was the result. When the torpedo hit the forward aircraft elevator jammed, and some fuel oil and aviation gasoline lines ruptured, but there was no appreciable loss of speed and overall fighting capacity appeared unimpaired. In this condition she should have no problems. However a damage control officer felt that the best method to dissipate the aviation gasoline fumes from one of the ruptured tanks was to open the ship's ventilation ducts and literally blow them away. In fact this action spread the fumes throughout the ship. Next the damage control party charged with disposing of the aviation gasoline from the ruptured tanks spilled large quantities of the dangerous spirit in the hangar deck in clumsy efforts to pump it over the side. At 1532 *Taiho* paid the penalty for the sloppy work of her damage control parties as the 29,800 ton ship suffered a terrible explosion. The enclosed hangar sides blew out, the flight deck was wrecked and the hull was perforated in several places. The ship began to settle rapidly. Ozawa, determined to go down with the ship, was only dissuaded by his longtime friend and chief of staff Capt Toshikazu Ohmae, who said, 'The battle is still going on and you should remain in command for the final victory'. He transferred to destroyer *Wakatsuki* as at 1828 the ship sank in position 12° 05′ N 138° 12′ E carrying all but 500 of her crew of 2150 (1751 ship's company plus air group and flag personnel) and thirteen aircraft with her. The unprocessed fuel oil played a major role in the fires which destroyed *Taiho* and *Shokaku*. (*Albacore* was lost on her next patrol and her crew never knew of this startling success.) At 1532 A and B Forces changed

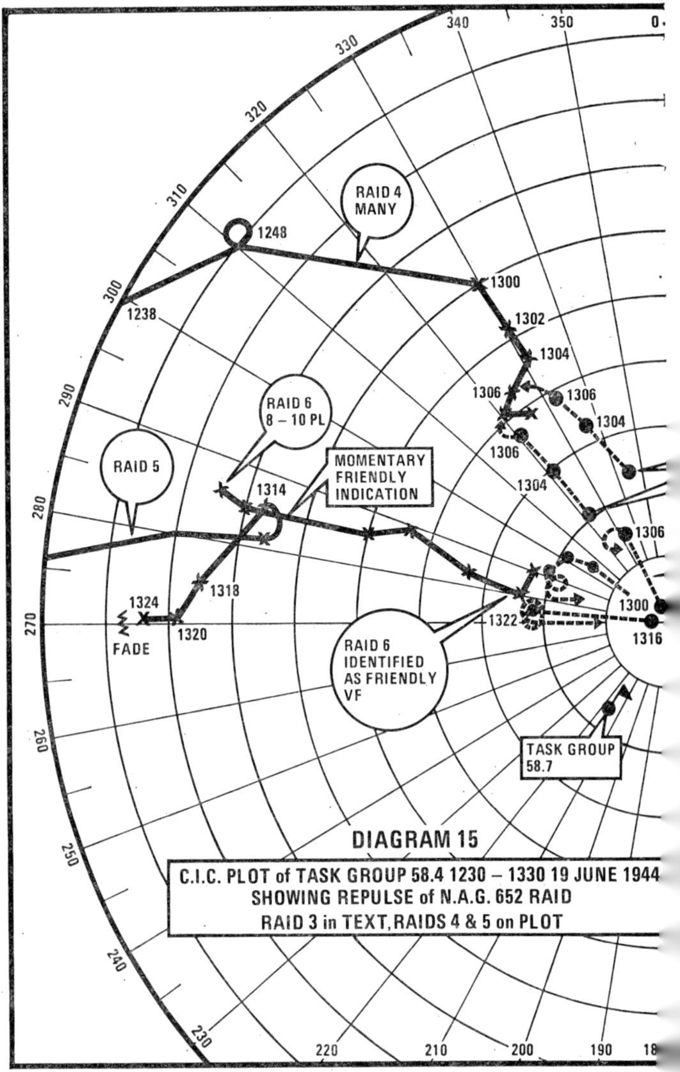

RAID 4
MANY

RAID 6
8 – 10 PL

RAID 5

MOMENTARY
FRIENDLY
INDICATION

FADE

RAID 6
IDENTIFIED
AS FRIENDLY
VF

TASK GROUP
58.7

DIAGRAM 15

C.I.C. PLOT of TASK GROUP 58.4 1230 – 1330 19 JUNE 1944
SHOWING REPULSE of N.A.G. 652 RAID
RAID 3 in TEXT, RAIDS 4 & 5 on PLOT

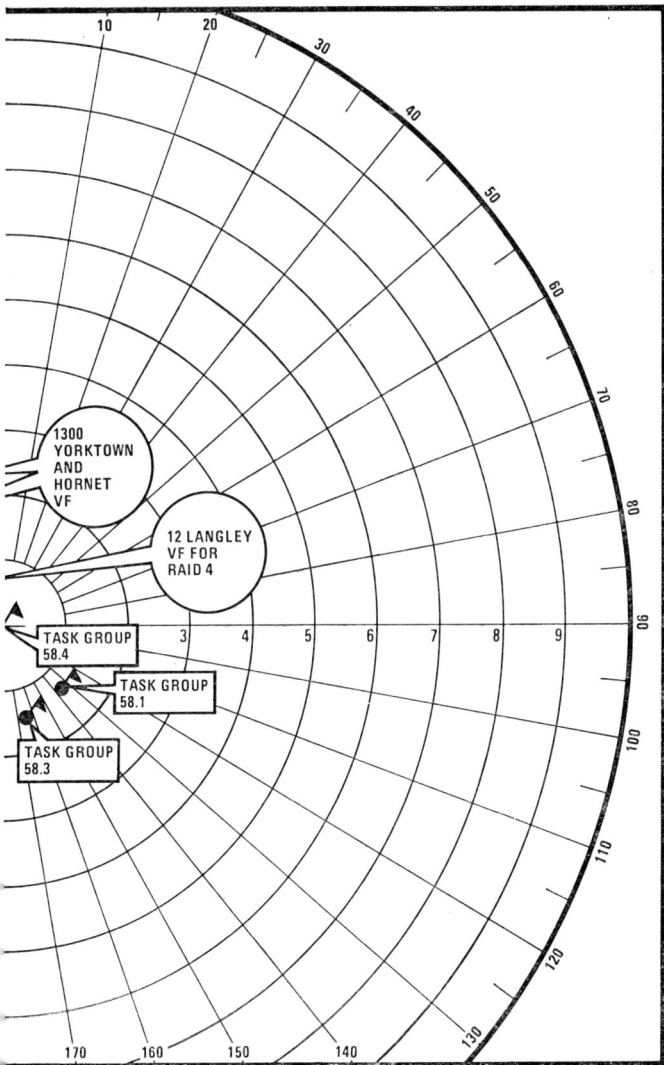

1300
YORKTOWN
AND
HORNET
VF

12 LANGLEY
VF FOR
RAID 4

TASK GROUP
58.4

TASK GROUP
58.1

TASK GROUP
58.3

10   20   30   40   50   60   70   80   90   100   110   120   130   140   150   160   170

3   4   5   6   7   8   9

course to northwest for a rendezvous with C Force and the Supply Groups.

At 1537 Mitscher signalled to his Task Group commanders, 'Please submit in *Shackle** code the number of enemy planes estimated destroyed by your unit.' The response confirmed the apparent victory.

Wrap-up on Guam

At 1600 USN TG 58.4 radars detected a bogey evaluated as a single at 342°/27 miles crossing from east to west. Four *Essex* Hellcats were vectored out, but were recalled at 1617 when the target had reached 305°/55 miles and continued to open. A fighter sweep by 12 *Essex* fighters over Guam reported many Japanese carrier type aircraft being shot down by US aircraft. These were part of Raid 4. Task Group 58.3, which contained flagship *Lexington*, changed course to the northwest at 1609 as the entire US disposition had drifted far eastward during the air battle and distance to the west had to be made if there was to be any chance of hitting the Japanese Fleet. Guam was southeast of *Lexington* about 30 miles at this time. When the first fighters were vectored at 1000, Mitscher's flagship was over 100 miles north by west of that island. While the fight over Guam continued the US force steamed northwest until 1640 when *Lexington* again changed course to the east to recover aircraft.

At 1600 Admiral Spruance signalled Mitscher:

'Desire to attack enemy tomorrow if we know his position with sufficient accuracy. If our patrol planes give us required information tonight no searches should be necessary. If not, we must continue searches tomorrow to ensure adequate protection for Saipan. Point option should be advanced to the westward as much as air operations permit.'

Point option is a moving point provided to aviators on missions from aircraft carriers. It is theoretically the position of the base carrier at any time. When it is set and aircraft are on missions then the carrier must remain on or near a constant course and speed so the aviators have no difficulty finding their ship. In case of a radical

---

* *Shackle* Code – A code in which numbers in an otherwise plain-text message are encoded in letter group substitutes. For example if the message to be sent was, 'Enemy aircraft destroyed, 25 fighters, 15 bombers' the message would be transmitted as follows, 'Bandits splashed shackle – AH DM – unshackle rats – MQ DM – unshackle hawks'. In this example AH=2, DM=5, MQ=1.

change of course the ship must break radio silence by voice radio or homing signals or run the unacceptable risk of losing the aircraft.

The pursuit of the Japanese Fleet was underway. If the '. . . to ensure adequate protection for Saipan' portion of the message seems overcautious in view of the results of the day's fighting, the performance of American reconnaissance to this point could not reassure Spruance that his only fear, the possibility of a flank attack by the Japanese was non-existent. The movement of point option as far westward as possible should leave no doubt of Spruance's thought at this moment.

Admiral Ozawa raised his flag in heavy cruiser *Haguro* at 1706. Though that ship was Fifth Squadron Flagship and equipped with an operations room, her facilities, particularly her communications equipment, were not adequate for handling the functions of fleet flagship. The fact that she was a squadron flagship probably had her signal facilities stretched to their maximum capacity when Ozawa arrived. The only ship which was convenient and also properly equipped was *Zuikaku* and she was not in sight at this time. To add to his difficulties *Taiho* had been the only ship in the force carrying a new flag officers' code for direct communications with Combined Fleet. Until Toyoda's headquarters received word that *Taiho* had sunk, with the codes, Ozawa and Toyoda were incommunicado. A change of codes to one common to all flag officers restored communications.

When he arrived on *Haguro* the tactical picture appeared to Ozawa as follows. He had lost many aircraft and had about 100 remaining in the seven surviving carriers. The air groups which were directed to attack contact '15–Ri' had proceeded on to Guam and he erroneously assumed they would be available for future action. His returning aviators reported many hits on American carriers and heavy destruction of the hated 'Grummans'. In the 1942 battles heavy air group losses were common in carrier battles. Based on the information now presented to Ozawa his optimistic plans for the next day were not unreasonable. The Guam aircraft would be ordered to return to their ships which would retire to the westward to refuel on the 21st and on the 22nd the fight would be renewed. In the meantime in accordance with orders issued by Ozawa the fleet would move northwestward. Orders for this movement were issued at 1820. At 1900 he issued an order for the next day's refuelling: 'From CMF to MF, Take a position at 0700 hours tomorrow, the

133

20th, as indicated in Battle Order no. 8. Location of Force A Grid HE–CHI–CHI–OO, Course 090°, speed 16 knots'.

Lexington again changed course to the northwest at 1705 continuing on that course until 1747 when air operations again required an eastward course. At 1748 TG 58.4 radars detected 10–15 aircraft at 205°/115 miles tracking on course 025° toward Guam, probably another remnant of Raid 4. By 1805 they had reached 205°/85 miles from *Essex* and Montgomery's groups was sending out 12 fighters from *Bunker Hill*. *Essex*'s fighters over Guam were also dispatched. The raid was tally-hoed at 1825 and several of the aircraft shot down. At 1830 *Lexington* again changed course to the northwest continuing on that course until about 1845 when she changed course to the southeast to recover the last big fighter patrols of the day. The last fight of the day was led, appropriately by Lt Cdr Brewer, who had first sighted Raid 1 at 1035 that morning. His four plane division was over Orote Field, Guam when they ran foul of a B6N escorted by about 16 Zekes. In spite of the odds several Japanese aircraft were shot down, but not before Brewer and two other Hellcat pilots (Lt (jg) J. L. Bruce and Ens. Thomas Tarr) were lost.

US Navy HF/DF stations indicated that the Japanese Fleet was within 100 miles of 10° 30' N, 136° 30' W at 1800. Commander Submarine Force Pacific advised Spruance of this find at 1957. In fact the Japanese Fleet was considerably to the north of this fix.

Victory and move Westward

At 2000 *Lexington* changed course to 260° and speed to 23 knots, maximum economical speed, to close the Japanese fleet which was assumed to be southwest of TF 58 retiring toward the Empire. The latter assumption was correct, but the Japanese were considerably to the north of Spruance's only fixes; *Cavalla*'s attack and the PB4Y sighting. At the same time Harrill's group, TG 58.4, was detached to cover Saipan and refuel. Harrill's failure to refuel his destroyers on the 17th now cost TF 58 three carriers. Of course, the heavy aircraft losses suffered by the Japanese and the sinking of *Shokaku* and *Taiho* meant there was no real risk in detaching Harrill's group, however, in 1942 a similar situation nearly cost the US Navy carrier *Enterprise*, when, on the eve of the Eastern Solomons battle USS *Wasp* (CV-7) was detached to fuel her destroyers, reducing the American carrier force to two ships. For this reason (the possible risks – which were also real – not the actual events), Harrill's handling of the fuel situation in his destroyers was questionable. In addition to refuelling, TG 58.4 would 'make minor strikes on Guam and Rota'. The other groups had refuelled on the 17th and Admiral Clark, who had accompanied Harrill on the Bonins raid, pointedly signalled Mitscher, 'Would greatly appreciate remaining with you. We have plenty of fuel.', to which Mitscher replied, 'You will remain with us all right – until the battle is over.' At the same time Task Group 58.7 was ordered to take station 270° from TG 58.3 at 25 miles. During the entire watch many small unidentified aircraft contacts passed close to TF 58 though none attacked.

In the ships of Task Force 58, particularly the aircraft carriers, the feeling of all hands was one of exultation. The fighter squadrons estimated that they had destroyed 318 Japanese aircraft in the eight hour fight.[*] Even considering the general tendency of men in combat to exaggerate their accomplishments no one doubted that the Japanese had launched an all out effort and that it had been thoroughly frustrated. For the first time in the war a major effort of the Japanese Naval Air Corps had failed to sink or damage a single US aircraft carrier. In 1942 raids on the scale of those launched on June 19 would have seriously damaged or sunk four or five of the US carriers. There was consensus that the quality of the Japanese carrier pilots, 'the flower of the Japanese Naval Air Force',[**] was poor and that their attacks were very badly executed. The Japanese fighters were not aggressive and their attack aircraft broke their defensive formations prematurely, making for easy pickings. This latter aspect of the air battle led to the popular name for the battle of June 19, 'The Turkey Shoot'. Lt Cdr Paul Buie, of Lexington's Fighting 16, overheard one of his pilots liken shooting Japanese planes to shooting turkeys and passed the anecdote on to Mitscher. It caught on throughout the Fleet. The US force had lost eighteen fighters of 296 engaged in interceptions. Two bombers and three torpedo planes also joined in the fight; twelve attack aircraft were

---

[*] See appendix for scores claimed by various fighter squadrons.

[**] TF 58 Intelligence Summary to CTF 58 OPLAN 7-44 contained the following estimate of Japanese Naval Aviators; 'The flower of the Japanese Naval Air Force has always been assigned to carrier duty. While only a small nucleus of present flying personnel on Japanese carriers has had combat experience, the others represent the best graduates of Naval Air Schools. All of the carriers are believed to be equipped with Type 0, Model 52, Zekes and they may use either Judy and Jill or Val and Kate as dive and torpedo bombers respectively.'

DIAGRAM 16
MOVEMENT of FORCES 0400 – 2400 19 JUNE 1944
SHOWING END of RAID 4 and AMERICAN AFTERNOON AIR SEARCHES and MOVEMENTS of SUBMARINE GROUP "PENTATHALON" and USS CAVALLA (1300 – 2100)

APPROXIMATE ALIGNMENT
T.F. 58 at 1330

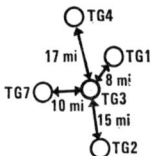

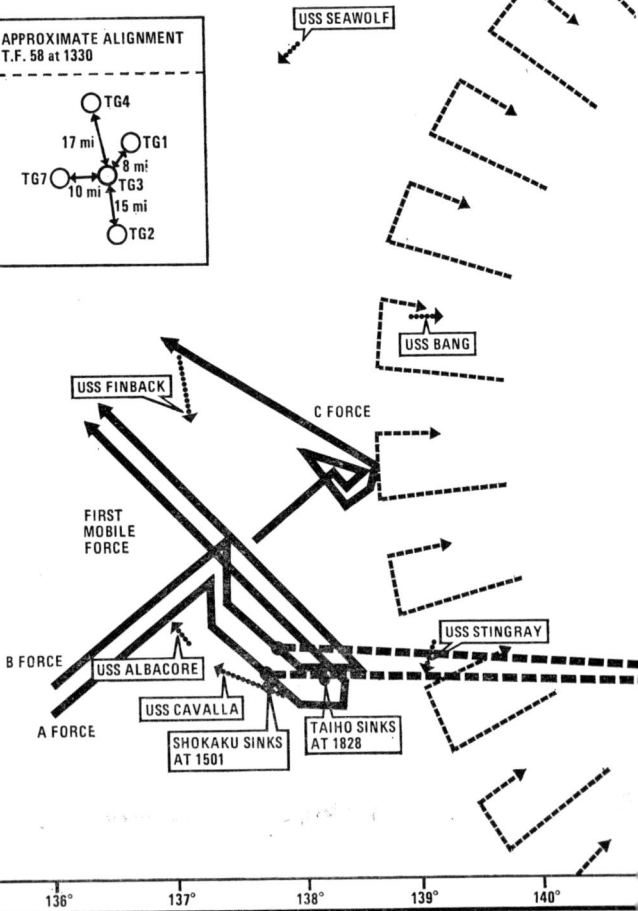

TG4
17 mi
TG1
8 mi
TG7
10 mi
TG3
15 mi
TG2

USS SEAWOLF

USS BANG

USS FINBACK

C FORCE

FIRST MOBILE FORCE

USS STINGRAY

B FORCE

USS ALBACORE

USS CAVALLA

TAIHO SINKS AT 1828

A FORCE

SHOKAKU SINKS AT 1501

136°   137°   138°   139°   140°

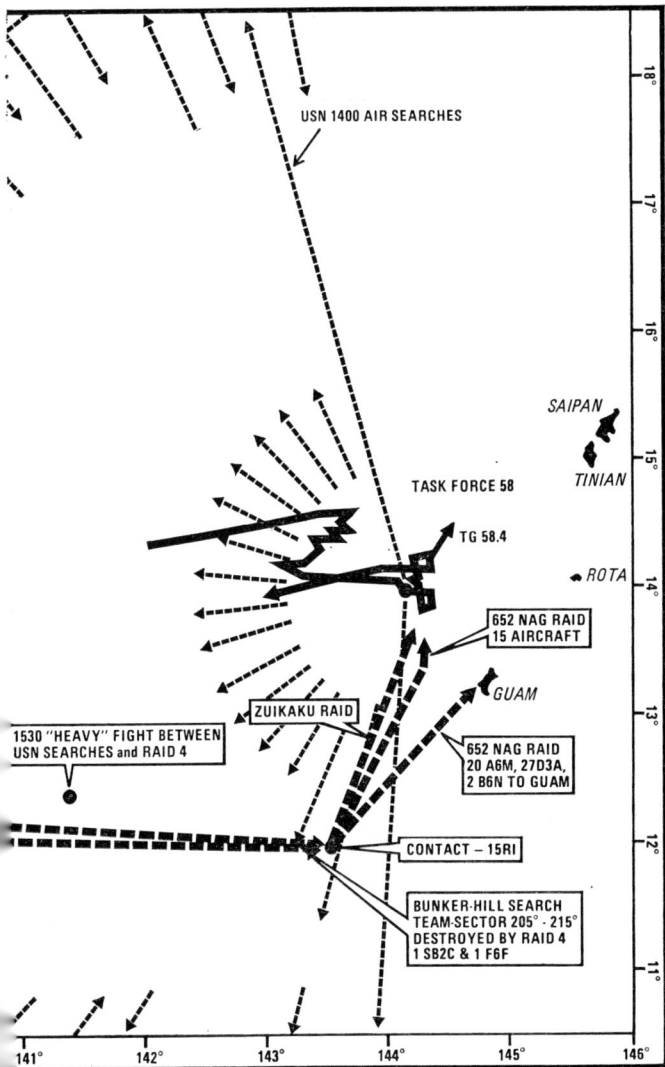

USN 1400 AIR SEARCHES

SAIPAN

TINIAN

TASK FORCE 58

TG 58.4

ROTA

652 NAG RAID
15 AIRCRAFT

GUAM

ZUIKAKU RAID

1530 "HEAVY" FIGHT BETWEEN
USN SEARCHES and RAID 4

652 NAG RAID
20 A6M, 27D3A,
2 B6N TO GUAM

CONTACT – 15RI

BUNKER-HILL SEARCH
TEAM-SECTOR 205° - 215°
DESTROYED BY RAID 4
1 SB2C & 1 F6F

137

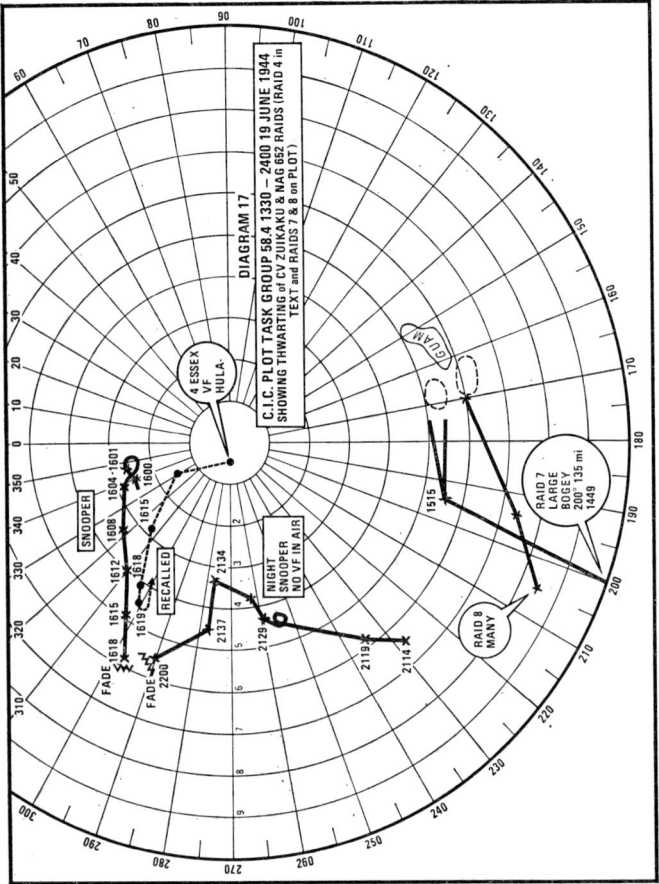

DIAGRAM 17

C.I.C. PLOT TASK GROUP 58.4 1330 — 2400 19 JUNE 1944
SHOWING THWARTING of CV ZUIKAKU & NAG 652 RAIDS (RAID 4 in
TEXT and RAIDS 7 & 8 on PLOT)

4 ESSEX
VF
HULA-

SNOOPER

RECALLED

NIGHT
SNOOPER
NO VF IN AIR

GUAM

RAID 7
LARGE
BOGEY
200° 135 mi
1449

RAID 8
MANY

1604-1601
1608
1600
1615
1612
1618
1615
1619
FADE 1618
FADE 2200

2134
2137
2129
2119
2114

1515
1515

lost, mostly over Guam. In all, twenty-seven aviators were lost. One of the interesting side lights of the battle was the role played by the Japanese air attack coordinator. As mentioned earlier, his transmissions were monitored throughout the fight and several vectors were results of information received by TF 58 communications intelligence personnel. When the air battle was over, Admiral Mitscher was asked if a CAP section should be sent to dispatch this unwitting ally. Mitscher vetoed the suggestion, 'No indeed, he did us too much good!'

At 2345 Admiral Ozawa signalled his ships:

'Mobile Force shall immediately proceed in a north-westerly direction and manoeuver in such a way as to be able to receive supplies on the 21st.'

Shortly after this dispatch was transmitted, Admiral Toyoda sent the following to his force commander:

'It has been planned to direct a running battle after reorganizing our forces and in accordance with the battle conditions.

1 On the 21st, Mobile Force shall reorganize its strength and take on supplies. Disabled vessels shall proceed to the homeland. Also, part of the aircraft carriers shall proceed to the training base (Lingga).

2 On the 22nd, according to the situation, you shall advance and direct your attack against the enemy task force, co-operating with the land-based air units. After this has been done, you shall dispatch your air units to land bases. Thereafter, operations shall be carried on under the commander of the 5 Base Air Force. The aircraft carriers shall proceed to their training base.

3 After the 22nd, according to the conditions, you shall manage most of your craft in mopping up operations around Saipan.'

The Japanese had not given up just yet!

June 20, The Battle; the Second Day; 'Mission Beyond Darkness'

Pursuit of the Japanese Fleet – an uneventful morning

During the midwatch the Japanese fleet proceeded northwest at 18 knots while Task Force 58 continued on 260°/23 knots. Admiral Mitscher ordered air searches launched at 0530 when TF 58 had reached 13° 42′ N, 141′ 05′ E to search sector 205°–325° to 325 miles hoping to find the *Shokaku* class carrier *Cavalla* had reported hitting. The idea of sending the first deck load out along the median of the search sector shortly after the searches were launched was considered by Mitscher, but rejected at 0443. The search, incredibly still of routine dimensions, found no enemy forces, missing the Japanese Mobile Force by about 75 miles, though they did encounter Jakes and Kates searching behind the Japanese fleet. They reported splashing two Jakes at 15° 45′ N 138° 05′ E and a Kate at 15° 38′ N, 135° 54′ E between 0900 and 0907. The search had landed at 1040. Curiously, in spite of heavy air losses, Ozawa's search effort that morning matched Mitscher's. At 0530 the battleships and cruisers of C Force, now at about 15° 25′ N, 135° 30′ E launched nine E13A (Jake) to search sector 040°–140° to 300 miles, followed by six carrier aircraft (probably Kates) from 3 S.F. at 0645 to search sector 050°–100° to 350 miles. The former group found nothing and lost three of its number, while the latter group sighted two American carrier planes (probably Mitscher's dawn search) at 0713.

Point option was set based on a 0530 position of 13° 15′ N, 141° 00′ E as 250°/15 knots. From this it can be seen that the US force was actually dropping behind instead of gaining on the Japanese.

A and B Forces changed course to north toward the rendezvous point at 0800.

Because of the fuel situation Mitscher signalled Spruance:

'Recommend that fleet oilers, protected by Task Group 58.4 head west as soon as possible.'

To which Spruance, who inferred from the reports of Jakes being shot down that heavy cruisers were 'possibly acting as an escort of the damaged *Zuikaku* class cv', replied:

'Damaged *Zuikaku* may be still afloat. If so, believe she will be most likely heading northwest. Desire to push our searches today far to westward if possible. If no contact with enemy fleet results consider it indication fleet is withdrawing and further pursuit after today will be unprofitable. If you concur, retire tonight toward Saipan. Will order out tankers with Task Group 58.4 and direct Task Group 58.4 remain in vicinity of Saipan. *Zuikaku* must be sunk if we can reach her. Advise.'

(Of course, the carrier referred to as *Zuikaku* in these dispatches w.

140

Shokaku) Mitscher and Spruance both agreed that the Japanese were likely retiring northwestward, but a course change could not be made immediately since search planes were airborne and point option had been given to them as previously indicated. During the forenoon watch Admiral Reeves suggested that the Japanese had slipped the net and that a sweep of Yap, Ulithi and Palau might be profitable, but Mitscher was still determined to press the pursuit. At 1100 Admiral Lee was asked to rotate his bearing to 330° from flagship *Lexington* preparatory to the course change anticipated after recovery of the morning air searches. Commander W. M. Widhelm, Mitscher's Air Operations Officer, projected the position of damaged '*Zuikaku*' on a northwest course at 15 knots and requested a special fighter-bomber air-search-strike. The twelve F6Fs manned by volunteers from *Lexington* would be fitted with 500 SAP★ bombs and belly tanks. They would fly out on bearing 340° to 450 miles, turn left 30 miles and then return, covering about a 20° sector. They would be escorted by eight F6Fs from *San Jacinto*. This flight took off at 1200 and found nothing, reaching its outer limit at 1500.

Search for the Japanese Fleet continues

At 1200, after recovering the last of the dawn search aircraft, TF 58 changed course to 330°. As mentioned previously, the disposition axis had been altered to that bearing an hour earlier. The US force was now at about 13° 15′ N, 139° 10′ E, having made good 261°/ 19.4 knots during the morning watches.

The last ships of Japanese First Mobile Force straggled into their fuelling rendezvous at 15° 20′ N, 134° 40′ E at 1230. The large area covered by the Japanese disposition and the loss of two large carriers, one of which was the fleet flagship, caused considerable confusion at the fuelling rendezvous. After several hours of 'milling about' while proper fuelling formations were being formed the fleet had to call off fuelling attempts because of the discovery of American scout aircraft. At 1300 Admiral Ozawa transferred his flag to carrier *Zuikaku*, where he learned the full extent of the previous day's disaster. He received the false information from Admiral Kakuta that many carrier aircraft had made it to Guam and were in proper fighting trim. Therefore, in spite of the previous day's losses Ozawa's resolve to renew the fight the next day was unchanged. *Chitose* and

★ SAP – Semi-armour piercing.

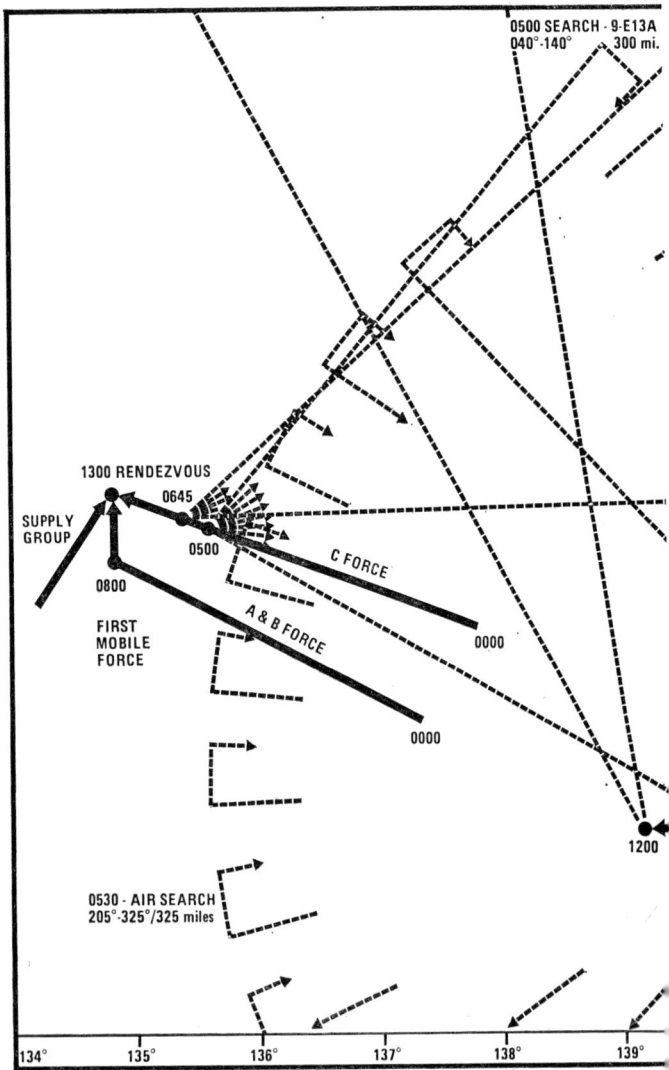

0500 SEARCH - 9-E13A
040°-140°   300 mi.

1300 RENDEZVOUS
0645
SUPPLY
GROUP
0500
C FORCE
0800
FIRST
MOBILE
FORCE
A & B FORCE
0000
0000
1200
0530 - AIR SEARCH
205°-325°/325 miles

134°   135°   136°   137°   138°   139°

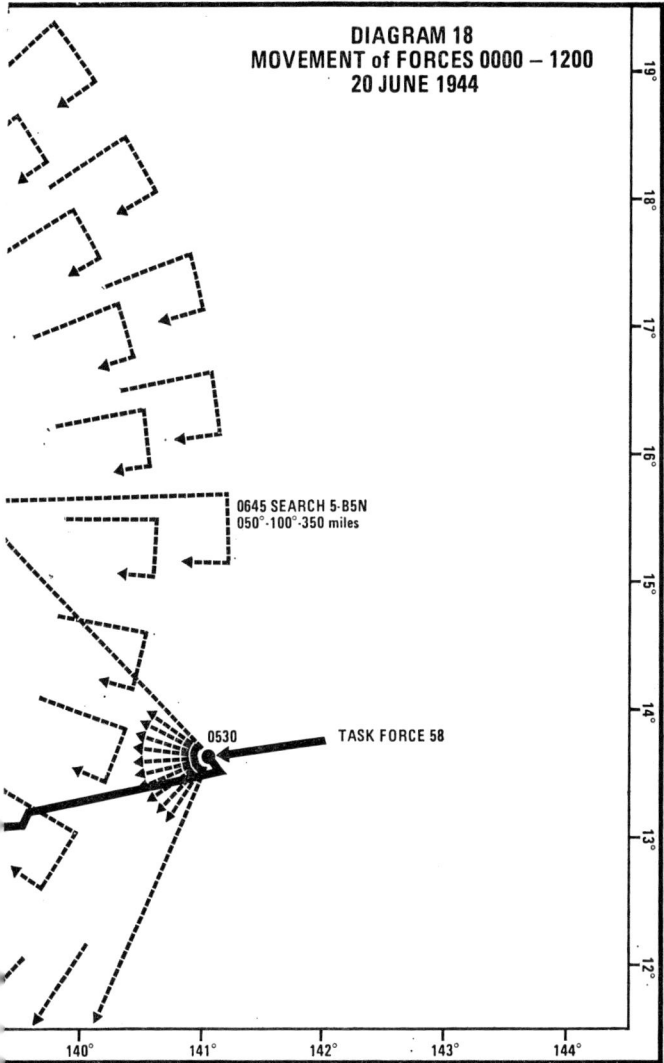

DIAGRAM 18
MOVEMENT of FORCES 0000 – 1200
20 JUNE 1944

0645 SEARCH 5-B5N
050°-100°-350 miles

0530

TASK FORCE 58

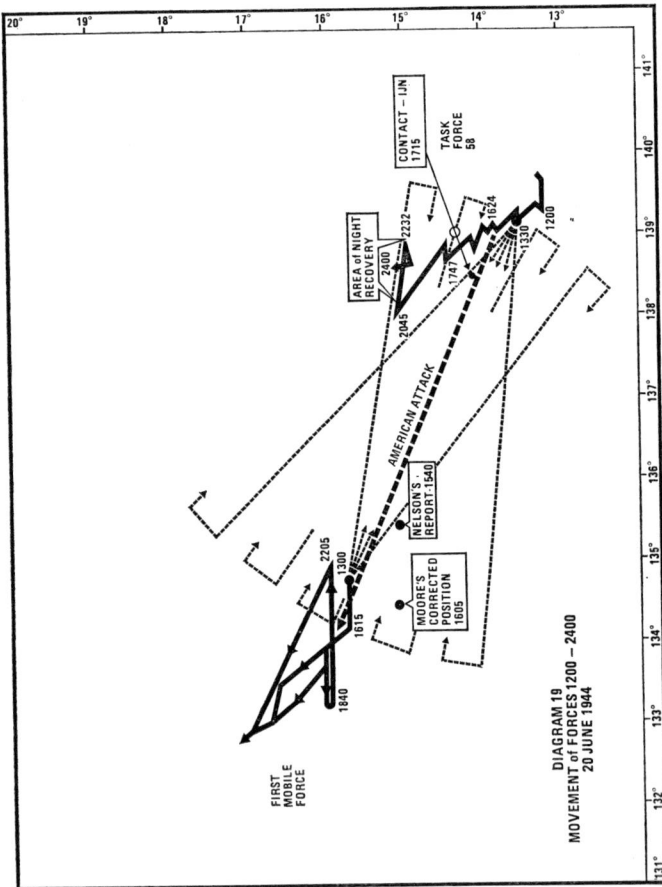

DIAGRAM 19
MOVEMENT of FORCES 1200 – 2400
20 JUNE 1944

FIRST
MOBILE
FORCE

MOORE'S
CORRECTED
POSITION
1605

NELSON'S
REPORT 1540

AMERICAN ATTACK

AREA of NIGHT
RECOVERY

CONTACT – IJN
1715

TASK
FORCE
58

2205
1300
1615
1640
2045
2400
2232
1747
1624
1330
1200

Zuiho launched three torpedo planes (probably B5N (Kate)) on a 300 mile search to cover sector 100°–130° at 1300.

Bataan's CAP splashed a G4M (Betty) at 1330 in 13° 41′ N, 138° 32′ E. The afternoon search of TF 58 was launched by *Enterprise* (8 VT, 4 VF) at 1330 to cover sector 275°–315° (30° to the right of previous routine searches) to 325 miles. Spruance signalled Mitscher at 1420:

'Would like to continue pursuit of enemy to northwestward tonight if this afternoon's operations give any indication it will be profitable. Please comment with particular reference to the fuel situation.'

To which Mitscher replied:

Some destroyers tomorrow morning will be very low on fuel. Propose to fuel them from large ships as opportunity affords, continuing pursuit of the enemy with remaining ships.'

Mitscher signalled Task Force 58 as follows at 1512: 'Indication that our birdmen have sighted something big. Speed 23.' It was a false alarm, though it turned out to be a good omen.

The Japanese Fleet is found

At 1540 Lt R. S. Nelson of *Enterprise*'s Torpedo Squadron 10, in a TBF (Avenger) at the outer edge of his search sector (295°–305°), in the afternoon searches launched at 1330 was the first American of the 98,618 officers and men assigned to Task Force 58 (FMF had about 48,000 officers and men) to see the ships of the Japanese First Mobile Force. Two minutes later he transmitted his first message which was received on flagship *Lexington* in a badly garbled form, probably because of interference from aircraft in adjoining sectors. Though it was not possible from the first message to know the location of the Japanese Fleet, there was little doubt that Nelson had a hot contact. At 1548 Mitscher sent the following to all ships, 'Have received following. Enemy fleet sighted 15° 02′ N, 135° 25′ E, speed 20, course 270. Reception was poor. Anybody heard transmission check position, course and speed. Anybody who had heard different contact CTF 58.' *Yorktown* responded, stating that she had received the following from plane 47V24, 'Enemy fleet sighted. Time 1540. Lat. 15–00, Long. 135–25. Course 270. Speed 20. About 10 ships.

Looks like two small carriers.' The minor difference in latitude convinced Mitscher that his searchers had found the Japanese and he signalled Spruance, at 1553, 'Expect to launch everything we have. We will probably have to recover at night.' This was followed with an order to the carriers to prepare for deck-load strikes. Curiously none of the contact reports were authenticated* and at least one was considered as possible enemy deception, though there is no evidence that in fact it was.

At 1557 Mitscher received his first clear contact report. It indicated that the Japanese force was disposed in three groups on a westerly course refuelling at slow speed. The position given, placed the Japanese over 200 miles to the west of the US fleet, at the edge of US aircraft strike range. When this latter information was received in flag plot, Mitscher asked Commander W. M. Wilhelm if the planes could make it. When, after checking his figures Wilhelm, who had led old *Hornet*'s dive bombers at Santa Cruz, said 'We can make it, but it's going to be tight', Mitscher replied, 'Launch them.'

Commander Task Force 58 now advised his force, 'Launch first deckload as soon as possible. Prepare to launch second deckload', followed immediately by the signal, 'Point option course 315°, speed 15'. These orders had been anticipated throughout the fleet. The aviators had their chartboards filled in with recognition signals, call signs, time of sunset, proper directional approach to base,** weather information and distance and bearing to nearest land. The only information missing was the enemy's position, course and speed and these were now appearing on the teletype screens in the ready rooms of the eleven carriers which were to send aircraft in the first raid.*** As the information came onto the screens the pilots realized the great range involved. The aircraft had been armed and fuelled since morning and their engines had been warmed-up periodically to insure that they were ready for instant launching. As soon as their engines were turned off they had been topped up again.

---

* Authentication – Plain text messages are checked to determine that the originator is 'friendly' by transmitting a coded group which must be responded to with a predetermined group, known as an authenticator. Each challenge has a specific response.

** During wartime aircraft would approach friendly formations on a designated bearing, which was changed regularly, to assist in recognition of friendly aircraft. Aircraft coming in on the proper bearing were assumed friendly until they were sighted or acted in a hostile way.

*** See appendix for make up of American attack group.

As the aviators headed for their aircraft, Mitscher received a depressing piece of intelligence. The Japanese fleet was sixty miles further west than originally plotted. Lt (jg) J. S. Moore, Nelson's wingman, had checked Nelson's navigation and found an error in longitude. Mitscher received this information at 1605.

The radio room on the Japanese heavy cruiser *Atago* of C Force was not an addressee to Moore's message, but listened in nonetheless and at 1615 passed it on to Ozawa stating that enemy reconnaissance aircraft 'were following them'. Based on this Ozawa called off further attempts to refuel on the 20th and ordered speed increased to 24 knots, maximum sustained speed for First Mobile Force.

At 1605 Commander TF 58 transmitted the first full report of the Japanese disposition to his carriers:

'There are two, possibly three, groups of enemy ships. One group, ten to fifteen miles to the north, consists of one large carrier, two or three cruisers, and eight destroyers. Southern group has two CVs, two AO and a destroyer on course due west. Third, consisting of one CV and many other ships is 60 miles west of the centre group. The primary objective is the carriers.'

The order to 'Start engines' was promptly given.

Mitscher and his staff debated whether the strike should be called off, but it was determined that the fleet could close about 75–100 miles during the attack, thus reducing the length of the return flight substantially. The decision to strike in spite of the range was made at about 1615. Mitscher, contrary to his usual practice, did not observe the take-off because of staff work required for the second raid.

The Flight to the Japanese Fleet
At 1621 TF 58 changed course into wind, speed 23 knots, and at 1624 the first aircraft began to roll down the flight decks of the American carriers. US Task Force 58 was at about 13° 58′ N, 138° 57′ E some 300 miles east of the Japanese First Mobile Force, which was in the vicinity of 15° 30′ N, 133° 55′ E.

On *Hornet* Cdr J. S. Arnold checked the blackboard at primary control on the ship's superstructure for last minute information. It contained Lt Moore's corrected position. Arnold plotted this new position and realized the impossible range for the strike. His reaction to this information typifies the determination of the American aviators to strike the Japanese carrier force while it was within range regardless of the cost;

'I had decided that if the enemy fleet finally was discovered even farther west than originally plotted it would be best to pursue and attack, retire as far as possible before darkness set in, notify the ship by key, then have all planes in the group land in the water in the same vicinity so that rafts could be lashed together and mutual rescues could be effected.'

At 1636 all aircraft were airborne and TF 58 changed course to the northwest, speed 23 knots, as the raiders formed up. Instead of the standard method of circling near the Task Groups the aircraft rendezvoused in task group formations en route climbing slowly to conserve fuel, taking nearly 30 minutes to close up. Air gunners closed their canopies to reduce air resistance and as the groups slowly reached 10,000 feet the pilots leaned their fuel mixture as much as possible, some below the safe minimum, enriching it only when the engine overheated to a dangerous degree. The raid consisted of 85 Hellcats with drop tanks, 54 Avengers (21 of which were torpedo equipped, the remainder carried four 500 lb bombs), 51 Helldivers with drop tanks and 26 Dauntlesses.*

At 1645 Commander TF 58 signalled Admiral Spruance, 'Have launched deckload strike. Expect to retain second deckload for tomorrow morning.' The excessive range and late hour were the two factors in this decision. The aircraft of that strike were disarmed and defuelled. At 1651 destroyer *Burns* in the screen of TG 58.1 opened fire on an aircraft identified as a Nell (G3M). (It was more probably a Frances.)

Original strike course was 279° (this was Air Group 16 course to target). At about 1715 Lt Cdr Ralph Weymouth, Commander Bomber Squadron 16, intercepted the following from the scouts, 'I've got a corrected position for you, a corrected position. Ready? One-three-three degrees three zero minutes east, One five degrees three zero minutes north; course two-seven-zero; speed one five. That's the main body. About fifteen or twenty miles southeast of them is a tanker force. Five tankers with half a dozen "cans"**. Got

---

* See Appendix for complete breakdown of American attack group. The American aerial torpedo was a 1920 lbs 22″ weapon.

** 'Cans' – US Navy slang for destroyers.

it?' Weymouth replied, 'Thanks, good work, out,' and plotted the new position. It was the corrected position referred to earlier and as mentioned before, plotted about 60 miles west of Nelson's original fix. Based on this new position Weymouth changed course to 284° continuing to climb, as one of his Dauntlesses turned back because of fuel system malfunction.

The usual chatter between aircraft was notably absent during this flight (radio discipline was a problem in aviation units throughout the war, with Midway – perhaps because of the odds – and Philippine Sea as exceptions). Perhaps the length of the flight and the fact that few of the pilots had ever seen a Japanese aircraft carrier group were the reasons.

As if to emphasize the major deficiency in US carrier operations *vis-à-vis* Japanese technique, at the time when Mitscher's aviators had finally found the Japanese and had a raid underway against a Japanese Fleet virtually stripped of aircraft, one of the aircraft of the Japanese 1300 air searches found Task Force 58, reporting two carriers and two battleships at 14° 20′ N, 138° 30′ E (Grid NI–I–2–KA) on course west at 1715. At 1720 Ozawa launched three pathfinders, followed by a tiny raid of seven torpedo planes. The pathfinders were unable to find the Americans, as the contact was somewhat west of TF 58's actual position and the raid returned, just before the American attackers arrived.

At 1754 the Japanese FMF, now aware that the US fleet was within strike range, assumed air defence formation and went to action stations. Their formations were well conceived to repel air attack, however their disposition was not. This paradox comes from the uneven distribution of heavy screen units required by the 'Straight line thrust' attack disposition of the previous day. C Force no longer stood between the US Fleet and the main body of A Force and B Force.

The assumption of air defence formation was timely, because at 1803 C Force radars detected American aircraft at 230° relative.★ Aircraft of NAG 653 encountered 24 American aircraft at 3000 metres altitude. The Japanese aircraft advised FMF of the approach

---

★ This bearing appears to be an error either as a true bearing or relative bearing. The actual bearing from C Force would have been about 090°. The primary reason this entry is of interest is the fact Japanese radars picked up American aircraft 20 minutes before the aircraft sighted Japanese ships, indicating about 40 miles radar range in actual operations.

of the Americans at 1825 stating that they were splitting into four groups. Records of the Japanese interceptions are very sketchy. There were forty fighters and twenty-eight fighter bombers in First Mobile Force after the 'Turkey Shoot' and it appears that the Japanese managed to scramble every one. In all, the Japanese had about seventy-five carrier aircraft of all types airborne during the American attack. The skill of their fighter and fighter-bomber pilots who did meet the American raiders was high and indicates that a large percentage of the survivors of the previous day's fight were veterans. At 1807 cruiser *Mogami* was ordered to transfer to C Force. Apparently this transfer took place after the American attack.

About the time the flight from NAG 653 ran across one of the American strike groups (1825) the first American groups approached FMF. The chatter over the radio began to pick up noticeably: 'Look at that oil slick.' 'Haven't got time to look around! We've got to attack immediately if we're going to get back home.' 'Is this the force to attack? My gas is half gone!' The first group encountered was the Supply Group of six fleet oilers, trailing oil indicating they had recently broken off fuelling (though they had not) and six escorting destroyers, which were on course 270° and falling astern of FMF which was now making best fleet speed, 24 knots.

THE AMERICAN ATTACKS

Attack on the Supply Group. Lt Cdr J. D. Blitch, Commander Bomber Squadron 14 (USS *Wasp*), decided that the US Fleet would have a great advantage in a stern chase if the Japanese 'train' was destroyed, causing them to retire at economical speeds. His air group struck the oilers disabling *Genyo Maru* and *Seiyo Maru*, both of which were later scuttled, after the Americans retired. Fleet oiler *Hayasui* was hit once and received two near misses suffering slight damage.

Attacks on 'A Force'. When the American attackers arrived, *Zuikaku* was at about 16° 20′ N, 133° 30′ E on course 320°, 24 knots, screened by heavy cruisers *Haguro* and *Myoko*, together with light cruiser *Yahagi* and seven destroyers. The two heavy cruisers were 1500 metres broad on each bow, while the light cruiser and destroyers were evenly distributed about the big carrier at 2000 metres. The carrier was recovering the afternoon search as the Americans approached. *Zuikaku* apparently had two four-plane divisions (*shotai*) of combat air patrol airborne as the American raiders approached. Both of these *shotai* reported attacking American aircraft between 1830–1930, but apparently not over A Force. *Zuikaku* probably launched the nine fighters remaining aboard (she had a total of 17 VF after the 'Turkey Shoot') as the Americans approached. About ten of these fighters were lost in the battle.

Lt Cdr Arnold had fought at Coral Sea where the US aircraft ganged up on light carrier *Shoho* while *Shokaku* and *Zuikaku* worked over old *Lexington* and old *Yorktown*. He was determined this would not happen this time and after scouting ahead of his group he picked *Zuikaku* escorted by an estimated '10 cruisers and 14–16 destroyers'. He noted that the other Japanese groups appeared to be under attack and chose Japan's most famous carrier as his target. His group was joined by TBFs from *Yorktown* (VT–1), SBDs from *Enterprise* (VB–10) and TBFs (Avenger) from *San Jacinto* (VT–51). Most of the TBFs were armed with four 500 lb bombs. Because of this and the fact that TBFs were not stressed for dive bombing they had to use the less accurate glide-bombing technique.

On signal, the Japanese formation opened fire with all of its weapons from the 8-inch guns of the two heavy cruisers to the 25mm and 13mm heavy machine guns mounted on all of the ships. The Japanese employed coloured bursting charges to assist director officers and the effect was similar to a fireworks display; red, white, yellow, pink, black, burgundy, lavender bursts together with the incendiaries filled the sky. *Zuikaku* managed to avoid the two torpedoes dropped, but she was hit by 'several' bombs and received five near misses. The hits caused aviation gasoline fires in the hangar deck, which quickly became unmanageable. The new bubble fire extinguishing equipment did not seem to slow the fires so the order was given to 'Abandon ship'. Before the order was executed the damage control parties reported progress and the ship was saved to fight again. The contrast between *Zuikaku*, an older ship with a veteran crew, and *Taiho*'s bungling efforts by 'green' damage control personnel is illustrative of the importance of proper training.

As mentioned earlier Cdr Arnold had felt he would fly east after the attack and crash land his air group in formation. He now decided to try to make it back to his carrier. Darkness was closing in as the groups which hit *Zuikaku* formed up, leaned out their mixtures and set course for Task Force 58.

Attacks on B Force. Admiral Joshima's B Force was about 20 miles southwest of *Zuikaku* on course 300°, speed 24 knots. Flagship *Junyo* *Hayataka* in USN action reports) was in the centre with battleship

Nagato broad on her starboard bow and heavy cruiser *Mogami* broad on her port bow, carrier *Hiyo* (*Hitaka* in USN action reports) was on *Junyo*'s port quarter and light carrier *Ryuho* on her starboard quarter; all were at 1500 metres while the eight screening destroyers were evenly spaced on a 2000 metre circle. Containing three carriers, this formation naturally drew many attackers. It also had the largest fighter contingent; thirty-eight fighters and fighter bombers of NAG 652 had survived the previous day's fight.

At 1823 Lt Cdr Weymouth overheard other attack groups, 'Ships there' and at about the same time passed the oil slick he had heard other groups mention. He changed course to 300° when he passed the oil slick. At 1835 Air Group 16 passed the Supply Groups. Ten minutes later they changed course to 310° to clear a large cumulus cloud. As the formation cleared the cloud Weymouth heard someone exclaim, 'Looks like the whole God damn Jap Navy!' Weymouth saw three groups. The 'main' group (B Force) 10 miles ahead, consisted of (in Weymouth's estimation) two 'Hayataka' class carriers, one light carrier, two *Kongo* class battleships, two to four heavy cruisers of the *Tone* and *Mogami** classes, four to six light cruisers and destroyers. The second group (A Force) twelve miles to the north, consisted of a *Shokaku* class carrier, three or four heavy cruisers and five or six destroyers. The third group (probably C Force) was thirty miles west, in Weymouth's estimation, too far to be identified or even counted.** Weymouth noted that the *Zuikaku* group was under attack by *Enterprise* and *Hornet* groups and decided to attack B Force. They were met by eight Zekes which were quickly distracted by the Hellcats as Weymouth pushed on. His group passed north of B Force and then turned to attack the 'southern *Hayataka*' (the southern CV was *Hiyo* but it seems that AG 16 concentrated most heavily on *Junyo*). All of the TBFs of the group were armed with four 500 lb bombs rather than torpedoes. The aircraft reached their push over point at 1904. The pilots estimated that they hit *Junyo* with seven 1000 lb bombs and nine 500 lb bombs, and that they hit *Hiyo* at least once. The Japanese records show that *Junyo* received two direct hits near the super

---

* CA – *Mogami* could be mistaken for a *Tone* class cruiser since her after turrets had been removed and replaced by an aircraft deck similar to the *Tone*

** After the battle the Air Combat Intelligence officers of Fifth Fleet did an extremely good job of reconstructing the actual Japanese disposition, in spite of the many conflicting descriptions such as Weymouth's.

Heavy cruiser *Maya* with No 3 8in (C turret) removed and increased AA.

Left: Superstructure of heavy cruiser *Maya* in May 1944. The canvas covered objects are triple 25mm machine guns. Note the Type 21 Radar on the foremast.

Below: Crew of *Zuikaku* at quarters on flight deck. The radar is Type 21.

Bottom: Part of First Mobile Force at Singapore in May, 1944. The three cruisers anchored in echelon are *Takao* class ships. The carrier at right is *Taiho*. Light cruiser *Noshiro* is in the centre background.

Above: May 11, 1944. Portions of First Mobile Force depart Singapore for Tawi-Tawi.

Below: Carriers *Junyo*, *Hiyo* and *Ryuho* (2 sf) as seen from heavy cruiser *Maya* en route for Tawi-Tawi in May, 1944. The aircraft is an E13A 'Jake'.

Above: A portion of First Mobile Force at Tawi-Tawi in May, 1944. The ship in the foreground is *Taiho*. *Shokaku* and *Nagato* are in the background. /US Navy

Below: May 13, 1944. Portions of First Mobile Force arrive at **Tawi-Tawi.** The triple AA mount is a 25mm machine gun.

Top: Aircraft Cruiser (*Koku Junyokan*) *Mogami* at Tawi-Tawi in May or June, 1944. Note at least four aircraft on deck and cv *Taiho* in background.

Above: First Mobile Force on June 15, 1944 as seen from cruiser *Maya*. The carrier in left background is *Taiho*. Battleship *Nagato* is in the centre and carrier *Shokaku* is in the right foreground.

Top: C Force on June 17, 1944. A portion of the force comprising from left to right the cruiser *Takao*, battleship *Kongo*, and battleship *Haruna* followed closely by a light carrier.

Above: Other ships of C Force seen on June 17, 1944. Just beyond the destroyer in the foreground is a light carrier and on the right is the battleship *Yamato*.

B Force, carriers *Junyo* and *Hiyo* underway as seen from cruiser *Maya*.

structure and six near misses, making air operations difficult, but her 'navigational powers were not impaired'. There is no indication in Japanese records whether *Hiyo* was hit in this attack. Air Group 16 withdrew through the Japanese disposition and was now attacked by four Zekes. In the attack the group had lost one Hellcat, one Avenger and one Dauntless. The survivors joined up at 1918 and set course 100° to return to the ship.

Light carrier *Ryuho* was the object of attention of four Avengers of VT–10 (*Enterprise*). These aircraft were bomb armed and escorted by VB–10 Hellcats. As they approached the Japanese formation they were met by one or two *Shotai* of Zekes, but the interceptors were driven off by the Hellcat escorts. In their glide bomb attacks the TBFs were taken under heavy fire by battleship *Nagato*, including her 16 in guns, but the aircraft managed to drop their weapons, claiming eight 500 lb bomb hits. The Japanese action report states: 'slight damage incurred by near misses, but fighting and navigational powers not impaired' in regard to the damage suffered by *Ryuho* during the battle.

Carrier *Hiyo* was not as lucky as her sisters. She had come under dive bombing attack by Air Group 16 as mentioned previously, but her damage, if any, from that attack had been superficial. The next attack was to be fatal.

Lt (jg) George Brown, leader of *Belleau Wood*'s torpedo planes (four Avengers with torpedoes), had vowed that he was going to get a hit on a Japanese carrier regardless of the cost. As his formation approached the Japanese fleet he entered a cloud, hoping to emerge close to the Japanese Fleet at attack level. In fact, as his group of three TBFs* emerged from the cloud at attack altitude they still had 5000 yards to run before they reached their drop position and the Japanese obviously saw the dreaded torpedo planes because they were immediately greeted by intense anti-aircraft fire from the screen of B Force. (There is no indication in Japanese logs that these aircraft were tracked on radar before emerging from cloud, though the facts indicate the possibility.) Brown picked *Hiyo*. His aircraft was hit and a bad fire started in the crew compartment. Brown climbed to an altitude sufficient for his two aircrewmen to bail out, which they promptly did. The other two aircraft were also buffeted and hit by Japanese gunfire as they fanned out to widen the torpedo spread,

---

* The fourth TBF had become separated in the approach.

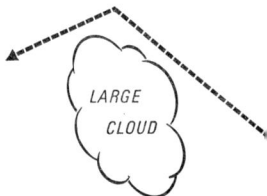

A FORCE LOG ENTRIES

1830 - 1st SHOTAI at 4000m
SIGHTS ENEMY CV
VB at 3500-4000m
WITH F6Fs at
4500-5000m
1st SHOTAI ATTACK
2nd SHOTAI ATTACK
ENEMY ENCOUNTERED,
9VF, 5VB, 1VT confirmed
3VF, 1VT probable
6 Japanese VF Lost

YAHAGI

MYOKO

B-FORCE

300°/24KT

NAGATO RYUHO
JUNYO
MOGAMI
HIYO

LARGE CLOUD

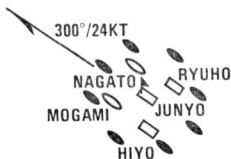

C-FORCE

TAKAO
CHITOSE
ATAGO
MUSASHI
300°/24KTS
KUMANO
CHIKUMA
YAMATO
ZUIHO TONE
SUZUYA
HARUNA
MAYA
KONGO
CHIYODA
CHOKAI

C-FORCE LOG ENTRIES

1754 - ASSUME AIR DEFENSE
FORMATION
1832 - 50 ENEMY AIRCRAFT
ATTACK CHIYODA
1838 - BOMB HIT CHIYODA
20 TBFs
ATTACK C FORCE
1846 - ENEMY WITH-
DRAW
1848 - 3 SBDs ATTACK
1910 - CEASE FIRE

1825 - 24 ENEMY AIRCRAFT BEARING 158
ALT. 3000m DIVIDE INTO 4 GROUPS

1830 - 20 ENEMY
AIRCRAFT
at 130° 5000m.
SPLIT to ATTACK
CHIYODA

1803 - RADAR CONTACT-
ENEMY AIRCRAFT
230° RELATIVE

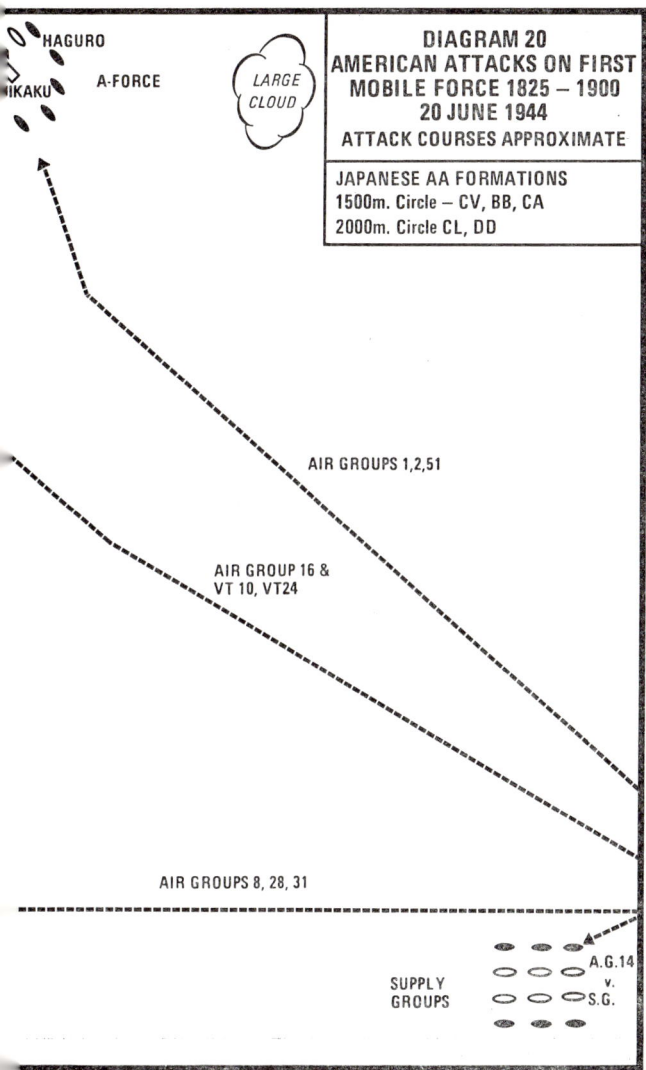

DIAGRAM 20
**AMERICAN ATTACKS ON FIRST
MOBILE FORCE 1825 – 1900
20 JUNE 1944**
ATTACK COURSES APPROXIMATE

JAPANESE AA FORMATIONS
1500m. Circle – CV, BB, CA
2000m. Circle CL, DD

HAGURO

ZIKAKU   A-FORCE

LARGE CLOUD

AIR GROUPS 1,2,51

AIR GROUP 16 &
VT 10, VT24

AIR GROUPS 8, 28, 31

A.G.14
v.
S.G.

SUPPLY
GROUPS

but Brown's aircraft seemed to take the brunt. The flames went out as he reached his drop point. After he dropped his weapon, he flew the length of the Japanese carrier drawing some of the anti-aircraft fire from his wingmen. Lt (jg) B. C. Tate and Lt (jg) W. R. Omark pressed on to their drop points. It seems that at least two of the three torpedoes hit *Hiyo*.

When the second torpedo hit *Hiyo*, she went dead in the water and lost all power. The big ship immediately began to list to port and fires spread rapidly from deck to deck. It seemed obvious she would not survive and the orders were passed to abandon ship. A destroyer stood by as the remainder of B Force continued westward.

Radioman E. C. Babcock and Gunner G. H. Platz, Brown's crewmen, watched the big carrier go down as they floated nearby. They would be rescued the next day by a float plane from cruiser *Boston*.

The three torpedo planes now headed back for TF 58. Omark was attacked by two Vals and a Zeke as he left the Japanese formation, but managed to drive them off. Tate's plane ran out of fuel and ditched but he was later rescued. Both pilots saw Brown's heavily damaged aircraft after the battle and reported he appeared to be severely wounded. (He was lost in the return flight.)

Attacks on C Force. Because of the attack disposition of the previous day Admiral Ozawa's three smallest carriers were the best protected ships in his force. The three light carriers were in three circular formations spaced 10 kilometres apart, on a 000°–180° axis, approximately ten miles south of B Force. The entire formation was on course 300°, speed 24 knots. From north to south they were formed as follows:

Chitose Unit: *Musashi, Atago, Takao* and three DDs.
Zuiho Unit: *Yamato, Chikuma, Tone, Kumano, Suzuya,* 3 DDs.
Chiyoda Unit: *Kongo, Haruna, Chokai, Maya, Noshiro,* 2 DDs.*

The entire group had but twenty-two aircraft, of which thirteen were fighters and fighter-bombers. As in the other formations the carriers were at the centre of each group, with the battleships and heavy cruisers on a 1500 metre circle and the light cruiser and destroyers at 2000 metres, evenly spaced. As the Americans approached, the carriers were in the process of recovering the sixteen

---

* Light cruiser and destroyer distribution is approximate only.

plane raid which had been launched at 1600 against the false contact. Seven of these aircraft were shot down in their landing circle by US aircraft and only two A6M were reported over the entire formation, one of which was shot down by US aircraft. The real defence of this group was its anti-aircraft guns, including the 46 CM (18-inch) guns of battleships *Yamato* and *Musashi*.

As mentioned previously the group from USS *Wasp* had attacked the oiler groups. The other three air groups from TG 58.2 (AG 28, AG 8, AG 31) had seen the oilers also, but their leader Lt R. P. Gift of VT-28 told the group, 'To hell with the merchant fleet. let's go get the fighting navy!' They picked light carrier *Chiyoda*'s group. They hit the carrier with two 500 lb bombs aft destroying two torpedo planes and damaging one fighter and one torpedo plane. Twenty *Chiyoda* crewmen were killed and thirty wounded. The ship also suffered splinter damage from several near misses. After her fires were put out she recovered her fighting and navigational powers. The attackers also hit *Haruna* on her deck aft and got several near misses on that often 'sunk' ship. It was necessary to flood the aft magazines and damage to her shaft brackets restricted her speed to 27 knots. Her fighting power was otherwise unimpaired. Heavy cruiser *Maya* (an excellent AA ship) suffered a near miss, which caused a fire on her port torpedo deck, but no serious damage. The only Japanese aircraft carriers which were not attacked were *Zuiho* and *Chitose*, the most heavily defended ships in the Japanese Fleet.

As the attackers withdrew they were attacked by six or seven Zekes, which were driven off by two Hellcats from *Bunker Hill*, but not before two Helldivers were lost.

Darkness was fast closing in as the Americans finished forming up for the flight back to TF 58. They encountered the seven B6N launched by *Zuikaku* at 1730. Both groups were so intent on getting to their respective carriers that they passed each other without firing a shot.

In the attack the Americans lost twenty aircraft to all causes, while the Japanese lost sixty-five carrier aircraft and fifteen floatplanes from all causes on June 20. Japanese First Mobile Force now had thirty-five carrier aircraft and 12 floatplanes, from a complement of 450 and 45 respectively.

Considering the long range and relative lack of coordination, the American attack was excellent in almost all respects; one fleet carrier sunk, another heavily damaged, three other carriers damaged moderately to lightly, a battleship and cruiser damaged and two oilers sunk and one damaged. Whether similar results could have been achieved on June 19 when the Japanese would have had more fighters and the vanguard shield is speculative. The primary criticism of the US attack is the small number of torpedo planes armed with their primary weapon. Of 57 torpedo planes launched only twelve carried torpedoes. All 48 Japanese torpedo planes in the attack groups of June 19 were torpedo armed.

The Japanese defenders fought well considering the odds. The most obvious criticism of their defence was the uneven distribution of the screen. The confusion involved in a redistribution of the screen while being pursued makes it difficult to criticize their formations in view of their initial decision to employ their attack disposition.

NIGHT RECOVERY

At 1900, as the American attackers withdrew Ozawa transferred heavy cruisers *Myoko* and *Haguro* and the bulk of 10th Destroyer Flotilla to C Force and ordered that force east to engage the Americans in night battle as the six remaining carriers headed for home.

On board light cruiser *Oyodo*, in the Inland Sea, Admiral Kusaka convinced Admiral Toyoda that the decision to retreat should be taken away from Ozawa. Having served as Admiral Nagumo's chief of staff at Midway, Kusaka knew from personal experience the difficulty of accepting defeat, even in the face of overwhelming evidence. The vigour of the American counterattack erased any hope that the optimistic reports of the survivors of June 19 were based on fact. If the Americans had been damaged on the 19th it had not substantially reduced their fighting capacity. The dispatch was received by Ozawa at 2045 and he ordered the carriers and their screens to continue northwest at 20 knots.

Task Force 58 opened the interval between groups to 15 miles for sufficient manoeuvering room in night recovery operations. At 1912 Mitscher signalled Spruance:

'After recovery of all planes tonight propose to have Task Groups 58.1, 58.2 and 58.3 take speed 19. Task Group 58.7 speed and distance optional.'

Mitscher intended that the battleships not be tied to the carriers while the latter were recovering aircraft, but that they close the

Japanese Fleet to be in position for surface action the next day. Spruance felt Task Force 58 should be kept concentrated, since it was a mathematical certainty the Japanese could not be overtaken that night, therefore the battleships would be in signalling range and from that position could easily move to destroy any cripples discovered by air search. He replied:

'Consider Task Force 58 should be kept tactically concentrated tonight and make best practical speed toward the enemy so as to keep them in air striking distance.'

As soon as the strike could be recovered the necessary arrangements for night searches would be made. The fuel status of all the destroyers was now critical, the average being about 33% while some were as low as 24%. This meant a high speed chase was out of the question. One destroyer division from each Task Group was ordered to trail its group to pick up downed pilots during the night landings and sweep the area the next morning for any they missed during the night and then to retire to refuel. At 2015 Mitscher signalled Spruance:

'Estimate that some undamaged Jap ships will retire tonight at 20 knots. Carriers should remain within 200 miles to strike enemy. Many of the planes launched today are now landing in water. Some destroyers will be out of fuel tomorrow and will require refueling. At what speed do you recommend that we steam tonight.'

After the attack on the Japanese Fleet the American pilots formed and started the long flight back to the carriers. They flew back in darkness at 120 mph, altitude 1000 feet with their throttles set at automatic lean allowing each gasoline tank to run dry before switching to the next tank. The flight back would take two and one half hours and most of the pilots were not night trained. Many had battle damage and some had no previous combat experience. The number of voice radio trasnmissions on the return flight was very high and covered the spectrum of human reaction to such predicaments: The matter of fact; 'I've got ten minutes of gas left Joe. Think I'll put her down in the water while I've still got power. So long Joe'; the forlorn, 'This is Forty-six Inkwell. Where am I please? Somebody tell me where I am!' and the ironic, 'Today the Navy is losing one of its best fighter pilots. I am going in.' One of the veteran pilots of Air Group 16 became so depressed by the voices on his radio that he turned the volume of his receiver off. Exhaustion and vertigo took their toll of the returning fliers. The Philippine Sea now contained several large thunder storms in the vicinity of Task Force 58. Some of the pilots mistook the lightning for lights of the Task Force while others feared that it was gunfire. By 2045 the first aircraft approached the force and course was changed to the east and speed to 22 knots. A night fighter from *Enterprise* was vectored to assist two groups in finding the force.

In both navies, ships were lighted for night landing. (See *Midway, The Japanese Navy's Story* p. 151, for Japanese use of lights in night flight operations.) As the planes approached, Admiral Clark's group turned on its lights. Next Mitscher ordered each task group flagship to turn on a searchlight. Truck lights and peacetime running lights were displayed in all ships. The destroyers and cruisers fired star shells to illuminate the carriers. The effect of this action on aviator morale was almost beyond calculation. Suffice it to say the pilots and aircrewmen knew that great risk was involved in this action by Mitscher. Now each pilot joined the nearest landing circle and at 2052 after it was obvious that it would be impossible for all the pilots to find their own ships, Mitscher ordered the planes to 'Land on any base you see. . . .' In the darkness and confusion there were some accidents and innumerable close calls. Aircraft on their final approach would be cut out at the last minute by some desperate pilot. One Hellcat came in low on the *Enterprise* and caught the second arresting wire, just as an Avenger came from nowhere skimming over the top of the fighter catching number 5 wire. Both aircraft landed safely amidst scrambling firefighters and flight deck personnel. A damaged Helldiver, with a badly wounded pilot landed on *Lexington*, crashing through the barrier into parked aircraft forward, several of which were still manned. Four other aircraft were destroyed and three men; a pilot, an aircrewman and a chockman were killed before the Helldiver came to a halt. *Lexington's* lights were out for ten minutes to indicate a foul deck. These incidents are illustrative of the events of the evening and the following quotation from the log of the Staff Duty Officer of Task Group 58.3 show how that evening was seen from one flagship:

2045 Executed turn 090
2056 Plane landed and guns firing
2057 Turn 095. Launched 1 VF (N)

2102 Executed Speed 23 knots

2100 *Knapp* picking up plane splashed in water astern of *Enterprise*

2123 Planes having trouble getting in landing circle in dark

2124 Plane crashed (SBD) hitting after island structure and crane

2126 Executed Speed 24 knots

2130 1 in water bearing 300, 500 yards from *Enterprise* – *Ingersoll* pick up pilot

2131 *Enterprise*, *Lexington*, *San Jacinto* and *Princeton* all landing planes. Plane in water 3000 yards from *Birmingham*, *Wadsworth* pick up

2135 *Lexington* tells *Cogswell* to stand clear

2135 Another in water

2137 Another in water from *Birmingham*

2145 *Cotten* picking up a pilot.

2146 *Cotten* picking up another pilot, starboard beam

2148 Port side of *Lexington* – man in water – *Cogswell* to pick up.

2150 Two planes just landed at same time and got away with it one forward of another

2155 Two or three on starboard bow of *Enterprise* in water, *Bronson* pick up

2200 Plane 500 yards astern of *Lexington*, *Cogswell* pick up

2201 Executed speed 22 knots

2207 *Wadsworth* told to pick up pilot and stay in that vicinity after daylight to pick up men in water

2215 DesDiv 90 told his boys to drop back and take intervals at 2 miles, speed 15 knots and search

2220 *San Jacinto* has 22 visitors

2221 *San Jacinto* reports 1 'VAL' with red lights on over formation

2223 *Dortch* says she has picked two up

2227 'Val' in our formation: order to fire given, flew directly over *San Jacinto* and *Enterprise*. Searchlight now on him

2230 Enemy carriers and many other ships badly damaged. This information just received from pilots

2231 CTG 58.3 informed CTF 58 that '*Val*' may be listening in on our circuit

2232 1 Night Chicken approaching on starboard side-hold fire

2237 CTG 58.3 ordered 'Hold Fire'. Val reported as disappearing

2244 'Val' reported flying over Task Group 58.2

2256 Last plane landed on *Enterprise*

2252 Executed 280 turn

2259 Executed Speed 16 knots

2348 Received word from *San Jacinto* and *Bunker Hill* that Jap plane tried to land twice on each carrier
2400 We have 17 visiting pilots aboard. We still have seven pilots not accounted for, but six reported in over base and are probably in water. Turner went in 20 miles from Jap force

The carriers were marked, in addition to peacetime running lights, with an individually coloured glow light, one foot square, visible from above. The flight deck was outlined with very small lights. When this was coupled with the starshells, searchlights, flares and aircraft running lights it is amazing that more aircraft were not lost in the confusion. Before the night was over about half of the aircraft which returned had landed on the wrong ship and some of the carriers had aircraft from as many as nine other ships aboard. During the height of the evening a Japanese aircraft was reported (see log above) attempting to land on several carriers. Some versions state that it was a 'Val' while others identify the type as 'Jill'. There is no evidence in Japanese records concerning this incident. At 2252 it was obvious that the last aircraft airborne had been recovered. Task Force 58 now changed course to retrace its path in an effort to recover as many downed aviators as possible. The sea was alight with the flashlights of the aviators, who were in rafts. Task Force 58 had lost six F6Fs, 35 SB2Cs and 28 TBFs in deck landing accidents or from crashing after running out of fuel in the return flight, for a total of 100 aircraft lost operationally. Sixteen pilots and 33 aircrewmen were lost together with two officers and four enlisted men on board the carriers. Fifty-one pilots and 50 aircrewmen were picked up that night. Further rescue operations saved 33 pilots and 26 aircrewmen.

At 2205 Ozawa ordered Kurita, whose detached force had reached 16° 05′ N, 134° 40′ E, finding no American ships, to change course to the northwest to rejoin his force as the Japanese fleet set course for Okinawa and home.

After asking Admiral Spruance to advise the 'Dumbos' of Task Force 58's position to facilitate rescue efforts, Mitscher sent the following message to his commander:

'Enemy fleet in four groups in approximate position at 1900 Lat. 15° 30′ N, Long. 133° 05′ E, apparently on course west. After recovery tonight expect to come to course 315° until we arrive at our 2045 position and then come to course approximately 280° in order to recover our downed pilots. Believe all enemy carriers and many other ships damaged and in confusion. Our carriers should proceed at 16 knots in order to retrieve as many pilots as possible.'

The low speed was to ensure that the destroyers could rejoin after conducting rescue operations. The Japanese fleet was heading northwest at 20 knots.

CHAPTER THREE

The Japanese Fleet Withdraws

A Saipan based PBM flying-boat, part of a 245°–295° 700 mile
search, found the Japanese Mobile Force at about 2300 on June 20
and after following it for $2\frac{1}{2}$ hours, reported that some of the
Japanese ships were trailing oil on course 330°, speed 15 knots. At
0200 *Bunker Hill* and *Enterprise* launched Avengers with long range
belly tanks to track the Japanese. They found 3 CVLs, 4 BBs, 12 CAs,
16 DDs – probably Kurita's reinforced van – in four groups between
17°–18° and 131°–132° on course northwest at 0522. The TBFs
tracked the Japanese force for about two hours.

Admiral Mitscher advised Spruance at 0450:

'With wind to easterly, it will not be possible to close enemy at
option speed greater than 15 knots. Enemy appears to be escaping
northwest with idea of fuelling. Some damage done. Yesterday,
anti-aircraft fire extremely heavy and accurate. Many planes
damaged. We hope to find a few crippled ships today.'

Point option was set as 280°, 15 knots. At 0600 a deckload of F6Fs
with 500 lb bombs was launched, with orders to fly to 225 miles on
course 285°, then 330° for 45 miles and then to return. It was not a
successful mission, failing to find the Japanese force.

Third Aircraft Carrier Squadron launched a four plane scout
mission at 0720, covering sector 090°–120° to 350 miles. This group
found no American ships.

At 0743 the Avengers broke contact with First Mobile Force, now
360 miles from Task Force 58, and returned to their ships. This was
the last contact between the two fleets in this operation.

Mitscher originally intended to launch a second strike as soon as
it could be organized, but it was now obvious the Japanese were far
beyond his strike range and at 0800 June 21 he advised Spruance:

'Report of special scouts equipped with special fuel tanks and

164

without bomb load, that enemy heading northwest, speed 20 knots distance 360 miles. Maximum range of plane with bomb load is 250 miles. Strike now in air ordered to hit cripples within range. If they go farther many of them will again make water landings. Air strikes cannot reach target at present range.'

At 1130 destroyer *Asagumo* dropped out of formation with fuel trouble. She was detached and ordered to follow Mobile Force at her best speed, 16 knots.

Monterey and *Cabot* were transferred to Task Group 58.1, as Task Group 58.2 (*Bunker Hill*, *Wasp* and their screen) joined the battle line at 1050. The force was joined by Spruance's flagship *Indianapolis* at 1126. The remaining groups steamed westwards at 15 knots searching for downed aviators. At 1205 the battle line slowed to 11 knots to refuel destroyers. The 1330 searches were sent to cover 250°–280° to 325 miles, finding nothing. At 1454 fuelling of battle line destroyers was complete and at 1516 speed was increased to 15 knots, course 280°. The Japanese launched an air search, composed of three aircraft, at 1440 to cover sector 115°–135°.

An afternoon search launched at 1500 found nothing and at 2030, when *Lexington* was at 16° N, 134° 40′ E, the bulk of Task Force 58 reversed course for Saipan. The battle line reached 133° 55′ E, the vicinity of the attack on First Mobile Force, picking up more aviators, before reversing course.

At 1645 Ozawa issued the necessary orders for entering Nakagasuku Bay, Okinawa and that evening dictated his resignation to his Chief of Staff, Captain Ohmae, for transmittal to Admiral Toyoda. Toyoda expressed his absolute confidence in Ozawa's ability for refusing to read the letter, saying, 'I am more responsible for this defeat than Admiral Ozawa and I will not accept his resignation'.

First Mobile Force entered Nakagasuku Bay (later Buckner Bay) in two groups; the vanguard (First Diversion Attack Force) arrived a 1300 followed at 1500 by the carriers (Mobile Force). The survivors of the three carriers were transferred to *Zuikaku* (*Taiho* and *Hiyo*) and *Maya* (*Shokaku*). The next day the supply groups departed at 0330 for the Inland Sea. At 0515 'A-Go' was dissolved and the carriers plus their destroyer screen returned to the administrative control of Commander Third Fleet (Admiral Ozawa) and returned to Japan. The battleships and cruisers, together with their destroyers, returned to Admiral Kurita's Second Fleet and, less *Haruna* and *Maya* (which

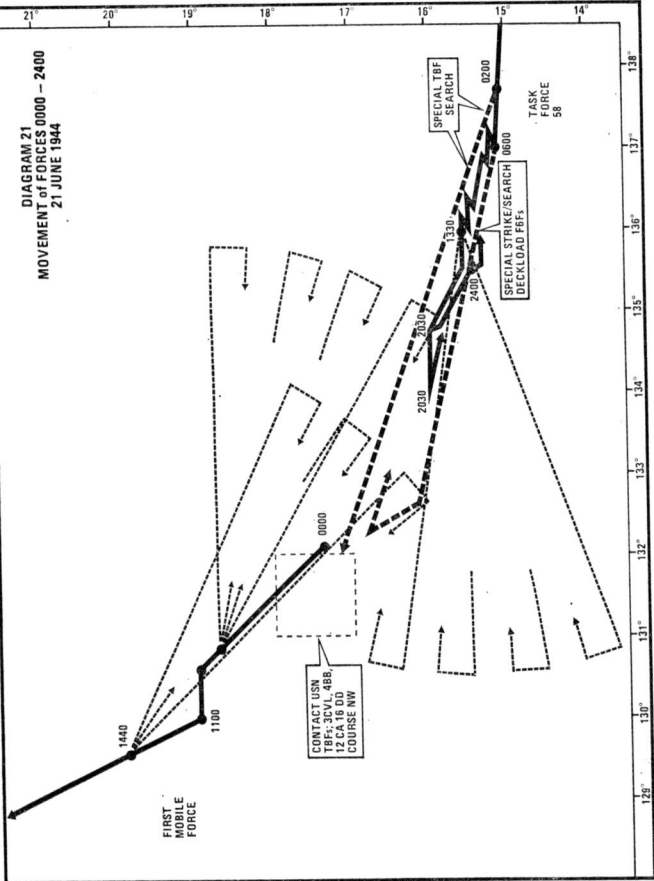

DIAGRAM 21
MOVEMENT of FORCES 0000 — 2400
21 JUNE 1944

SPECIAL TBF
SEARCH

TASK
FORCE
58

SPECIAL STRIKE/SEARCH
DECKLOAD F6Fs

0200

0600

0330

2400

2030

2030

0000

1440

1100

CONTACT USN
TBFs: 3CVL, 4BB,
12 CA 16 DD
COURSE NW

FIRST
MOBILE
FORCE

proceeded to Japan for repair to battle damage), returned to Singapore.

Between June 27 and July 5 the American task groups returned to Eniwetok. Saipan would be secured by July 9 and the remainder of the Marianas by the end of August.

CHAPTER FOUR

Conclusion

'Our Imperial Combined Fleet is now powerless. Prepare at once to reform the Cabinet so we can seek peace.' (Sign which appeared in Japanese Navy Headquarters after the fall of Saipan, p. 507 *The Rising Sun*, Toland.)

'The enemy had escaped. He had been badly hurt by one aggressive carrier air strike at the one time he was within range. His fleet was not sunk.' CTF 58 Action Report Serial 00388.

'The opinion expressed in the narrative that the covering force should have proceeded earlier to the westward in search of the approaching Japanese fleet is not concurred in.' ComFifth Fleet endorsement to CTF 58 Action Report Serial 00388.

The Battle of the Philippine Sea presents an apparent paradox; strong dissatisfaction on the part of victor and vanquished alike.

The Japanese frustration is readily understandable. Twenty months after the victory at Santa Cruz, the Japanese carrier force's best effort had been completely thwarted. To add to their distress is the fact that Admiral Ozawa had handled his fleet in excellent fashion. He took his fleet to the most advantageous tactical position possible, just inside his own strike range and outside American search and strike range, launched raids that would have been devastating in 1942 and had lost just one of his carriers to the superior US carrier force. In view of Ozawa's skill and the results obtained was a Japanese victory possible? Probably not. Two things worked against Admiral Ozawa. First, of course, was American superiority in numbers. Second, US Navy radar fighter direction subjected raiders to long periods of attention by combat air patrol, and Japanese strike tactics attacked American strength. The remarkable strides in American radar technique were unknown to the Japanese and would not be known until after the defeats of Formosa and Leyte.*

---

* War College Analysis of Leyte Gulf – '. . . the failure of the Japanese to realize (a) the excellence of Allied radar, (b) the Allied capability of long-range interceptions, and (c) the method of conducting such

The performance of Japanese search aircraft was outstanding. From the beginning of the operation Admiral Ozawa was better advised by his reconnaissance units than Admiral Mitscher was by his. The importance of this aspect should not be lost when one realizes that American *strategic* reconnaissance was as good as the Japanese. It was only when the battle reached the tactical phase that the Japanese Fleet 'disappeared'. The two bad plots (3–Ri and 15–Ri) on June 19 were minor errors comparable to Nelson's crucial error on June 20.

In the areas of submarine and anti-submarine warfare the Japanese performance was disastrous. The Japanese '*Battle Lessons*' contain the following interesting comment regarding Japanese submarine and anti-submarine operations:

'(g) It is admitted that the antisubmarine defence (especially during a battle) should be re-examined. Since a battle of a fleet is now mainly carried out by its planes, the fleet frequently stays in the same combat area to launch or receive the planes. Therefore, the antisubmarine defence must be carried out more strictly than ever before. In spite of this situation the fleet observes practically no other precaution than posting lookouts for submarines in a circular fleet formation, and cruises unconcerned at a high speed with the blind trust that the submarine danger is not much to worry about. This is indeed a serious misconception which makes us really worried.

'In *A-Go* three of our carriers were sunk by enemy submarines all at once.* It was indeed regrettable that this could not be avoided. At least each fleet should post a small carrier against enemy submarines around the formation, and tighten its antisubmarine defence measures, and during a battle the guard ships should advance ahead of the carriers at will and fire guns for warning for enemy submarines. These measures should be adopted at once, but a most

---

long-range interceptions.' The Japanese Battle Lessons says, 'The enemy attempted a thorough-going interception of our attacking planes by using accurate radio instruments and by disposing a powerful fighter plane formation about 100 nautical miles in advance of the carriers'. This was written after Formosa and Leyte when the Japanese had finally realized the extent of Allied radar superiority.

* The Japanese thought that *Hiyo* was finished off by submarines, but there is no evidence of this in any American submarine action reports.

urgent problem for antisubmarine defence is development of efficient antisubmarine weapons.

'During *A-Go*, enemy submarines were sighted, yet our submarines engaged in the battle very little, out of proportion to damages done to them. This was admittedly due to lack of improvement in the radio instruments of submarine detection at the base, while the enemy submarines were equipped with improved radars. Furthermore, in order to avoid confusion among our submarines, their field of operation was restricted to the water east of the line joining the archipelago. This was very regrettable. It would admittedly have been better if the submarines had not been subjected to restriction to the operational field and ordered about where to go according to the development of the battle.'

The very poor tactics combined with an inadequate ratio of destroyers to large combatants and with the reduction of antisubmarine air patrols on the 19th to produce a debacle. Interestingly, in spite of the insights of '*Battle Lessons*', the Japanese ASW effort at Leyte Gulf was even poorer when incorrect formations were employed in known submarine waters. Perhaps the underlying (and seemingly never learned) lesson of this fact is the necessity of operational units putting such studies as '*Battle Lessons*' into practical application. Japanese submarine operations waivered from very poor to very good during the Pacific War and '*A-Go*' was one of the best examples of the former. Their principal effort was tied to the route their planners hoped the Americans would take and the axis of their main picket line (in itself a good tactic) was anchored to a US advance base, a blunder which resulted in the most spectacular ASW score of the war.

In light of Admiral Toyoda's statement at the beginning of the section on Japanese tactics it would seem that the Japanese would have had a better chance of some modest success had they concentrated their entire effort on the first contact rather than trying to pay attention to all discovered targets. It should be remembered that only two of the four raids hit the American defences head on. Although these were thoroughly defeated, had the Japanese raiders come in in four waves in fairly rapid succession some might have broken through. American interception techniques, however, make even such small expectations seem remote. The ranges involved in the Japanese attacks prevented the massing for one gigantic raid though this might have been a successful alternative. Tactically the Japanese air attack commanders showed the effects of the drop in ten years' experience when they orbited at 100 miles range. Since most of the Japanese aviators were killed and few survived the war one can only speculate on the reason for this decision (closing up the formation of inexperienced flyers is the most likely reason) but it was fatal.

Much has been written about Japanese obsession with 'decisive battles', but when faced with their strategic situation the alternatives seem even less promising. Attrition war could have but one ending, therefore destruction of or severe damage to the American carrier force seemed the only way of slowing the Allied advance and negotiating a favourable settlement – the only Japanese hope at this stage.

One of the interesting aspects of the Japanese planning which has not been mentioned in the text is the 'tailoring' of their Operations orders for their opponent's supposed psychological make-up. After the war Admiral Ozawa was asked: 'During the course of the war, did the Japanese make any effort to study the personal characteristics of our commanders and to vary their tactics in accordance with the commander they believed opposed them in any particular operation?' He replied: 'We always tried to adopt the operation plan according to the characteristics of the *United States* commander.' Spruance's 'known caution' led to the adoption of outranging tactics. Students of this battle and the Battle for Leyte Gulf might feel that the Japanese were very successful in this important area of operational planning.

American frustration is more difficult to understand in view of the margin of US victory and can be explained only in view of the 'black show-brown shoe' schism. Rarely in history has so convincing a victory generated such dissatisfaction among the ranks of the victors and it seems more than mere coincidence that the ranks split almost uniformly along line-officer-aviator lines (with Arleigh Burke as an articulate and important defector from the line-officer ranks) regarding the merits of Admiral Spruance's decision. The reasons for the line-officer-aviator split have been discussed in the introductory chapter and need not be dwelt upon further.

If Task Force 58 had changed course at 0130 on June 19, 1944 as suggested by Admiral Mitscher it would have reached a position of about 14° 20′ N, 141° 45′ E at the time of the launch of dawn air searches, well within search range of Kurita's C Force and also within strike range of that force by the time they might reasonably assumed to be discovered, but the main body (A and B Forces) would have been at the edge of these searches and the range even at 0800 would have still been about 240–250 miles, at the edge of 'safe' strike range. Once the Japanese force was found then Mitscher would have to decide whether to strike the vanguard force, comfortably within range, or attempt to close the range on the main body, a process which would take about three hours if a 270°/15 knot Point Option could be maintained. The natural inclination likely would have been to hit the force which was within range with the first deck load (about 110 VF, 85 VB, 75–90 VT) and then close the second group (A and B Forces) and hit it with the second deck load (same number of VF and somewhat reduced VB/VT). This would have the effect desired by the Japanese; drawing the main American blow to the better defended CVLs of C Force, but the first deckload likely would have sunk or heavily damaged all three in spite of any heavy AA they would encounter. The strike probably would have arrived over the Japanese vanguard between 0830–0900 had it followed along the median line of the 0530 search, a common American practice. It can be reasonably assumed that the Japanese would have found Task Force 58 at least as early as the Americans found Mobile Force, in which event the same strikes actually launched by the Japanese on the 19th would have been sent against the Americans. If the Japanese were slow finding the Americans then C Force would have been in a Midway condition – loaded and fuelled aircraft on deck. If they were prompt then the raids would have passed each other, probably unmolested. When Japanese aircraft began appearing on TF 58 radar further moves west would end so fighters could be launched into the easterly wind. The flight decks would be spotted with the second deck load which would have to be flown off or struck below (American radar practically eliminated the Midway situation where the raiders came in in large formations at high altitude). The fighter force would be reduced by 110 aircraft and perhaps 220 if the second deck load was aloft. How much this would have reduced the score is speculative. So is the question of whether the Japanese raiders might have hit or sunk any US carriers had the American fighter force been reduced. Obviously the fewer American fighters involved in interceptions the more Japanese raiders could break through and the more raiders that break through the higher the probability of damage. Beyond this general statement, speculation is built upon speculation. Japanese tactics in the battle indicate the possible difficulty of closing the range. At 0807, 'The A Force (and B Force) in order to keep about 400 miles from the enemy reversed course . . .' suggesting Ozawa's reaction to an American move westward. Of course, such tactics would keep the Japanese at the edge of effective range against the transports which remained at Saipan and very likely would have accomplished Spruance's stated goal of insuring the safety of the landing force, but the possibility of closing the range sufficiently to attack A and B Force on June 19 would be greatly reduced once the Japanese raids began to come in. A strike on the 19th against these forces might have crippled a ship or two and increased the bag on the 20th. Whether American moves westward would have altered Ozawa's movements sufficiently to change the effect submarines had on the fighting of June 19 is likewise speculative but not beyond the realm of possibility. The thoroughness of American submarines' dispositions indicate Ozawa could not avoid contact with submarines and still close the American force. To this point we have discussed what might have happened had the Americans moved westward in view of known Japanese movements. The problem is that the Japanese did not act in the manner Spruance or Mitscher expected (the carrier admirals also expected decoy or flanking tactics). Spruance supposed, in fact was convinced (and no one doubted) there was a second Japanese force at large and felt that the carriers should not go outside effective support range of Saipan until the Japanese dispositions had been ascertained. Mitscher's response to this line of reasoning has been quoted at length earlier particularly in regard to one of the Japanese carrier squadrons slipping around Task Force 58, but part deserves re-examination at this point: 'It could be defeated or beaten off by our forces concentrated primarily for the defense of the amphibious operation, or it would be outflanked by our Fast Carrier Task Force in a sudden reverse to the south *if our main carrier force was not then engaged with the main Japanese Fleet*', language anticipating Leyte Gulf.

Let us assume that after refuelling on the 17th, when in the vicinity of 12° N 132° 20' E, First Mobile Force had split into two or three groups (in accordance with their alternative task organizations) sending one group along the route actually followed. The second group proceeded to the vicinity of Yap and thence in a straight line toward Guam to be in strike range of Saipan on the morning of the 19th. A third group could reach a point about three hundred miles northwest of Saipan at the same time. Assume further that the same indications presented to Admiral Spruance were the only indications received (the possibility of the second group remaining undiscovered is remote because of the PB4Y searches). Spruance assents to the move west. At dawn Task Force 58 is at 14° 20′ N, 141° 45′ E or about 250 miles west of Saipan and discovers the Japanese Centre Force about 240 miles west of its position. The first deck load is sent out and the second readied. Now the word that the transports at Saipan are under attack is received. Should the bombers be recalled? They would be 3–4 hours in the air and with a 270°/15 knot Point Option the entire force would be 300 miles west of Saipan before it could reverse course. Even after recovery at 300 miles Task Force 58 would have to close about 50 miles (two hours at best) to be in strike range of Saipan. If on the other hand the raiders were recalled immediately it would be two to three hours before relief reached the beaches. This presents a most interesting hypothetical question. Task Force 58 is proceeding east recovering and refuelling its strike groups in contemplation of an attack on Japanese Task Groups at Saipan while another group is astern and within strike range presumably sending off a deck load strike. The Midway analogy unravels when one remembers American radar and the size of the Japanese individual groups. The important point is the suggestion made elsewhere that carriers have no flanks is demonstrably rebutted by such hypothetical arguments. It is true that, unlike battleships and cruisers, carriers can react in the first instance to unexpected contingencies much quicker than surface ships and in some instances divert committed forces to newly discovered threats, but once their aircraft are sent on extended missions then the carrier is nailed to a Point Option and can be flanked. Also, the appearance of attackers when flight decks are crowded with armed and fuelled aircraft is analogous to flanking the enemy.

At Saipan the Americans had one CVE group (TG 52.14) with about 40 fighters and 30 torpedo planes embarked, together with seven old battleships, three cruisers and eight destroyers (5 with the BB/CA and 3 with the CVEs), to meet the Japanese group(s). The remaining CVE groups were with the retirement groups 200 miles to the east of Saipan. The CVE groups' handling of the Japanese raids on June 17 indicate the altogether logical presumption that they were not as well equipped as the fast carriers to meet this type of contingency however their reaction at Samar should indicate they would be no 'pushover'.

If A and/or B Force should arrive unmolested at a point 200 miles from Saipan what would be their prey if they could defeat Task Group 52.14 and the old battleships? *Cambria* (APA–36), *Hercules* (AK–41), *Jupiter* (AK–43), *Elliott* (DMS–14) and 17 LSTs together with numerous small landing craft (LCI, LVT etc.) were at the Saipan beaches during the battle. Minor elements were called in from the retirement groups as needed by the troops ashore and on the 19th 'additional assault shipping was dispatched to the objective for unloading'. At daylight on the 18th the Marines had approximately seven days' rations and two units of fire and due to estimates of losses expected in unloading (up to 50% of the supplies) the position ashore 'was not regarded favourably'. The same day Aslito Field was captured and several severe Japanese counterattacks were repulsed. At dawn on the 19th Japanese landing barges attempted an attack on US shipping remaining at Saipan. It was broken up by LCIs and LVTs which destroyed 13 of the attackers. This same day the 106th Infantry was landed and by 1800 the US troops controlled the south 20% of the island. On the 20th 'enemy resistance began to show signs of weakening' and 'on June 21 the USS *Rocky Mount* and the bulk of the transports of Task Force 52 returned to Saipan'.

The carrier admirals' view was substantially similar to the Japanese attitude; the one organization which constituted a threat to the American advance was the Japanese carrier fleet and the sooner it could be eliminated the sooner the war would end. Admiral Clark said, 'A chance of a century was missed. Had we sunk the entire Japanese fleet, as I am sure we could have done, the war in the Pacific might have ended in a matter of days, rather than some fifteen months later.' Fact or hyperbole? In my opinion more the latter than the former. The loss of Saipan led to the downfall of the Tojo government and its replacement by one whose primary function was to find an honourable way out of the war. Whether the destruction of three or four more carriers (or all nine for that matter) would have tilted the balance further is speculative given the nature of Japanese politics and the 'unconditional surrender' formula of the Allies.

After the Battle of Jutland in May 1916 Admiral Jellicoe, the British commander, was severely criticized for failing to exploit the tactical advantages of numbers (28 British battleships v. 16 German battleships) and position (twice the British Fleet 'capped the German "T" '*) presented during the battle. His justification for his actions was the vital importance to the Allied war effort of the preservation of the British Battle Fleet. In his mind, and the mind of most Admirals of the World War I period the 'Battle Fleet' had become the end of sea-power rather than an important means for achieving that end. In fact, Winston Churchill stated that Jellicoe was the only person who could lose the war in one day, though Churchill did disagree with Jellicoe's handling of his fleet. Because of the obsession with the almighty 'Battle Fleet', Jutland was fought in a vacuum. Neither force had any concern but destruction or crippling of the other. The German Fleet escaped relatively intact, and by its continued existence threatened the British Fleet. The uproar over the Philippine Sea battle compared with that in the Royal Navy (among Admiral Beatty's** supporters) but the objective facts vary widely. First, in the Pacific war the carriers were the combat arm of a vast amphibious force and clearly were not the end of American sea-power, but one of the means for bringing that power to bear upon the Japanese. Conversely the Japanese carrier force was not Japanese sea-power, but merely an arm of that power. Land-based naval air power, anti-submarine forces and merchant shipping were the other arms (granted the last two were very weak) of Japanese sea-power. As the Allies approached the Philippines and the Japanese home islands, land-based naval aircraft became the primary method for defending Japanese bases and because of geography would have become so even if the carriers had survived.

At the Marianas a large amphibious operation was underway and though a large portion of the shipping had retired, the landing was in a critical stage and ships which were quite important to the success of the enterprise ashore remained in what Spruance considered, not unreasonably, an exposed position should the carriers go too far to the west. Second, in 1942 four of Japan's best carriers were

---

* Cap T – In battleship tactics if one force forms the horizontal component of a 'T' and the other force the vertical component, the latter is unable to fire the guns of any ship except the lead ship while ships in the other column can theoretically fire all of their guns.

** Commander Battle Cruiser Fleet and advocate of a more aggressive use of the Battle Fleet. He was also motivated by a power play (as were the carrier admirals) since he succeeded Jellicoe as Commander Grand Fleet.

destroyed at Midway, but many of the pilots were picked up by the ships in the screen and formed a cadre around which were built the air groups of the carriers which fought the battles at Eastern Solomons and Santa Cruz Islands. After Santa Cruz most of the veteran pilots were gone and the carriers disappeared. After Philippine Sea the carriers continued to exist as they did after Santa Cruz (and as did the German Battle Fleet) but in a disarmed condition (unlike the German Battle Fleet). The air groups were rebuilt and committed in the Formosa* air battle in an even worse state of training than in June. At Leyte Gulf the carrier force was acknowledged as expendable following the air defeats of June and September (Formosa).

Commander-in-Chief, US Fleet, Admiral Ernest King, stated that although everyone, including Spruance, would have preferred to move west, the stage that the landing had reached dictated a more conservative policy. He also alluded to the Japanese forces in the Inland Sea as a flanking force. The only combat ready force in the Inland Sea at this time was Fourth ACS (Battleship/aircraft carriers *Ise* and *Hyuga*). Its air group (NAG 634) had commenced training in early May and was even less prepared for combat operations than the other three groups. The number of aircraft assigned to this group was 20 D4Y and 20 E16A (Paul) floatplanes for scouting. It is very unlikely that this force could have sortied at the same time as FMF and remained undetected though it is not impossible. Certainly had they not sortied until the battle began they would have presented no threat on the 19th.

Long after the battle (in 1952) Admiral Spruance stated to Admiral Morison, 'As a matter of tactics I think that going after the Japanese and knocking their carriers out would have been much better and more satisfactory than waiting for them to attack us; but we were at the start of a very important and large amphibious operation and we could not afford to gamble and place it in jeopardy. The way Togo waited at Tsushima for the Russian fleet has always been in my mind. We had somewhat the same basic situation, only it was modified by the long-range striking power of the carriers.'

This seems a fair appraisal of the situation. When participants in a victorious operation split into camps to argue over whether an

---

* In early October 1944, Task Force 38 attacked Formosa and the Japanese committed their carrier aircraft previously earmarked for 'Sho-Go' (the plan which resulted in the battle of Leyte Gulf) and lost between 5–600 aircraft. American losses were modest though two cruisers were hit with torpedoes.

even greater victory could have been achieved, politics is usually one of the reasons. At Midway, Spruance, the surface officer, had won the greatest victory in US Naval history using aircraft carriers. It is true that he was a 'substitute' and the staff of Admiral Halsey did the detail work but it was Spruance who made the most important tactical decision of any American naval officer in the war. Miles Browning, Halsey's chief of staff, suggested that immediate launch of the American planes (at the very edge of safe combat range) had a good chance of catching the Japanese carriers with decks loaded with armed and fuelled aircraft. Spruance concurred and ordered an immediate attack with all available aircraft. In view of American aircraft losses at Midway the latter portion of the order was almost as important as the former. Miles Browning suggested; Admiral Spruance ordered! Admiral Fletcher,* who commanded the *Yorktown* group delayed his launch for two hours and when he did send his aircraft out he sent a deckload rather than all available aircraft. The important decision was Spruance's, the line-officer.

Admiral Clark's thought on June 17 seems much more promising and in retrospect it seems unfortunate that he did not put his view to Mitscher (who liked it when he heard of it after the battle) and Spruance (who apparently never discussed it). A fighter courier could have maintained radio security. Both American commanders had good intelligence on Japanese fleet strength. The prospect of splitting the carrier force in front of the enemy therefore should not have been cause for rejecting such a proposal out of hand. Had the Japanese been able to isolate TG 58.1 and TG 58.4 as suggested by Admiral Ozawa's Dispatch Operation Order No. 16 of June 18, they still would be facing seven carriers, ten cruisers and 28 destroyers equipped with 223 fighters, 77 dive bombers and 91 torpedo bombers (total 391), very nearly Mobile Force's total air strength. Even if the Japanese pilots had been good, a stand-off would have probably resulted in the American main body swaying the outcome. Conversely, had the Japanese gone after the main body they would have faced eight carriers, seven battleships, eleven cruisers and 41 destroyers with 247 fighters, 120 dive bombers and 102 torpedo planes embarked. The Clark–Harrill groups would have been in position to force the Japanese into a fighting retreat or seriously limiting the line they could choose for withdrawal in the likely

---

* Admiral Fletcher was a non-aviator.

event of defeat. Of course, the Japanese could have chosen a southern line of retirement toward Mindanao Strait and Singapore to reduce their losses, rather than the northern route they actually followed.

Superlatives apply to US submarines and anti-submarine forces. *Albacore* and *Cavalla*'s successes are the stars in the American submarine forces's crown. From the beginning of *A-Go* they harassed Japanese destroyers, sank Japanese supply ships and reported Japanese movements. In fact they so completely frustrated Japanese screening ships that at least one mishap, the loss of *Shiratsuya*, can be traced to the fear of American submarines. Similarly the exploits of uss *England* were only a part of the important role played by US anti-submarine forces.

The worst single aspect of American operations was tactical aerial reconnaissance. In view of the Japanese effort the American carrier admirals come off poorly. It is amazing that US carriers continued to conduct routine air searches for two days while the Japanese scout forces were constantly in contact with the US carriers and the Japanese were sending large air strikes against the carriers. Only on the 20th when it was more and more obvious that the Japanese might slip the net completely did any US air searches go beyond the standard 325 mile range, and those aircraft were sent on a highly speculative mission. The TBFs from *Enterprise* which had been conducting the regular 0200 radar night search for several days before the battle were earmarked for air strikes on the 19th and airborne most of the day, therefore unavailable for night searches on the 20th.* This seems to be uneconomical use of such valuable aircraft but everyone assumed that the Japanese fleet would be found on the 19th.

In the air the American aviators clearly established what had been suspected for some time. The Japanese pilots were no longer of full combat quality. Conversely the American fliers were top notch. They were directed by fighter director officers who showed that the lessons of 1942 had been thoroughly learned and converted into practical doctrine. As in all carrier battles the victory (and defeat) were accomplished (or suffered) by the junior officers in the aircraft, directed by the junior officers in the CICs.

Not only was the Battle of the Philippine Sea the last great carrier

---

* US Naval Air Operations says that 10 VT of VT 10 were in bombing missions on the 19th.

battle of World War II but one of the last great fleet actions in history and like many of those actions it was one which left a lingering controversy. The ultimate result of the controversy before and after the battle was the rule in the US Navy that aviator admirals would be served by line officers as chief of staff and vice versa and the recognition that aviators could command fleets of ships. Spruance had shown at Midway that line officers could command carrier forces.

PART II

APPENDICES

Forces Involved in the Battle of the Philippine Sea

A. The Two Navies in May 1944

In May 1944, after two and a half years of hard fighting, the surface forces of the Japanese Navy were relatively intact (nine of twelve battleships and 14 of 18 heavy cruisers in commission at the beginning of the war were still in commission) and the carrier fleet had been built back to December 1941 strength through completion of one large carrier, *Taiho*, and conversions. The destroyer situation was critical, however. The carrier air groups, though woefully trained, were at full strength. Retrospectively the Japanese situation appears impossible. However, one should remember that at the time First Mobile Force was the most powerful carrier fleet the Japanese mustered during the war and was still the second most powerful carrier force in the world.

The Japanese fleet was composed of excellent ships. Their carriers were well equipped and could operate their aircraft in times which compared favourably with their American counterparts in spite of inferior training. With the exception of *Taiho*, *Shokaku* and *Zuikaku* their carriers were slower than American carriers. Except for *Yamato* and *Musashi* their battleships were quite old, however they all had good speed (important for carrier operations – older American battleships were too slow to operate with fast carriers) and fire power and had been lavishly modernized in the 1930s. The Japanese may have had the best heavy cruiser force in the world during the war. The ships were all fast and well armed. They were also relatively homogeneous and all had served with distinction. Japanese light cruisers were designed as destroyer flotilla flagships and did not compare favourably with American light cruisers (which were heavy cruisers with 6-inch guns). When the war began the

Japanese had the best destroyer force in the world. By June 1944 constant fighting had reduced Japanese destroyer strength to about thirty first rate ships. Their *Akitsuki* class destroyers were actually closer to USS *Atlanta* class AA cruiser in function than conventional destroyers.

The most remarkable aspect of the US Fleet was its newness. One of the carriers had been in commission on December 7, 1941. All of the battleships were less than five years old and only four of the cruisers were pre-war construction. The destroyers were also new ships as a whole. This influx of ships was a result of fantastic industrial production which, in spite of little or no quality control, produced excellent ships. The lack of quality control did result in ships being accepted which would have been returned to builders during peacetime and in one major disaster when 1 cruiser *Pittsburgh* lost her bow in a typhoon. Conversely, *Franklin* and *Bunker Hill* took amazing punishment without sinking.

The American carriers all had excellent speed and aircraft handling characteristics. Because of their speed the US carriers were generally better in handling their aircraft than the Japanese ships (though not appreciably) but this was achieved in the case of the CVLs by reduction of the original airgroups from about 45 aircraft in late 1943 to 32 in May 1944. The American battleships were all new, fast, well armed and homogeneous. The cruisers were excellent. The American anti-aircraft cruisers were particularly important ships. By 1944 the American destroyers had established their ability to fight the Japanese destroyers on a ship to ship basis, and, more important, now outnumbered the Japanese about three to one.

B Tactical Organization of the US Forces

The US Navy, like all large navies, functions within administrative as well as tactical organizations at one and the same time. Under the Major Fleet commands the most important administrative organization is the type command. For example, all destroyers in the Pacific would be under the 'Commander Destroyer Force, Pacific' and all aircraft carriers in the Pacific were commanded by Admiral Pownall, 'Commander Air Force, Pacific Fleet'. The function of the type commander is primarily training, personnel and material. The carriers were also organized into carrier divisions for administrative purposes. For examples the Fast Carriers of Task Force 58 were assigned to Carrier Divisions 1, 3, 4 and 13.

The major tactical command in the US Navy is the numbered fleet, such as Fifth Fleet, whose function in the operations described in this book was the capture of the Marianas. The Fleet was subdivided into specialized Task Forces, such as Task Force 58, the Fast Carrier Force. These Task Forces were further subdivided into Task Groups, which were further subdivided into Task Units.

One of the most important organizational aspects of the Pacific war was introduced in the Marianas; the Third and Fifth Fleet parallel organizations. Under this reorganization Admiral Spruance's Fifth Fleet staff would conduct the Marianas operation with the Central Pacific Force while Admiral Halsey's Third Fleet staff prepared plans for the next operation. Thus at Leyte Gulf the Fast Carrier Force (essentially the same force that fought at Philippine Sea) became Task Force 38. The ships were constantly in action but the staffs changed from operation to operation. This had the benefit of putting constant pressure on the Japanese.

Commander in Chief Pacific Fleet, Admiral C. W. Nimitz, USN at Pearl Harbor, Hawaii

Fifth Fleet, Admiral R. A. Spruance, USN, in USS *Indianapolis* (CA–35)

I *TASK FORCE* 58 (*Fast Carrier Task Force*). Vice Admiral M. A. Mitscher in USS *Lexington* (CV–16)

A TASK GROUP 58.1 (Carrier Task Group One), Rear Admiral J. J. Clark (Commander Carrier Division 13) in USS *Hornet* (CV–12)

i TASK UNIT 58.1.1 (Carrier Unit)

CV–12	*Hornet*, Capt W. D. Sample		
Air Group 2	1 TBM–1C (Avenger)	Lt Cdr J. D. Arnold
VB–2	33 SB2C–1C (Helldiver)	Lt Cdr G. B. Campbell
VF–2	36 F6F–3 (Hellcat)	Lt Cdr W. A. Dean
VT–2	14 TBM–1C 4 TBF–1C	Lt Cdr L. M. D. Ford
VF(N) 76 (det B)	4 F6F–3N —	Lt R. L. Reiserer
	92 Total	

The American command structure for the operation was as follows:

TG 50.1
FLEET FLAG
INDIANAPOLIS
Adm. R.A.SPRUANCE

TF 57
Forward Area CenPac
R. Adm. HOOVER

TF 59
Shore-Based Air
Force, Forward Area
Maj. Gen. HALE, USA

TF 58
Fast Carrier Forces
V.Adm. HITSCHER

TG 58.1
2 CV
2 CVL
3 CA
2 CL(AA)
14 DD

TG 58.2
2 CV
2 CVL
2 BB
3 CL
14 DD

TG 58.3
2 CV
2 CVL
5 BB
16 DD

TG 58.4
1 CV
3 CL
2 CL(AA)
14 DD

TF 51
Joint Expeditionary Force
ROCKY MOUNT (AGC)

Hqdrs. Support Aircraft
Capt. Whitehead

TU 53.1.15
Preliminary Bombardment
Unit (GUAM)
BatDiv FOUR

TG 51.1
Joint Expedition-
ary Force Reserve
R. Adm.BLANDY

TG 51.2
Defence Group 1

TG 51.3
Defence Group 2

TG 51.4
Garrison Group 1

TG 51.5
Garrison Group 2

TG 51.6
Garrison Group 3

TF 53
Southern Attack Force
R.Adm. CONOLLY
Force Flag
APPALACHIAN (AGC)

TG 53.2
South. Attack Group

TG 53.4
South. TransGroup
7 APA   16 LST
1 AP   2 PC
2 AKA   4 SC
1 LSD   5 LCC
1 DD   9 LCI(G)

TG 53.5
Fire Support Group
(Units 53.5.1,
53.5.4, 53.5.6)
1 BB   1 CL
2 CA   9 DD

TF 52
Northern Attack Force
V.Adm. TURNER

TG 52.2
West. Landing Group

TG 53.1
Northern Attack Gr.

TG 53.3
Northern TransGr.
9 DD   2 LSD
1 APD   2 LCT
9 APA   9 LCI(G)
2 AP   3 PC
3 AKA   6 SC
16 LST   3 DMS
1 APH   2 AM

TG 53.5
Fire Support Group
(Units 53.5.1,
53.5.3, 53.5.5,
53.5.7)
3 BB   1 CL
2 CA   12 DD

TF 56
Expeditionary Troops
Lt. Gen.H.M.SMITH, USMC

TG 55.3
Reserve Landing Force
Maj. Gen. Ralph SMITH, USA

TG 52.3
TransGroup ABLE
10 APA   2 AP
3 AKA   2 LSD
2 AK

TG 52.4
TransGroup BAKER
9 APA   4 AP
3 AKA   2 LSD

TG 52.5
Tractor Flotilla
2 PC(S)
40 LST

TG 52.6
Control Group
4 PC(S)   4 PC
6 SC   3 APC
25 LCI   37 LCT
11 LCC

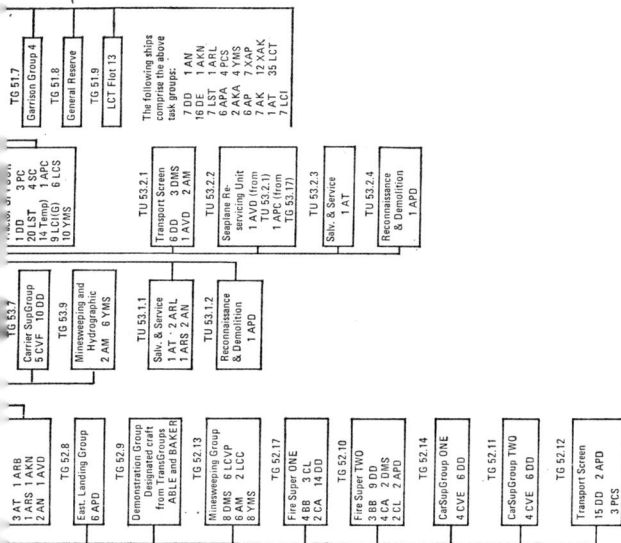

ORIGINAL ORGANIZATION OF FORCES
MARIANAS ISLANDS OCCUPATION
Made from various Op-plans
of Commanders concerned
JUNE-JULY 1944

TG 51.7

Garrison Group 4

TG 51.8

General Reserve

TG 51.9

LCT Flot 13

The following ships
comprise the above
task groups:

7 DD	1 AN
16 DE	1 AKN
7 LST	1 ARL
6 APA	4 PCS
2 AKA	4 YMS
6 AP	7 XAP
7 AK	12 XAK
1 AT	35 LCT
7 LCI	

TU 53.2.1

Transport Screen
6 DD   3 DMS
1 AVD   2 AM

TU 53.2.2

Seaplane Re-
servicing Unit
1 AVD (from
TU 53.2.1)
1 APC (from
TG 53.17)

TU 53.2.3

Salv. & Service
1 AT

TU 53.2.4

Reconnaissance
& Demolition
1 APD

TG 53.7

Carrier SupGroup
5 CVE   10 DD

TG 53.9

Minesweeping and
Hydrographic
2 AM   6 YMS

TG 53.1.1

Salv. & Service
1 AT · 2 ARL
1 ARS 2 AN

TG 53.1.12

Reconnaissance
& Demolition
1 APD

1 DD	3 PC
20 LST	4 SC
14 Templ	1 APC
9 LCI(G)	6 LCS
10 YMS	

3 AT   1 ARB
1 ARS 1 AKN
2 AN   1 AVD

TG 52.8

East. Landing Group
6 APD

TG 52.9

Demonstration Group
Designated craft
from TransGroups
ABLE and BAKER

TG 52.13

Minesweeping Group
8 DMS   6 LCVP
6 AM   2 LCC
8 YMS

TG 52.17

Fire Super ONE
4 BB   3 CL
2 CA   14 DD

TG 52.10

Fire Super TWO
3 BB   9 DD
4 CA   2 DMS
2 CL   2 APD

TG 52.14

CarSupGroup ONE
4 CVE   6 DD

TG 52.11

CarSupGroup TWO
4 CVE   6 DD

TG 52.12

Transport Screen
15 DD   2 APD
3 PCS

CV-10 *Yorktown*, Capt R. E. Jennings (Rear Admiral Davison, COMCARDIV 2, on board)

Air Group 1	1 F6F-3	Cdr J. M. Peters
VB-1	40 SB2C-1C	Lt Cdr J W. Runyan,
	4 SBD-5	USNR
	(Dauntless)	
VF-1	41 F6F-3	Lt Cdr B. M. Strean
VT-1	16 TBM-1C	Lt Cdr W. F. Henry
	1 TBF-1C	
VF(N) 77	4 F6F-3N	Lt A. C. Benjes
(det B)	—	
	107 Total	

CVL-24 *Belleau Wood*, Capt John Perry

Air Group 24		Lt Cdr E. M. Link
VF-24	26 F6F-3	Lt Cdr Link
VT-24	6 TBM-1C	Lt Cdr R. M. Swenson
	3 TBF-1C	
	—	
	35 Total	

CVL-29 *Bataan*, Capt V. H. Schaeffer

Air Group 50		Lt Cdr J. C. Strange, USNR
VF-50	24 F6F-3	Lt Cdr Strange
VT-50	9 TBM-1C	Lt Cdr L. V. Swanson
	—	
	33 Total	

ii TASK UNIT 58.1.2 (Support Unit)
Cruiser Division 10, Rear Admiral L. H. Thebaud

CA-69 *Boston*, Capt E. E. Herrmann	VCS-10(B), 1 OS2N1	
	1 OS2U3	
CA-68 *Baltimore*, Capt W. C. Calhoun	VCS-10(A), 1 OS2U3	
	1 OS2N1	
CA-70 *Canberra*, Capt A. R. Early	VCS-10(C), 2 OS2N1	

iii TASK UNIT 58.1.3 (Screen Unit)
CLAA-95 *Oakland*, Capt W. K. Phillips (CRUDIV 11)

DD   *Izard* (DD–589), *Charrette* (DD–581), *Conner* (DD–582),
          Bell (DD–587), *Burns* (DD–588)
Destroyer Division 92, Capt W. M. Sweetser
          Boyd (DD–544), *Bradford* (DD–545), *Brown* (DD–546),
          Cowell (DD–547)
Destroyer Division 11, Capt E. G. Fullinwider
          Maury (DD–401), *Craven* (DD–382), *McCall* (DD–400)

B TASK GROUP 58.2 (Carrier Task Group Two), Rear Admiral
    A. E. Montgomery (COMCARDIV 3) in *Bunker Hill* (CV–17)
i TASK UNIT 58.2.1 (Carrier Unit)
CV–17 *Bunker Hill*, Capt T. P. Jeter

Air Group 8	1 F6F–3	Cdr R. L. Shifley
VB–8	33 SB2C–1C	Lt Cdr J. D. Arbes
VF–8	37 F6F–3	Lt Cdr W. M. Collins
VT–8	13 TBF–1C	Lt Cdr K. F. Musick
	5 TBM–1C	
VF(N) 76	4 F6F–3N	Lt Cdr E. P. Aurand
(det A)	—	
	93 Total	

CV–18 *Wasp*, Capt C. A. F. Sprague

Air Group 14	1 F6F–3	Cdr W. C. Wingard
VB–14	32 SB2C–1C	Lt Cdr J. D. Blitch
VF–14	34 F6F–3	Lt Cdr E. W. Biros, USNR
VT–14	15 TBF–1C	Lt Cdr H. S. Roberts, USNR
	3 TBF–1D	
VF(N) 77	4 F6F–3N	Lt J. H. Boyum
(det C)	—	
	89 Total	

CVL–26 *Monterey*, Capt S. H. Ingersoll

Air Group 28		Lt Cdr R. H. Mehle, USNR
VF–28	21 F6F–3	Lt Cdr Mehle
VT–28	8 TBM–1C	Lt R. P. Gift, USNR
	—	
	29 Total	

CVL–28 *Cabot*, Capt S. J. Michael
  Air Group 31   Lt Cdr R. A. Winston
    VF–31 24 F6F–3   Lt Cdr Winston
    VT–31   1 TBF–1C   Lt E. E. Wood, USNR
         8 TBM–1C
         —
       33 Total

ii TASK UNIT 58.2.2 (Support Unit)
Cruiser Division 13, Rear Admiral L. T. DuBose
CL–63 *Mobile*   VCS–13(C), 1 OS2N1
                1 OS2U3
CL–60 *Santa Fe*   VCS–13(A), 2 OS2N1
CL–80 *Biloxi*   VCS–13(D), 2 OS2U3

iii TASK UNIT 58.2.3 (Screen Unit)
CLAA–54 *San Juan*, Capt G. W. Clark (CRUDIV 11)
Destroyer Squadron 52, Capt G. R. Cooper
    Owen (DD–536), *Miller* (DD–535), *The Sullivans* (DD–
     537), *Stephen Potter* (DD–538), *Tingey* (DD–539)
Destroyer Division 104, Cdr H. B. Bell
    Hickox (DD–673), *Hunt* (DD–674), *Lewis Hancock* (DD–
    675), *Marshall* (DD–676)
Destroyer Squadron 1, Capt E. R. McLean
    Macdonough (DD–351), *Dewey* (DD–349), *Hull* (DD–350)

C TASK GROUP 58.3 (Carrier Task Group Three), Rear
 Admiral J. W. Reeves (COMCARDIV 4) in USS *Enterprise*
 (CV–6)
i TASK UNIT 58.3.1 (Carrier Unit)
CV–6 *Enterprise*, Capt M. B. Gardner
  Air Group 10   Cdr W. R. Kane
    VB–10 21 SBD–5   Lt Cdr J. D. Ramage
    VF–10 31 F6F–3   Lt R. W. Schumann
    VT–10   9 TBF–1C   Lt Cdr W. I. Martin
         5 TBM–1C
    VF(N) 101 3 F4U–2   Lt Cdr R. E. Harmer
    (det C)   (Corsair)
         —
       69 Total

CV–16	*Lexington*, Capt E. W. Litch		
	Air Group 16	1 F6F–3	Cdr E. M. Snowden
	VB–16	34 SBD–5	Lt Cdr R. Weymouth
	VF–16	37 F6F–3	Lt Cdr P. D. Buie
	VT–16	17 TBF–1C	Lt N. A. Sterrie, USNR
	VF(N) 76	4 F6F–3N	Lt W. H. Abercrombie,
	(det C)	—	USNR
		94 Total	

CVL–30	*San Jacinto*, Capt H. W. Martin		
	Air Group 51		Lt Cdr C. L. Moore
	VF–51	24 F6F–3	Lt Cdr Moore
	VT–51	6 TBM–1C	Lt Cdr D. J. Melvin
		2 TBM–1D	
		—	
		32 Total	

CVL–23	*Princeton*, Capt W. H. Buracker		
	Air Group 27		Lt Cdr E. W. Wood
	VF–27	24 F6F–3	Lt Cdr Wood
	VT–27	9 TBM–1C	Lt Cdr S. M. Haley,
		—	USNR
		33 Total	

ii TASK UNIT 58.3.2 (Support Unit)
Cruiser Division 4 (Unit Assigned)

CA–35	*Indianapolis*, Capt E. R. Johnson	VCS–4(C),	4 SOC1

Cruiser Division 12, Rear Admiral R. W. Hayler

CL–57	*Montpelier*, Capt H. D. Hoffman	VCS–12(C),	2 SOC1
CL–55	*Cleveland*, Capt A. G. Shepard	VCS–12(A),	1 SOC1

Cruiser Division 13, Unit Assigned

CL–62	*Birmingham*, Capt T. B. Inglis	VCS–13(B),	2 OS2U3

iii TASK UNIT 58.3.3 (Screen Unit)

CLAA–96 *Reno*, Capt R. C. Alexander (CRUDIV 11)

Destroyer Squadron 50, Cdr C. F. Chillingworth
        Clarence K. Bronson (DD–668), *Cotten* (DD–669), *Dortch*
        (DD–670), *Gatling* (DD–671), *Healy* (DD–672)

Destroyer Division 90, Cdr F. L. Tedder
        Anthony (DD–515), *Wadsworth* (DD–516), *Terry* (DD–513),
        Braine (DD–630)

D TASK GROUP 58.4 (Carrier Task Group Four), Rear Admiral W. K. Harrill (Commander Carrier Division 1) in USS *Essex* (CV–9)

i TASK UNIT 58.4.1 (Carrier Unit)

CV–9	*Essex*, Capt R. A. Ofstie		Cdr D. McCampbell
	Air Group 15	1 F6F–3	
	VB–15	36 SB2C–1C	Lt Cdr J. H. Mini
	VF–15	38 F6F–3	Lt Cdr C. W. Brewer
	VT–15	15 TBF–1C	Lt Cdr V. G. Lambert
	VF(N) 77	4 F6F–3N	Lt R. M. Freeman
	(det A)	—	
		99 Total	

CVL–27	*Langley*, Capt W. M. Dillon		
	Air Group 32		Lt Cdr E. C. Outlaw
	VF–32	23 F6F–3	Lt Cdr Outlaw
	VT–32	7 TBF–1C	Lt D. A. Marks
		2 TBM–1C	
		—	
		32 Total	

CVL–25	*Cowpens*, Capt H. W. Taylor		
	Air Group 25		Lt Cdr R. H. Price
	VF–25	23 F6F–3	Lt Cdr Price
	VT–25	3 TBF–1C	Lt R. B. Cottingham,
		6 TBM–1C	USNR
		—	
		32 Total	

ii TASK UNIT 58.4.2 (Support Unit)

Cruiser Division 11, Rear Admiral L. J. Wiltse

CLAA–54	*San Juan*, Capt L. J. Hudson	

Cruiser Division 14, Rear Admiral W. D. Baker

CL–64	*Vincennes*, Capt A. D. Brown	VCS–14(A), 2 OS2U
CL–81	*Houston*, Capt W. W. Behrens	VCS–14(B), 2 OS2U
CL–89	*Miami*, Capt J. G. Crawford	VCS–14(C), 1 OS2U
		1 OS2N

iii TASK UNIT 58.4.3 (Screen Unit)

Destroyer Squadron 12, Capt W. P. Burford

Lansdowne (DD–486), *Lardner* (DD–487), *McCalla* (DD–488), *Case* (DD–370)

Destroyer Division 24, Cdr J. L. Melgaard
>Lang (DD–399), Sterrett (DD–407), Wilson (DD–408), Ellet (DD–398)

Destroyer Squadron 23, Capt T. B. Dugan
>Charles Ausburne (DD–570), Stanly (DD–478), Dyson (DD–57)

Destroyer Division 46, Cdr R. W. Cavenagh
>Converse (DD–509), Spence (DD–512), Thatcher (DD–514)

E TASK GROUP 58.7 (Heavy Surface Strike Group), Vice-Admiral W. A. Lee

i TASK UNIT 58.7.1 (Battle Line)

Battleship Division 6, Vice-Admiral Lee

BB–56	Washington, Capt R. R. Cooley	VO–6(B), 2 OS2U3★
BB–55	North Carolina, Capt F. P. Thomas	VO–6(A), 2 OS2U3★

Battleship Division 7, Rear Admiral O. M. Husvedt

BB–61	Iowa	VO–7(A), 2 OS2N1★
BB–62	New Jersey	VO–7(B), 2 OS2U3★

Battleship Division 8, Rear Admiral G. B. Davis

BB–58	Indiana, Capt T. J. Keliher	VO–8(A), 2 OS2U3★

Battleship Division 9, Rear Admiral E. W. Hanson

BB–57	South Dakota	VO–9(A), 2 OS2N1★
BB–60	Alabama	VO–9(B), 2 OS2U3★

ii TASK UNIT 58.7.2 (Support Unit)

Cruiser Division 6, Rear Admiral C. T. Joy

CA–45	Wichita, Capt J. J. Mahoney	VCS–6(D), 4 SOC3
CA–36	Minneapolis, Capt Harry Slocum	VCS–6(B), 4 SOC1
CA–38	San Francisco, Capt H. E. Overesch	VCS–6(C), 3 SOC1
		1 SOC2
CA–32	New Orleans, Capt J. E. Hurff	VCS–6(A), 2 SOC1
		1 SOC2
		1 SOC3

iii TASK UNIT 58.7.3 (Screen Unit)

Destroyer Division 12, Cdr K. F. Poehlmann
>Mugford (DD–389), Ralph Talbot (DD–390), Bagley (DD–386)

★ All BB VO squadrons were assigned six aircraft but four were all that were embarked (two on each ship in the division). The other two were put ashore at Majuro.

Destroyer Division 89, Cdr E. B. Taylor
>   *Halford* (DD–480), *Guest* (DD–472), *Bennett* (DD–473), *Fullam* (DD–474), *Hudson* (DD–475)

Destroyer Division 106, Cdr Thomas Burrowes
>   *Twining* (DD–540), *Monssen* (DD–798), *Yarnall* (DD–541),★ *Stockham* (DD–683)★

2 *US Submarine Forces participating in Operation Forager*
   A Task Force 17 Patrol Submarines, Vice-Admiral C. A. Lockwood
   i 'Dunker's Derby' (Bonin Islands) *Plunger* (SS–179) Lt Cdr E. J. Fahy; *Gar* (SS–206) Cdr G. W. Lautrup; *Archerfish* (SS–311) Cdr W. H. Wright; *Plaice* (SS–390) Cdr C. B. Stevens; *Swordfish* (SS–193) Cdr K. E. Montrose
   ii 'Convoy College' (SE of Formosa) *Pintado* (SS–387) Lt Cdr B. A. Clarey; *Pilotfish* (SS–386) Lt Cdr R. H. Close; *Tunny* (SS–282) Cdr J. A. Scott
   iii 'Pentathlon' (Marianas) *Albacore* (SS–218) Cdr J. W. Blanchard; *Seawolf* (SS–197) Lt Cdr R. B. Lynch; *Bang* (SS–385) Cdr A. R. Gallaher; *Finback* (SS–230) Lt Cdr J. L. Jordan; *Stingray* (SS–186) Lt Cdr S. C. Loomis
   iv 'Speedway' (Ulithi-Philippines) *Flying Fish* (SS–229) Lt Cdr R. D. Risser; *Muskallunge* (SS–262) Cdr M. P. Russillo; *Seahorse* (SS–304) Lt Cdr S. D. Cutter; *Pipefish* (SS–388) Lt Cdr W. N. Deragon; *Cavalla* (SS–244) Lt Cdr H. J. Kossler (Surigao Strait); *Growler* (SS–215) Cdr T. B. Oakley
   B Seventh Fleet Submarines, Rear Admiral R. W. Christie
   i (Mindanao Area) *Hake* (SS–256) Cdr J. C. Broach; *Bashaw* (SS–241) Lt Cdr R. E. Nichols; *Paddle* (SS–263) Lt Cdr B. H. Nowell
   ii (Tawi-Tawi) *Harder* (SS–257) Cdr S. D. Dealey; *Haddo* (SS–255) Cdr C. W. Nimitz Jr; *Redfin* (SS–272) Cdr M. H. Austin; *Bluefish* (SS–222) Cdr C. M. Henderson
   iii (Luzon) *Jack* (SS–259) Cdr A. E. Krapf; *Flier* (SS–250) Cdr J. D. Crowley

3 *Long Range Patrol Aircraft available to US Naval Forces*
   i AVD–10 *Ballard*, Lt Cdr G. C. Nichandross, USNR
>   Air Group Lt Cdr W. J. Scarpino

★ Destroyers *Yarnall* and *Stockham* were picket ships on June 19, 1944 and placed approximately 20 miles to the west of TG 58.7.

vp–16 5 PBM–5 (Mariner)
ii Shore based air Manus
vB–101 12 BB4Y–1 (Liberator) Cdr J. A. Miller

4 *Escort Carriers and Combatant Ships (cruiser size and larger) assigned to Fifth Fleet which were not assigned to Task Force 58 (see Table of Organization for entire strength of Fifth Fleet)*
  i Task Group 52.14
    Fanshaw Bay (cve–70), 16 FM–2 (Wildcat), 12 TBM–1C
    Midway (cve–63), 12 FM–2, 9 TBM–1C
  ii Task Group 52.11
    Kitkun Bay (cve–71), 12 FM–2, 8 TBM–1C
    Gambier Bay (cve–73), 16 FM–2, 12 TBM–1C
    Nehenta Bay (cve–74), 12 FM–2, 9 TBM–1C
  iii Task Group 53.7
    Sangamon (cve–26), 22 F6F–3, 1 TBF–1C, 8 TBM–1C
    Suwannee (cve–27), 22 F6F–3, 1 TBF–1C, 8 TBM–1C
    Chenango (cve–28), 22 F6F–3, 1 TBF–1C, 8 TBM–1C
    Corregidor (cve–58), 14 FM–2, 8 TBM–1C, 4 TBM–1
    Coral Sea (cve–57), 14 FM–2, 2 TBF–1, 6 TBF–1C, 4 TBM–1C
  v Task Group 52.17
    bb–43 *Tennessee*; bb–44 *California*; bb–45 *Colorado*; bb–46 *Maryland*; ca–33 *Portland*
  vi Task Group 52.10
    bb–38 *Pennsylvania*; bb–42 *Idaho*; bb–40 *New Mexico*; cl–48 *Honolulu*; cl–49 *St. Louis*

C Tactical Organization of the Japanese Forces

Japanese Naval forces (warship and aircraft) were also organized both administratively and tactically. The basic administrative unit was the *Kantai* (Fleet) and the basic tactical entity was the *Butai* (Force). Most of the first class combatant ships of the Japanese Navy were in the Second and Third Fleets. The Second Fleet, commanded by Vice-Admiral Kutira, was composed of First Squadron (*Ichi Sentai*), Second, Third, Fourth, Fifth and Seventh Squadrons and Second Destroyer Flotilla. Vice-Admiral Ozawa's Third Fleet was composed of First Aircraft Carrier Squadron (*Ichi Koku Sentai*), Second, Third and Fourth ACS and Tenth Destroyer Flotilla. This administrative organization had the advantage of placing ships with similar training, procurement problems etc. in the same unit to facilitate the handling of these routine functions. The major difference in this administrative organization and the US Navy's 'type commands' was the assignment of a destroyer flotilla to each administrative 'fleet'. Apparently this caused no great problems. The Second and Third Fleets were combined administratively as *Dai Ichi Kido Kantai* (The First Mobile Fleet). This latter organization was formed in March 1944 in recognition of the primacy of the aircraft carrier in the combatant arm of the Navy and allowed for development of common doctrine for carrier operations.

The basic administrative unit for shore based naval aircraft in the Japanese Navy was the *Koku Kantai* (Air Fleet). Admiral Kakuta, Commander First Air Fleet, was charged with the deployment and employment of the shore based contingent of the Japanese Naval Air Forces. Tactically *Ichi Koku Kantai* (1st Air Fleet) became *Konkyo Koku Butai* (6th Base Air Force). The Japanese Submarines were administratively assigned to Sixth Fleet, commanded by Admiral Takaki. Their tactical designation was *Senken Butai* (Advance Expeditionary Force).

All the Japanese forces participating in *A-Go* were under the command of C-in-C Combined Fleet (*Rengo Kantai*), Admiral Toyoda. Admirals Ozawa, Kakuta and Takagi had tactical command of the forces assigned to them while Admiral Toyoda exercised overall command of the operation from the operations room of light cruiser *Oyodo* in the Inland Sea.

The Japanese command structure was fairly conventional and much clearer than it was to become at Leyte Gulf. Three aspects of Japanese organization bear comment. First Combined Fleet prepared extremely detailed operations orders (unlike the US Navy practice where CINCPACFLT would issue a basic directive and allow his fleet commanders to work out the details). Though this is not unusual (for example the Italian Navy's SUPERMARINA drafted the operation order for Matapan) the American method seems to be more economical than the Japanese. Second, Combined Fleet, rather than one of the commands at the scene had overall command of the operation. In this operation this would not have any great effect, however at Leyte Gulf this type of command structure would cause great difficulty to both sides. The third deficiency was the multiplicity of 'hats' worn by many Japanese flag officers. For example, Admiral Ozawa as Commander First Mobile Fleet had administrative responsibility for all the major combatants not assigned to area fleets. As Commander Third Fleet he had administrative charge of the carrier force. His role as Commander Mobile Force charged him with tactical command of the bulk of the major combatants of the fleet. In addition to these functions he was also

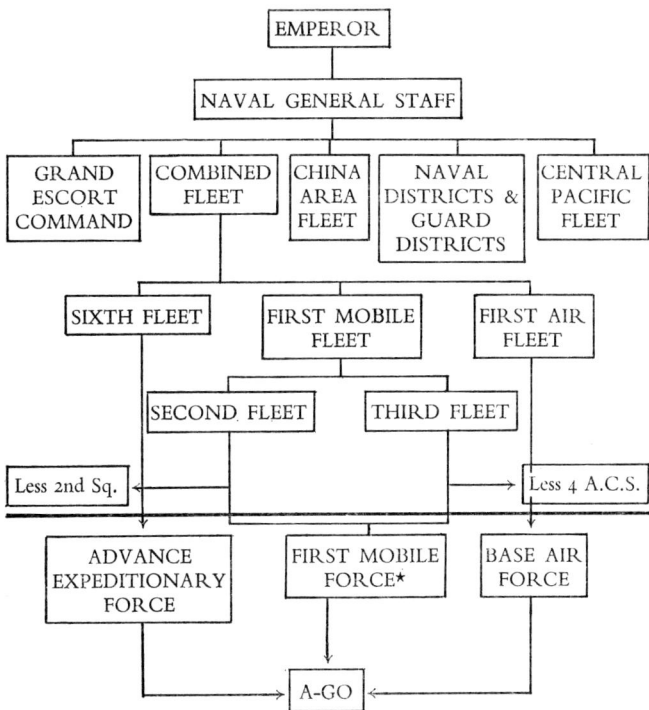

Commander First Aircraft Carrier Squadron and during the battle, Commander A Force. Likewise, Admiral Kurita served as Commander Second Fleet, Commander C Force and Commander Fourth Squadron (Cruisers). The requirement that the Fleet Commander also have the responsibility for one of the squadrons in that fleet seems cumbersome and unduly burdensome for the staff

★ *Dai Ichi Kido Butai* – Tactical designation for *Dai Ichi Kido Kantai*.

whose primary function must be the tactical and administrative handling of the entire fleet.

Commander-in-Chief, Combined Fleet, Admiral Soemu Toyoda in CL *Oyodo*

I FIRST MOBILE FORCE (*Dai Ichi Kido Butai*)

Vice-Admiral (*Chu-sho*) Jisaburo Ozawa in cv *Taiho*, Commanding A 'A' FORCE, Vice-Admiral Ozawa

i Carrier Group

First Aircraft Carrier Squadron (*Ichi Koku Sentai*), Vice-Admiral Ozawa

Naval Air Group 601 (601 *Kokutai*) assigned, Lt Cdr (*Sho-sa*) Akira Tarui

cv *Taiho*

VF	27	A6M5a 'Zeke' (*Rei-sen*; Zero Fighter)
VB	27	D4Y1 'Judy' (*Suisei*; Comet)
VS	3	D4Y1c 'Judy'
VT	18	B6N1 'Jill' (*Tenzan*; Heavenly Mountain)
	—	
	75	Total

cv *Shokaku*

VF	27	A6M5a
VB	27	D4Y1
VS	3	D4Y1c
VT	18	B6N1
	—	
	75	Total

cv *Zuikaku*, Rear Admiral (*Sho-sho*) T. Kaizuka

VF	27	A6M5a
VB	27	D4Y1
VS	3	D4Y1c
VT	18	B6N1
	—	
	75	Total

i:Heavy Screen Group

Fifth Squadron (Cruiser), Vice-Admiral Shintaro Hashimoto

CA *Myoko*, Capt (*Tai-sa*) H. Ishiwara   VS 2 E13A 'Jake'

CA *Haguro*, Capt K. Sugyira   VS 2 E13A

iii Destroyer Screen
Tenth Destroyer Flotilla (less DG 4), Rear Admiral S. Kimura
CL *Yahagi*, Capt M. Yoshimura   VS 2 E13A
Tenth Destroyer Group★
DD *Asagumo*
17th Destroyer Group, Capt T. Tanii
DD *Urakaze, Isokaze*
61st Destroyer Group,★ Capt S. Amano
DD *Hatsuzuki, Wakatsuki, Akizuki, Shimozuki*

B 'B' FORCE, Rear Admiral Takaji Joshima in CV *Junyo*
i Carrier Group
Second Aircraft Carrier Squadron, Rear Admiral Joshima
Naval Air Group 652 assigned, Lt Cdr Jyotaro Iwami
CV *Junyo*

VF	18 A6M5a
VFB	9 A6M5a
VB	9 D4Y1
VB	9 D3A2
VT	6 B6N1
	—
	51 Total

CV *Hiyo*

VF	18 A6M5a
VFB	9 A6M5a
VB	18 D3A2
VT	6 B6N1
	—
	51 Total

CV *Ryuho*

VF	18 A6M5a
VFB	9 A6M5a
VT	6 B6N1
	—
33	Total

★ Destroyers *Tanikaze* (DG 10) and *Minazuki* (DG 61) lost at Tawi-Tawi prior to sortie.

ii Heavy Screen Group
BB *Nagato*,* Rear Admiral Y. Kobe   VO 2 F1M 'Pete'
CA *Mogami*,** Capt R. Tooma   VS 6 E13A

* *Nagato* assigned from First Squadron.
** *Mogami* under direct administrative control of COMMANDER FIRST
MOBILE FLEET and assigned to B Force screen for this operation.

iii Destroyer Screen
Fourth Destroyer Group,* Capt K. Takahashi
DD *Michishio, Nowaki, Yamagumo*
27th Destroyer Group**
DD *Shigure, Samidare, Hayashimo, Hamakaze, Akishimo*★★★

* 4DG assigned from Tenth Destroyer Flotilla.
** 27DG assigned from Second Destroyer Flotilla.
*** DDS *Shiratsuya* and *Harusame* of 27 DG sunk prior to battle.

C 'C' FORCE, Vice-Admiral Takeo Kurita in CA *Atago**
  i Carrier Group
  Third Aircraft Carrier Squadron, Rear Admiral Sueo Obayashi
    in *Chitose*
  Naval Air Group 653 assigned, Lt Cdr Masayuki Yamagami
  CVL *Chitose*, Capt Y. Kishi

VF	6 A6M5b
VFB	15 A6M5b
VT	3 B6N1
VT	6 B5N2 'Kate'

30 Total

  CVL *Chiyoda*, Capt E. Zyo

VF	6 A6M5b
VFB	15 A6M5b
VT	3 B6N1
VT	6 B5N2

30 Total

* At 1800K June 20, 1944 Number 4 Battle Disposition was ordered and
First Diversionary Strike Force formed (Tactical designation of Second Fleet
as a Battleship force). At 1807 *Mogami* was ordered to transfer to the Vanguard
(C FORCE) and at 1900 Fifth Squadron and some of the destroyers were also
transferred. The CVLs were ordered to join the CVs and their light screen.

CVL *Zuiho*, Capt K. Sigiura
VF	6	A6M5b
VFB	15	A6M5b
VT	3	B6N1
VT	6	B5N2

30 Total

ii Heavy Screen Group
First Squadron (Battleship), Vice-Admiral Matome Ugaki
BB *Yamato* (Z), Rr Adm N. Morishita   VO 3 F1M
BB *Musashi* (CT), Rr Adm T. Inoguchi   VO 3 F1M
Third Squadron (Battleship), Vice-Admiral Yoshio Suzuki
BB *Kongo* (CY), Rr Adm T. Shimazaki   VS 2 E13A
BB *Haruna* (CY), Rr Adm K. Shigenaga   VS 2 E13A
Fourth Squadron (Cruiser), Vice Admiral Kurita
CA *Atago* (CT), Capt D. Araki   VS 2 E13A
CA *Takao* (CT), Capt S. Onodo   VS 2 E13A
CA *Chokai* (CY), Capt K. Ariga   VS 2 E13A
CA *Maya* (CY), Capt R. Ooe   VS 2 E13A
Seventh Squadron (Cruiser), Vice Admiral Kazutaka Shiraishi
CA *Kumano* (Z), Capt S. Hitomi   VS 3 E13A
CA *Suzuya* (Z), Capt W W. Takahashi   VS 3 E13A
CA *Chikuma* (Z), Capt S. Norimitsu   VS 5 E13A
CA *Tone* (Z), Capt H. Mayuzumi   VS 5 E13A

iii Destroyer Screen
Second Destroyer Flotilla (less 27DG), Rear Admiral Mikio Hayakawa
CL *Noshiro*, Capt S. Kajiwara   VS 2 E13A
31st Destroyer Group, Capt T. Fukuoka
DD *Naganami, Asashimo, Kishinami, Okinami*
32nd Destroyer Group, Cdr (*Chu-sa*), K. Aoki
DD *Tamanami, Hamanami, Fujinami, Shimakaze*★

2 *Supply Forces*
A First Supply Force
AOS   *Hayusui, Nichiei, Maru, Kokuyo Maru, Seiyo Maru*

★ DDS *Hayanami* lost prior to battle (32DG); CT – *Chitose* screen; CY – *Chiyoda* screen; Z – *Zuiho* screen.

DDS *Hibiki, Hatsushimo, Yunagi, Tsuga*
B Second Supply Force
AOS *Genyo Maru, Azusa Maru*
DDS *Yukikaze, Uzuki*

3 *Advance Expeditionary Force (Senken Butai)*, Vice-Admiral Takeo
    Takagi ashore at Saipan
  SSS   I–5; I–10; I–38; I–41; I–53; I–184; I–185; RO–36; RO–41;
        RO–42; RO–43; RO–44; RO–47; RO–68; RO–104;
        RO–105; RO–106; RO–108; RO–112; RO–113;
        RO–114; RO–115; RO–116; RO–117

4 *Base Air Forces*
Vice-Admiral Kakuda at Tinian No. 1 airfield
A Air Flotilla 61; Rear Admiral Ueno at Peleiu
i Naval Air Group 121, Cdr Iwao (48 vs)
    Tinian No. 1   vs–10 D4Y1
    Peleiu   vs–10 D4Y1
ii Naval Air Group 261, Cdr Ueda (72 vf)
    Saipan No. 1   vf–80 A6M5
iii Naval Air Group 263, Cdr Tamai (72 vf)
    Guam No. 1   vf–80 A6M5
    Yap   vf–40 A6M5
iv Naval Air Group 265, Cdr Urata (72 vf)
    Peleiu   vf–40 A6M5
    Guam No. 1   vf–15 A6M5
v Naval Air Group 321, Cdr Kubo (72 vfn)
    Tinian No. 1   vfn–15 J1N 'Irving' ('*Gekko*'–Moonlight)
vi Naval Air Group 343, Cdr Takenaka (72 vf)
    Tateyama   vf–40 N1K 'George' ('*Shiden*'–Violet
                            Lightning)
vii Naval Air Group 521, Cdr Kamei (96 vb)
    Guam No. 2   vb–80 P1Y "Frances' ('*Ginga*'–Milky
                            Way)
    Tinian No. 2   vb–40 P1Y
viii Naval Air Group 523, Cdr Wada (96 vb)
    Yap   vb–40 D4Y1
    Tinian No. 1   vb–40 D4Y1
ix Naval Air Group 761, Cdr Matsumoto (72 vb)
    Peleiu   vb–40 G4M 'Betty'

x Naval Air Group 1021, Cdr Kurihara (12)
    Tinian No. 1   VR–20 L2D 'Tabby' (Licence built DC–3)

B Air Flotilla 22; Rear Admiral Sumikawa at No. 1 Harushima
  i Naval Air Group 151, Cdr Nakamura (24 VS)
    Harushima No. 1   VS–20 D4Y1
  ii Naval Air Group 202, Cdr Netaba (96 VF)
    Harushima No. 1   VF–40 A6M5
    Mereyon   VF–40 A6M5
 iii Naval Air Group 251, Cdr Shibata (48 VF)
    Takeshima   VF–20 J1N
  iv Naval Air Group 253, Cdr Okasawara (96 VF)
    Takeshima   VF–80 A6M5
  v Naval Air Group 301, Cdr Yagi (96 VF)
    Yokosuka   VF–40 J2M 'Jack' ('*Raiden*'–Thunderbolt)
  vi Naval Air Group 503, Cdr Masuda (48 VB)
    Kaedeshima   VB–40 D4Y1
 vii Naval Air Group 551, Cdr Takahashi (48 VT)
    Harushima No. 1   VT–40 B6N1
    Harushima No. 2   VT–40 B6N1
viii Naval Air Group 755, Cdr Kusumoto (48 VB)
    Guam No. 1   VB–40 G4M

C Air Flotilla 26; Rear Admiral Arina at Davao No. 1
  i Naval Air Group 201, Cdr Nakano (96 VF)
    Davao No. 1   VF–80 A6M5
  ii Naval Air Group 501, Cdr Sakata (48 VF, 48 VB)
    Lasang   VF/VB–40 A6M5/D4Y1
 iii Naval Air Group 751, Cdr Ohtani (48 VB)
    Davao No. 2   VB–40 G4M

D Air Flotilla 23; Rear Admiral Ito at Sorong
  i Naval Air Group 153, Cdr Inoguchi (24 VS, 48 VF)
    Sorong   VS–20 D4Y1
    Sorong   VF–40 A6M5
  ii Naval Air Group 753, Cdr Umedami (48 VB)
    Menado   VB–40 G4M

Note on Base Air Force Air Groups – The air strengths in the Base
Air Force table of organization are paper strengths in the *A-Go* plan.

The parenthetical figure is the 'Fixed Number' of aircraft assigned to each air group according to Japanese Monograph No. 90, pp. 7–11 while the figure opposite the air station represents the 'Assigned Strength' as it is given in *Campaigns of the Pacific War*, p. 238. The approximate strength actually in the zone of operations during the battle according to Morison, p. 219 was: Chichi Jima–4; Saipan–35; Tinian–67; Guam–70; Truk–67; Yap–40; Palaus–134; Davao–25; Cebu–40; Halmahera–42; Sorong–16. The types and organizations to which they were assigned is unknown though it can be assumed they bore a ratio to the paper strength and the formations listed above participated in the operation.

APPENDIX TWO

Ship's Characteristics

	CV **Fleet Aircraft Carriers**	*Koku Bokan*
	USN (7)	IJN (5)
	Essex class (6 ships)	*Taiho* class (1 ship)
Displacement (s)	27,100 tons	29,300 tons
Displacement (f)	33,000 tons	36,809 tons
Dimensions	876′ × 93′ × 28.5′	852′ × 90′ × 31′
Machinery	4 Shafts Geared Turbines	4 Shafts Geared Turbines
	150,000 SHP 33 Knots	160,000 SHP 33 Knots
Armament	12–5″/38 (4× 2, 4× 1) 2 dir.★	12–100 mm (3.9″)/60, dir.
	68–40 mm (17× 4)	51–25 mm (17× 3)
	52–20 mm (52× 1)	
Air Group	Rated 100 aircraft	Rated 53 aircraft
Air Complement	36 VF/36 VB/18 VT (90)	27 VF/27 VB/18 VT/3 VS (75)
Armour	Belt 2.5″–4″; F.D. 1.5″	Belt 2.5″; F.D. 3.75″
	Hangar Deck 3″; Main 1.5″	
Complement	3448 including air group	1751 exclusive of air group and flag personnel
Radar	SK–1 air search (1)	21 Air/Surface (2)
	SC–2 air search (1)	13 air search (2)
	SM height finding (1)	
	SG surface search (1)	
	Mk–4 Fire control (2)	
	Mk–3 IFF	
Ships in battle	*Essex, Yorktown, Hornet, Lexington, Bunker Hill, Wasp*	*Taiho*
	Enterprise class (1 ship)	*Shokaku* class (1 ship)
Displacement (s)	19,900 tons	25,675 tons
Displacement (f)	25,500 tons	29,800 tons
Dimensions	827.5′ × 114′ × 28′	844′ × 85′ × 29′
Machinery	4 Shafts Geared Turbines	4 Shafts Geared Turbines
	120,000 SHP 34 Knots	160,000 SHP 34 Knots

★ dir. = director.

Armament	8–5″/38 (8 × 1) 2 directors	16–5″/40 (8 × 2) 4 directors
	40–40 mm (10 × 4)	70–25 mm
	40–20 mm (40 × 1)	
Air Group	Rated 81 aircraft	Rated 84 aircraft
Air Complement	36 VF/36 VB/18 VT (90)	27 VF/27 VB/18 VT/3 VS (75)
Armour	Belt 4″; Main deck 3″	Belt 8.5″; Main deck 6.75″
	Hangar deck none; Mag 3″	
	Lower decks 1″	
Complement	2919 including air group	1660 exclusive of air group
Radar	SK–1 air search (1)	21 Air/Surface (1)
	SC–2 air search (1)	
	SM height finding (1)	
	SG surface search (1)	
	Mk–4 Fire control (2)	
	Mk–3 IFF	
Ships in battle	Enterprise	Shokaku, Zuikaku

		Hiyo class (2 ships)
Displacement (s)		24,140 tons
Displacement (f)		27,500 tons
Dimensions		719.5′ × 88′ × 27′
Machinery		2 Shafts Geared Turbines
		56,250 SHP 25.5 Knots
Armament		12–5″/40 (6 × 2) local control
		40–25 mm (11 × 3, 7 × 1)
Air Group		Rated 53 aircraft
Air Complement		27 VF/18 VB/6 VT (51)
Armour		Belt 1″ over eng spces only
Complement		1224 exclusive of air group
Radar		21 Air/Surface (1)
Ships in battle		Hiyo, Junyo

CVL Light Fleet Aircraft Carriers

	USN (8)	IJN (4)
	Independence class (8 ships)	Ryuho class (1 ship)
Displacement (s)	11,000 tons	13,360 tons
Displacement (f)	15,100 tons	15,300 tons
Dimensions	622 × ′71′ × 26′	707′ × 64′ × 22′
Machinery	4 Shafts Geared Turbines	2 Shafts Geared Turbines
	100,000 SHP 33 Knots	52,000 SHP 26.5 Knots
Armament		8–5″/40 (4 × 2) 2 directors
	26–40 mm	42–25 mm
	40–20 mm	6–13 mm

Air Group	Rated 45	Rated 31
Air Complement	24 VF/9 VT (33)	27 VF/6 VT (33)
Armour	Belt 5″; Main deck 3″;	
	Magazines 3″; Lower d. 1″	
Complement	1569 including air group	
Radar	SK–1 air search (1)	13 air search (1)
	SC–2 air search (1)	
	SG surface search (1)	
	Mk–3 IFF	
Ships in battle	Princeton, Belleau Wood,	Ryuho
	Bataan, Cowpens, Monterey,	
	San Jacinto, Cabot, Langley	

		Zuiho class (1 ship)
Displacement (s)		11,262 tons
Displacement (f)		13,950 tons
Dimensions		712′ × 59′ × 22′
Machinery		2 Shafts Geared Turbines
		52,000 SHP 28 Knots
Armament		8–5″/40 (4 × 2) 2 directors
		48–25 mm
Air Group		Rated 30 aircraft
Air Complement		21 VF/9 VT (30)
Complement		
Radar		13 air search (1)

		Chiyoda class (2 ships)
Displacement (s)		11,180 tons
Displacement (f)		13,600 tons
Dimensions		631′ × 68′ × 24′
Machinery		4 Shafts Geared Turbines
		56,800 SHP 29 Knots
Armament		8–5″/40 (4 × 2) 2 directors
		30–25 mm
Air Group		Rated 30
Air Complement		21 VF/9 VT (30)
Complement		
Radar		21 Air/Surface (1)
Ships of class		Chitose, Chiyoda

BB **Battleships**

		Senkan
	USN (7)	IJN (5)
	Iowa class (2 ships)	*Yamato* class (2 ships)

Displacement (s)	48,500 tons	64,170 tons
Displacement (f)	57,450 tons	71,659 tons
Dimensions	887′× 108′× 36′	863′× 128′× 35′
Machinery	4 Shafts Geared Turbines 212,000 SHP 33 Knots	4 Shafts Geared Turbines 150,000 SHP 27.5 Knots
Armament	9–16″/50 (3×3)	9–46 cm (18.1″)/45 (3×3) 6–155 mm (6.1″)/60 (2×3) 2 directors
	20–5″/38 (10×2) 4 directors	Y–24–5″.40 (12×2) 4 directors M–12–5″.40 (6×2) 4 directors
	I. 60–40 mm; 60–20 mm N.J. 64–40 mm; 60–20 mm 3 aircraft; 2 catapults	Y–74–25 mm M–115–25 mm 6 aircraft; 2 catapults
Armour	Belt 12.25″/Turret 17.5″ Decks: Upper 1.5″; Main 4.75″;0.75″; Lower 5.6″+0.75″	Belt 16″/Turret 25.5″ Decks: Sloped 9.06″; Flat 7.87″
Complement	2700	2500
Radar	SK–2 air search (1) SG surface search (1) MG–8 Fire control (2) Mk–4 Fire control (4) *Iowa* only SC–2 Air (1)	21 Air/Surface (2) 22 Surface (2) 13 Air (2)
	South Dakota class (3)	*Nagato* class (1)
Displacement (s)	38,000 tons	39.130 tons
Displacement (f)	44,374 tons	46,356 tons
Dimensions	670′× 108′× 36′	738′× 113′× 31′
Machinery	4 Shafts Geared Turbines 130,000 SHP 28 Knots	4 Shafts Geared Turbines 82,300 SHP 25 Knots
Armament	9–16″/45 (3×3)	8–41 cm (16.1″)/45 (4×2) 16–14 cm (5.5″)/50 (16×1) 8–5″/40 (4×2) 4 directors
	S.D. 16–5″/38 (8×2) 4 dir *Ind Ala* 20–5″/38 (10×2) 4 Directors S.D. 68–40 mm *Ind Ala* 56–40 mm 40–20 mm	22–25 mm
Armour	Belt 12.25″; Turrets 18″ Decks: Upper 1.5″; Main 5″+0.75″; Lower 5.75″+0.75″	Belt 12″; Turrets 14″ Deck: 3.5″
Complement	2500	1368

Radar	SK–1 Air (1) *Ind Ala* only	21 Air/Surface (1)
	SC–2 (S.D.) Air (1)	22 Surface (2)
	SG (1); Mk 8 (2); Mk 4 (4)	13 Air (1)
	North Carolina (2 ships)	*Kongo* (2 ships)
Displacement (s)	38,000 tons	31,720 tons
Displacement (f)	46,770 NC; 45,374 t (W)	36,314 tons
Dimensions	729′ × 108′ × 35′	728′ × 95′ × 32′
Machinery	4 Shafts Geared Turbines	4 Shafts Geared Turbines
	121,000 SHP 28 Knots	136,000 SHP 30.5 Knots
Armament	9–16″/45 (3 × 3)	8–36 cm (14.2″) 50 (4 × 2)
	20–5″/38 (10 × 2) 4 directors	8–6″/50 (8 × 1)
		12–5″/40 (6 × 2) 2 directors
	60–40 mm	H–34–25 mm
	56–20 mm	K–20–25 mm
Armour	Belt 12″; Turrets 16″	Belt 8″; Turrets 11″
	Decks: Upper 1.5″; Main	Decks: Lower 2.75″; Main
	3.7″–4.7″–1.5″; Lower	4.75″
	4.75″–0.75″	
Complement		
Aircraft	3 with two catapults	2 with one catapult
Radar	SK Air (1)	21 Air/Sirface (1)
	SG Surface (1)	22 Surface (2)
	Mk–8 Fire control (2)	13 Air (1)
	Mk–4 Fire control (4)	
Ships of class in battle	*North Carolina, Washington*	*Kongo, Haruna*

Heavy Cruisers

		Junyokan (I o)
	USN 8	IJN 11
	Baltimore class (3 ships)	*Tone* class (2 ships)
Displacement (s)	13,600 tons	11,215 tons
Displacement (f)	17,070 tons	14,070 tons
Dimensions	673′ × 71′ × 26′	661′ × 63′ × 21′
Machinery	4 Shafts Geared Turbines	4 Shafts Geared Turbines
	120,000 SHP 33 Knots	152,200 SHP 35 Knots
Armament	9–8″/55 (3 × 3)	8–8″/50 (4 × 2)
	12–5″/38 (6 × 2)	8–5″/40 (4 × 2)
	48–40 mm	57–25 mm
	24–20 mm	
		12–24″ T.T. (4 × 3)
	2 catapults 4 aircraft	2 catapults 5 aircraft
Armour	Belt 6″; Turrets 3″–6″	Belt 4″; Turrets 3.2″
	Decks: Main 3″; Lower 2″	Decks 2.5″

Complement	1750	850
Radar	SK Air (1)	21 Air/Surface (1)
	SG Surface (1)	
	Mk-4 Fire control (2)	
	Mk-8 Fire control (2)	
Ships of class in battle	*Baltimore, Boston, Canberra*	*Tone, Chikuma*

	Wichita class (1 ship)	*Suzuya* class (2 ships)
Displacement (s)	9,324 tons	12,400 tons
Displacement (f)	13,700 tons	13,887 tons
Dimensions	614′ × 62′ × 25′	669′ × 66′ × 19′
Machinery	4 Shafts Geared Turbines	4 Shafts Geared Turbines
	100,000 SHP 32.5 Knots	152,000 SHP 34.75 Knots
Armament	9-8″/55 (3 × 3)	10-8″/50 (5 × 2)
	8-5″/38 (8 × 1)	8-5″/40 (4 × 2)
	20-40 mm	30-25 mm
	20-20 mm	
		12-24″ T.T. (4 × 3)
	2 catapults 4 aircraft	2 catapults 3 aircraft
Armour	Belt B″; Turrets 3″-6″	Belt 4″; Turrets 1.5″
	Decks: Main 3″; Lower 2″	Decks: 1.5″
Complement	1200	850
Radar	SC-2 Air (1)	22 Surface (1)
	Mk-4 Fire control (2)	
	Mk-8 Fire control (2)	
Ships of class in battle	*Wichita*	*Suzuya, Kumano*

	New Orleans class (3 ships)	*Mogami* class modified (1)
Displacement (s)	9,950 tons	12,206 tons
Displacement (f)	13,500 tons	13,700 tons
Dimensions	588′ × 62′ × 25′	669′ × 66′ × 19′
Machinery	4 Shafts Geared Turbines	4 Shafts Geared Turbines
	107,000 SHP 32.7 Knots	152,000 SHP 35 Knots
Armament	9-8″/55 (3 × 3)	6-8″/50 (3 × 2)
	8-5″/38 (8 × 1)	8-5″/40 (4 × 2)
	16-40 mm	30-25 mm
	19-20 mm	
		12-24″ T.T. (4 × 3)
	2 catapults 4 aircraft	2 catapults 11 aircraft
Armour	Belt 5″; Turret 3″-5″	Belt 4″; Turrets 1.5″
	Decks: Main 3″; Lower 2″	Decks: 1.5″

Complement	1200	850
Radar	SK Air (1)	21 Air/Surface (1)
	SG Surface (1)	
	Mk–4 Fire control (2)	
	Mk–8 Fire control (2)	
Ships of class in battle	New Orleans, San Francisco, Minneapolis	*Mogami* (sometimes referred to as a *Junyokan-koku,* i.e. Aircraft Cruiser)
	Indianapolis class (1 ship)	*Atago* class (4 ships)
Displacement (s)	9,800 tons	13,160 tons
Displacement (f)	12,575 tons	14,989 tons
Dimensions	610′ × 66′ × 24′	664′ × 68′ × 21′
Machinery	4 Shafts Geared Turbines	4 Shafts Geared Turbines
	107,000 SHP 32.75 Knots	133,100 SHP 34.25 Knots
Armament	9–8″/55 (3 × 3)	10–8″/50 (5 × 2) except Maya 8–8″/(4 × 2)
	8–5″/38 (8 × 1)	Takao/Atago 8–5″/40 (4 × 2)
		Chokai 4–4.7″ (4 × 1)
		Maya 12–5″ (6 × 2)
	16–40 mm	Takao/Atago 26–25 mm
	22–20 mm	Maya 39–25 mm
		Chokai No machine guns
Armour	Belt 3″–4″; Turrets 3″	Belt 4″; Turrets 1.5″
	Decks 2″–2″	Decks 1.5″
Complement	950	773
Radar	SK Air (1)	21 Air/Surface (1)
	Mk–4 Fire control (2)	13 Air (1)
	Mk–8 Fire control (2)	
Ships of class in battle	Indianapolis	Atago, Maya, Chokai, Takao
		Myoko class (2 ships)
Displacement (s)		13,380 tons
Displacement (f)		14,980 tons
Dimensions		662′ × 68′ × 21′
Machinery		4 Shafts Geared Turbines
		130,250 SHP 33.75 Knots
Armament		10–8″/50 (5 × 2)
		8–5″/40 (4 × 2)
		24–25 mm
		2 catapults 3 aircraft
Armour		Belt 4″; Turrets 1.5″
		Decks 2.5″–5″

Complement		773
Radar		21 Air/Surface (1)
		22 Surface (2)
		13 Air (1)
Ships of class in battle		Myoko, Haguro

Light Cruisers

		Junyokan Nito
	USN 13 (9 CL, 4 CLAA)	IJN 2
	Cleveland class (9 ships)	*Agano* class (2 ships)
Displacement (s)	10,000 tons	6,652 tons
Displacement (f)	13,755 tons	7,710 tons
Dimensions	610′ × 66 × 25′	594′ × 49.8′ × 18.5′
Machinery	4 Shafts Geared Turbines	4 Shafts Geared Turbines
	100,000 SHP 33 Knots	100,000 SHP 35 Knots
Armament	12–6″/47 (4 × 3)	6–15 cm (5.9″)/40 (3 × 2)
	12–5″/38 (6 × 2)	4–3″/60 (2 × 2)
	Cleve. 8–40 mm	52–25 mm (8 × 3, 28 × 1)
	Birm., Mob., Mia 28–40 mm	
	Mont., S.F., Vin., Bil. and	
	Hou. 24–40 mm	
	Mia. 10–20 mm	
	Cle., Mont. 17–20 mm	8–24″ T.T. (4 × 2)
	Others 21–20 mm	1 catapult 2 aircraft
	2 catapults 4 aircraft	
Armour	Belt 5″; Turrets 3″–5″	Belt 2.25″; Turrets 1″
	Decks: Main 3″; Lower 2″	Decks 0.75″
Complement	1426	
Radar	SC Air (1)	21 Air/Surface (1)
	SG Surface (1)	13 Air (1)
	Mk–4 Fire control (2)	
	Mk–8 Fire control (2)	
Ships of class in battle	*Cleveland, Santa Fe, Mobile, Biloxi, Houston, Montpelier, Birmingham, Vincennes, Miami*	*Yahagi, Noshiro*

	Atlanta class (2 ships)
Displacement (s)	6,000 tons
Displacement (f)	8,100 tons
Dimensions	541.75′ × 53.25′ × 26.5′
Machinery	4 Shafts Geared Turbines
	75,000 SHP 33 Knots

Armament	16–5″/38 (8 × 2)
	8–40 mm
	11 to 19–20 mm
	8–21″ T.T. (4 × 2)
Armour	Belt 3.5″; Turrets 1.5″–1″
	Decks 2″
Complement	810
Radar	SG Surface (1)
	SC Air (1)
	Mk–4 Fire control (2)
Ships of class in battle	San Juan, San Diego

	Oakland class (2 ships)
Displacement (s)	6,000 tons
Displacement (f)	8,200 tons
Dimensions	541.5′ × 53.25′ × 26.5′
Machinery	4 Shafts Geared Turbines
	75,000 SHP 33 Knots
Armament	12–5″/38 (6 × 2)
	16–40 mm
	16–20 mm
	6–21″ T.T. (3 × 2)
Armour	Belt 3.5″; Turrets 1.5″–1″
	Decks 2″
Complement	
Radar	SC Air (1)
	Mk–4 Fire control (2)
Ships of class in battle	Oakland, Reno

Destroyers

	USN 69	Kuchikukan
		IJN 23 (19 DD, 4 DLAA)
	Fletcher class (46 ships)	Akitsuki AA escorts (4 ships)
Displacement (s)	2,050 tons	2,701 tons
Displacement (f)		3,470 tons
Dimensions	376.5′ × 39.5′ × 17.75′	440′ × 38′ × 13.5′
Machinery	2 Shafts Geared Turbines	2 Shafts Geared Turbines
	60,000 SHP 37 Knots	52,000 SHP 33 Knots
Armament	5–5″/38 (5 × 1)	8–10 cm (3.9″) 60 (4 × 2)
		auto.
	6–10 40 mm	15–25 mm
	10–21″ T.T. (5 × 2)	4–24″ T.T. (4 × 1)

Complement	300	
Radar	SC Air (1)	21 Air/Surface (1)
	SG Surface (1)	22 Surface (1)
	Mk–4 Fire control (1)	
Ships of class in battle	Izard, Charrette, Conner, Bell, Burns, Boyd, Bradford, Brown, Cowell, Owen, Miller, The Sullivans, Stephen Potter, Tingey, Hickox, Hunt, Lewis Hancock, Marshall, Clarence K. Bronson, Cotten, Dortch, Gatling, Healy, Caperton, Cogswell, Ingersoll, Knapp, Terry, Anthony, Wadsworth, Braine, Charles Ausburne, Stanly, Dyson, Converse, Spence Thatcher, Halford, Guest, Bennett, Fullam, Hudson, Yarnall, Twining, Stockham, Monssen	Hatsuzuki, Wakatsuki, Akitsuki, Shimozuki

	Livermore class (4 ships)	Shimakaze class (1 ship)
Displacement (s)	1,630 tons	2,567 tons
Displacement (f)	2,515 tons	
Dimensions	341.5′ × 36′ × 10′	391′ × 35′ × 12′
Machinery	2 Shafts Geared Turbines	2 Shafts Geared Turbines
	50,000 SHP 37 Knots	75,000 SHP 39.75 Knots
Armament	4–5″/38 (4 × 1)	4–5″/40 (2 × 2)
	4–40 mm	14–25 mm
	6 to 7–20 mm	
	5–21″ T.T. (5 × 1)	15–24″ T.T. (5 × 3)
Complement	276	
Radar	SC Air (1)	22 Surface (1)
	SG Surface (1)	13 Air (1)
	Mk–4 Fire control (1)	
Ships of class in battle	McCall, Lansdowne, Lardner, McCalla	Shimakaze

	Craven class (8 ships)	Yugumo class (9 ships)
Displacement (s)	1,500 tons	2,077 tons
Displacement (f)		
Dimensions	341.5′ × 36′ × 10′	391′ × 35′ × 12′

Machinery	2 Shafts Geared Turbines 49,000 SHP 36.5 Knots	2 Shafts Geared Turbines 52,000 SHP 35.5 Knots
Armament	4–5″/38 (4×1) Helm, Gridley, Patterson, Craven 4–1.1″; 16–21″ T.T. (4×4) Balance 4–40 mm; 8–21″ T.T. (4×2)	4–5″/50 (4×2) 15–25 mm 8–24″ T.T. (4×2)
Complement	250	228
Radar	SC Air (1) SG Surface (1) Mk-4 Fire control (1)	13 Air (1) 22 Surface (1)
Ships of class in battle	Maury, Craven, Gridley, Lang, Sterrett, Wilson, Ellet, Helm	Naganami, Asashimo, Okinami, Kishinami, Hayashimo, Akishimo, Hamanami, Tamanami, Fujinami

	Mahan class (1 ship)	Kagero (4 ships)
Displacement (s)	1,500 tons	2,033 tons
Displacement (f)		
Dimensions	341.5′ × 35.5′ × 10′	388.75′ × 35.5′ × 12.3′
Machinery	2 Shafts Geared Turbines 49,000 SHP 36.5 Knots	2 Shafts Geared Turbines 52,000 SHP 35.5 Knots
Armament	4–5″/38 (4×1) 8–40 mm 6 to 7–20 mm 4–21″ T.T. (4×1)	4–5″/50 (2×2) 14–25 mm 8–24″/T.T. (4×2)
Complement	172	240
Radar	SC Air (1)	22 Surface (1) 13 Air (1)
Ships of class in battle	Case	Hamakaze, Urakaze, Nowake, Isokaze

	Farragut class (3 ships)	Asashio class (3 ships)
Displacement (s)	1,396 tons	1,961 tons
Displacement (f)		
Dimensions	341.5′ × 34.25′ × 9′	388′ × 34′ × 12′
Machinery	2 Shafts Geared Turbines 42,800 SHP 36.5 Knots	2 Shafts Geared Turbines 50,000 SHP 35 Knots
Armament	4–5″/38 (4×1) 4–40 mm 6 to 7–20 mm 8–21″ T.T. (4×2)	4–5″/50 (2×2) 14–25 mm 8–24″/T.T. (4×2)

Complement	250	200
Radar	SC Air (1)	unk
Ships of class in battle	MacDonough, Dewey, Hull	Yamagumo, Michishio, Asagumo

Shiratsuya class (2 ships)

Displacement (s)	1,580 tons
Dimensions	352.75' × 32.5' × 11.5'
Machinery	2 Shafts Geared Turbines
	42,000 SCP 34 Knots
Armament	4–5"/50 (2 × 2)
	13 to 21–25 mm
	4–13 mm
	8–24"/T.T. (4 × 2)
Complement	180
Radar	22 Surface (1)
	13 Air (1)
Ships in battle	*Shigure, Samidare*

APPENDIX THREE

Aircraft Characteristics

With some exceptions the performance differential between 1944 aircraft of the two navies was not greatly different from that of 1942. Japanese aircraft were still generally more lightly armoured, more manoeuvrable and faster than their American counterparts. American machines were still more heavily gunned and armoured than the Japanese.

In the important fighter category the Americans enjoyed the widest superiority. The American fighter force was composed of 448 F6F-3, 24 F6F-3N and 3 F4U-2. The F6F-3 (Hellcat) was heavily armed (6–.50 cal mgs), heavily armoured and faster than the latest Japanese carrier fighters. The Hellcat could also dive faster. The A6M-5 (Zeke), the famous 'Zero', was the only Japanese aircraft type which was slower than its American opposite. It could climb faster and was more manoeuvrable than the Hellcat, but lacking armour and self-sealing fuel tanks, was less durable than the F6F. The A6M-5b assigned to NAG 653 were the first Zekes with armoured glass and automatic fire extinguishing equipment in their fuel systems. Such equipment had long been standard in US aircraft.

	USN F6F-3 'Hellcat'	IJN A6M5a/A6M5b 'Zeke'
Manufacturer	Grumman	Mitsubishi/Nakajima
Engine	1–2000 hp Pratt × Whitney R2800–10 Double Wasp Radial	1–1130 hp Nakajima-Sakae 21 Radial
Span/Length/Height	42' 10"/33' 6.5"/13'	36' 1"/29' 9"/9' 2"
Weight:		
Empty/Loaded	9042 lb/11,381 lb	4175 lb/6047 lb
Crew	One	One
Maximum speed	376 mph at 17,300'	351 mph at 19,685'
Cruise speed	168 mph	230 mph

Service ceiling	38,400'	35,100'
Range normal	1090 miles	1194 miles
Armament	6–.50 cal mgs	A6M5a: 2–20 mm/1–12.7 mg
		2–7.7 mm mg
		A6M5b: 2–20 mm/1–12.7 mg
		1–7.7 mm mg
Numbers involved	F6F–3, 448: F6F–3N, 24	A6M5a (VF) 135
	Total 472	A6M5a (VFB) 27
		A6M5b (VF) 18
		A6M5b (VFB) 45
		───
		Total 225

SB2C (Helldiver) comprised 174 of the American dive bomber force. With good air speed and capable of taking amazing punishment this aircraft seems, on paper, to have been an excellent replacement for the older Dauntless, however the consensus in the US Navy was otherwise. The Helldiver could carry a 1000 lb bomb internally. In contrast, the Japanese D4Y, though slow in reaching full scale production, had good performance characteristics and was considered a successful type. It carried a 500 kg (1102 lb) bomb internally and its overall dimensions were not much greater than Zeke. Both sides employed 1942 dive bomber types. The USN still had two squadrons of SBD–5 (Dauntless). One of the most successful aircraft designs in the US Navy history they were still favoured by many dive bomber pilots. The Japanese employed 27 D3A2 (Val). Somewhat faster than Dauntless they were lightly armoured and operationally a very successful type in spite of their ungainly appearance. Originally the Japanese CVLs were to carry dive bombers (Judys) as well as fighters and torpedo planes. The 'hot' characteristics of Judy on the small slow CVLs made the Japanese adopt an expedient which would later become the heart of the 'kamikaze' attack forces; the fuel drop tank mechanism was modified so that seventy-two (see above) of the A6M assigned to 652 and 653 NAG could carry a 250 kg (55 1lb) bomb.

	USN	IJN
	SB2C–1C 'Helldiver'	D4Y–1 'Suisei (Comet)' Judy
Manufacturer	Curtiss	Yokosuka
Engine	1–1900 hp Wright	1–1200 hp Aichi Atsuta
	R2600 Cyclone	12 cylinder inverted vee
	Radial	in line liquid cooled

	USN	IJN
Span/Length/Height	49' 9"/36' 8"/13' 2"	37' 9"/33' 4"/10' 9.5"
Weight:		
Empty/Loaded	10,400 lb/14,042 lb	5,514 lb/8,270 lb
Crew	Two	Two
Maximum speed	294 mph at 16,700'	343 mph at 15,585'
Cruise speed	158 mph	265 mph
Range	1925 miles	2417 miles
Armament	2–20 mm/1–.50 mg 1000 lb bomb load	1–7.9 mg/2–7.7 mm mg 1650 lb bomb load
Number involved	174 Total	90 D4Y–1 VB 9 D4Y–1C VS — 99

	USN SBD-5 'Dauntless'	IJN D3A2 'Val'
Manufacturer	Douglas	Aichi
Engine	1–1200 hp Wright R1820–60 Cyclone Radial	1–1300 hp Mitsubishi Kinsei 54 Radial
Span/Length/Height	41' 6"/33'/12' 11"	47'/33' 7"/10' 11.25"
Weight:		
Empty/Loaded	6,533 lb/9,353 lb	5,772 lb/8,378 lb
Crew	Two	Two
Maximum speed	252 mph at 13,800'	267 mph at 20,340'
Cruise speed	144 mph	184 mph
Service ceiling	24,300'	34,450'
Range	1115 miles	970 miles
Armament	2–.50 mg 2–.30 mg 1000 lb bomb load	2–7.7 mm mg 817 lb bomb load
Number involved	59	27

Both sides employed torpedo planes that had remarkable performance characteristics compared with pre-war torpedo plane types. The USN employed 190 TBF/TBM 'Avenger'. Well armed and armoured, and with good speed they could carry one 1921 lb (22") torpedo internally. The Japanese utilized two torpedo types, B5N (Kate) and B6N (Jill). The latter type was a new very high performance torpedo bomber and could carry a 1764 lb (18") torpedo externally. Like all Japanese aircraft they were poorly armoured. Eighteen B5Ns were embarked in *Chitose*, *Chiyoda* and *Zuiho* and were employed principally as reconnaissance aircraft in this battle.

With good speed by 1942 standards, they could not be used as first line attack aircraft in 1944 because they now suffered the worst of two worlds; low speed (by 1944 standards) and poor armour. They could carry a 1764 lb torpedo.

	USN TBF/TBM Avenger	IJN B6N-1 'Tenzan' (Heavenly Mountain) 'Jill'
Manufacturer	Grumman/General Motors	Nakajima
Engine	1–1850 hp Wright R2600–8 Double Cyclone Radial	1–1850 hp Mitsubishi-Kasei 25 Radial
Span/Length/Height	54′ 2″/40′/16′ 5″	48′ 10.25″/35′ 7.5″/12′ 5.5″
Weight:		
Empty/Loaded	10,080 lb/15,905 lb	7,105 lb/11,464 lb
Crew	Three	Three
Maximum speed	271 mph at 12.000′	299 mph at 16,076′
Cruise speed	145 mph	207 mph
Range	1215 miles	2142 miles
Armament	3–.50 cal mg/1–.30 cal mg	2–7.7 mm mg
	1–1921 lb torpedo	1–1764 lb torpedo
Number involved	97 TBF-1C 88 TBM-1C 2 TBM-1D 3 TBF-1D ——— 190 Total	81 Total

	IJN B5N2 'Kate'
Manufacturer	Nakajima
Engine	1–1000 hp Nakajima-Sakae 11 Radial
Span/Length/Height	50′ 11″/33′ 9.5″/12′ 2″
Weight:	
Empty/Loaded	4643 lb/8157 lb
Crew	Three (Two as VT)
Maximum speed	235 mph at 11,810′
Cruise speed	161 mph
Range	1404 miles
Armament	2–7.7 mm mgs 1–1764 lb torpedo
Number involved	18 Total

Numbers aside, the aircraft of the two fleets were not mismatched. In 1942, in expert hands, the more nimble Japanese aircraft had performed well against the more rugged and heavily armed American planes. In 1944 in inexpert hands their manoeuvrability could not be exploited and the sacrifice of protection required for their 'hot' characteristics made them death traps when confronted with the more skilful American fighter pilots. Also, the Japanese employed a larger portion of obsolescent (Val and Kate) types than the Americans (Dauntless). One aspect that defies tabulation was the operational age of many of the aircraft in the US Fleet. A good portion had been in combat for ten months. The engines were in need of overhauls and would not peform at their rated output. They were 'gas greedy, some of them dangerously so' and could not match their handbook air speed.

Because of the lighter construction of Japanese aircraft they could attack and search at greater ranges than American carrier aeroplanes. American aircraft could attack to about 200–250 miles while the Japanese could strike to 300–350 miles. In the area of search the Japanese routinely searched to ranges of 560 miles while American searches were generally 325–350 miles, outside Japanese strike range.

Other aircraft: USN

FM-2 Fighter–'Wildcat'; 1–1200 hp; 38′× 28′ 9″; 318 mph at 19,400′; 6–.50 cal mgs; 1 man

PBM-5 Patrol Flying Boat–'Mariner'; 2–1700 hp; 118′× 80′; 198 mph at 18,000′; 5–.50 cal mgs; 9 men

PB4Y-1 Land Based Patrol Bomber–'Liberator'; 4–1200 hp; 110′× 67′ 3″; 279 mph at 26,500′; 8–.50 cal mgs; 9–10 men

SOC-1 Scout and observation seaplane 'Seagull'; 1–600 hp; 36′× 31′ 5″; 165 mph at 5000′; 2–.30 cal mgs; 2 men (23 on CA/CL: 16 SOC1; 2 SOC2; 5 SOC 3).

OS2U Observer Scout seaplane 'Kingfisher'; 1–450 hp; 35′ 10″× and 33′ 10″; 164 mph at 5500′; 2–.30 cal mgs; 2 men (34 on OS2N BB/CA/CL: 12 OS2N1; 22 OS2U3)

4U-2 Night Fighter–'Corsair'; 1–2450 hp; 40′ 11″× 33′ 8″; 446 mph at 26,000′; 6–.50 cal mgs; 1 man

Other aircraft: UJN

G4M2 Land based bomber–'Betty'; 2–1800 hp; 82′× 65′ 7″; 272

mph at 15,900′; 4–7.7 mm mgs, 2–20 mm mgs; 7 men; 1–1764 lb torpedo

F1M   Observation Float Seaplane–'Pete'; 1–875 hp; 36′ 1″× 29′ 1.75″; 230 mph at 11,285′; 3–7.7 mm mgs; 2 men (9 carried by BB)

N1K   Land based Fighter–'George'; 1–1820 hp; 39′ 4.5″× 29′ 1.75″; 363 mph at 19,355′; 2–7.7 mm mgs; 4–20 mm mgs; 1 man

J2M   Land based Fighter–'Jack'; 1–1800 hp; 35′ 5.25″× 31′ 9.74″; 371 mph at 17,880′; 2–7.7 mm mgs; 2–20 mm mgs; 1 man

J1N   Long range escort fighter–'Irving'; 2–1130 hp; 55′ 8.5″× 39′ 11.5″; 329 mph at 19,685′; 1–20 mm mg; 6–7.7 mm mgs; 2–3 men

P1Y   Medium bomber–'Frances'; 2–1820 hp; 65′ 7″× 49′ 2.5″; 340 mph at 19,355′; 1–7.7 mm mgs; 1–20 mm mgs; 3 men; 1–1764 lb torpedo

E13A   Reconnaissance seaplane–'Jake'; 1–1060 hp; 47′ 7″× 37′ 1″; 234 mph at 7155′; 1–7.7 mm mg; 1–20 mm mg; 3 men (43 carried on BB/CA/CL)

Radar and Combat Information Centre

Next to the aeroplane and submarine, nothing had a greater impact on naval warfare in World War II than radar (*RA*dio *D*irection *A*nd *R*anging). A primitive radio locating device at the beginning of the war, by 1944, it could detect formations of aircraft at great distances, provide information for an accurate plot of the progress of enemy air raids and provide shipboard gunfire control.

In October 1940 the British Tizard mission came to the United States for an exchange of radar (RDF in the RN during World War II) information. One of the interesting operational techniques the British imparted to the Americans was the use of a radar-equipped carrier as a fighter direction ship. The concept of a central clearing house for the collection, evaluation and dissemination of combat information predated radar (see *The Grand Fleet*, Jellicoe, Admiral, pp. 43–44). Most of the techniques which were later used by the US Navy in 1944–45 with great success were learned during this mission.

In an air attack situation Combat Information Centre (CIC or 'Combat' in the USN) in the following fashion. One section of the compartment contained radar consoles which were manned by radar operators. These men operated the cathode ray tube scopes which contained built in range and bearing cursors. When they had determined the range and bearing of a target and evaluated it (friendly, enemy, unknown, ship, aircraft, etc.) they advised a radar plotter by means of a sound powered telephone set. The plotters then located the target on a plexiglass display in the form of a compass rose which contained ten equal range circles for any convenient scale, with the centre representing the tracking ship, thus presenting a relative movement plot (see diagrams 10, 13, 15 and 17 for examples of CIC plots). Any information which might be useful was put in a box or circle next to the position of the 'Raid' and it was given a designation: 'Raid 1' etc. Location of own aircraft was also shown. In another section of the CIC the status of all aircraft under the control of the ship was shown on a large plexiglass display. This 'status board' contained such information as number of aircraft airborne, take off time, fuel and ammunition state and any other information of value in determining the use of interceptor. In addition to this all tactical and combat information radio nets were monitored. Any tactical signals effecting the battle situation such as a formation change or screen reorientation, were noted. A plot of the formation was kept which showed course, speed and axis of the formation together with all ships plotted on station. A communications status board showed all ships and air units by names or unit designations, voice call sign and CW (morse) call sign. Such items as challenge-response codes etc. were also shown on the Communications status board. The centre of this activity in an air attack was the Fighter Director Officer. It was his duty to observe the progress of enemy raids on the radar plotting boards, determine the number of fighters available, their fuel and ammunition status and place them in a position to intercept the incoming raid. He had the responsibility of rotating all fighters on board for refuelling and re-arming, insuring that all aircraft were well armed and fuelled while at the same time sufficient aircraft were airborne to meet incoming raids. A raid often lasted for an hour with a constant flow of information being given to him, digested and acted upon.

Generally American radar was divided into three broad functional groups: air search, surface search and fire control. The two most important air search types employed in 1944 were SC and SK.

The concept of 'Flag Plot' referred to in Admiral Jellicoe's book was well known to the Japanese. All Japanese ships equipped as flagships (i.e. all BB, CV, CA, CL) had operations rooms similar to the flag plot on US ships and the Japanese certainly used fighter director officers for control of combat air patrol (CAP), but they apparently never married the operations room and the radar plot. An officer, either a pilot or the anti-aircraft commander controlled the fighters by radio telephone using radar as his primary means of plotting enemy raids. By 1944 all Japanese combatant ships were equipped with at least one of the three types of standard radar equipments available: Type 21 combination air/surface warning, Type 13 air warning and Type 22 surface warning. Some ships particularly large conbatants, carried all three types. Japanese radars were about equal in sophistication to radars in service in the US Navy in 1940-41. They had no fire control radar though Type 22 was later modified to provide range and bearing information to the gunnery computers in surface firing. Admiral Ozawa had little confidence in the level of training of his radar technicians.

Because of the two year lead in equipment development and operational experience the US Navy had a clear superiority in both equipment and technique in this very important aspect of carrier warfare.

Generally two types of scope presentations were available during World War II; the A-Scope and the PPI Scope. The former was the basic type presentation (many variants* existed but for simplicity the basic will be shown) that all nations first developed as follows:

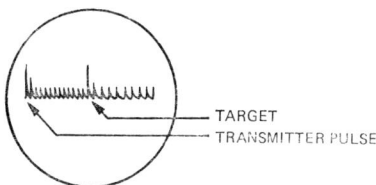

This type of presentation was always the best form for use in fire control.

The PPI (Plan Position Indicator) 'presented a semi-persistent, up to the minute geographical radar picture in polar coordinates. The relative positions of friendlies and enemies, of ships and land masses could be seen at a glance. By marking the positions of targets from time to time and connecting these, their courses and speeds could be estimated directly from the scope.' The advantage of this equipment over the A-Scope in plotting air raids should be obvious.

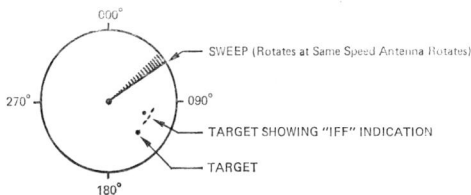

* Such as 'J' scope, 'B' scope etc.

US Shipboard Radar

In June 1944 the US Navy was Radar rich. The equipment fell into three broad categories: air search, surface search and fire control. The search sets were developed by the Bureau of Ships and (during World War II) were generally designated by a two letter symbol followed by a number for modifications (e.g. SC–2) though early models such as CXAM were not so designated. The fire control sets were developed by the Bureau of Ordnance and were given Mark numbers (Mk. 1).

US Navy Search Radars

DESIGNATION	FUNCTION	FREQUENCY	RANGE	REMARKS
SC (SC and SC–2)	Air	400mcs 75cm w/l	60 miles on aircraft	First tested in June 1941 on USS *Semmes*. First US RADAR small enough for installation on destroyers. No height finding. A-Scope only. SC & SC–1; non-directional IFF and A-Scope. SC–2; directional IFF and PPI scope. Bearing error 2° at 100 mi. (7 miles).
SG	Surface	3000mcs 10cm w/l	Horizon	First tested in May 1941 on USS *Semmes*. First installed in a fleet unit (USS *Augusta*) in April 1942. First USN microwave radar. Also first to use multicavity nagnetron for increase in output. Modifications of this type were SE, SF, SJ, SO, SP, SS, ST. A-Scope only. Sp could be used to detect low flying torpedo planes with some success.
SA (as SC)	Air	400mcs 75cm w/l	Same as SC	Modified SC. Initial contract Jan. 1942. Destroyer installation. Non directional IFF; A-Scope.

DESIGNATION	FUNCTION	FREQUENCY	RANGE	REMARKS
SK (SK and SK-3)	Air	400mcs 75cm w/1	100 miles on aircraft	Modified SC receiver with CXAM antenna and PPI scope. Initial contract April 1942. Best USN air search radar 1943 to end of war. Bearing error 2° at 100 miles (7 mi). SK-2 exceeded performance expectations in the battle.
SM (also known as CXBL)	Height Finding			Could give height information and because of definition of scope presentation gave good information as to composition and vertical formation of attackers. First cv equipped with this system cv-16. All were so equipped in this battle.

Identification, Friend or Foe (IFF)

The Mark III IFF equipment was installed in all carriers. It had the advantage over earlier equipment (some of which was still installed in destroyers) of being directional. It was mounted atop the SC-2 and SK radar antennas and had seven codes. Different codes were assigned to fighters than those given to torpedo planes, dive bombers and other type aircraft so the fighter directors could pick out their CAP from other friendly contacts on their radar. In action reports there was fairly widespread belief that Mk III was compromised since raids 3 and 4 showed Mk III indications. This could have been the returning search aircraft (see Diagram No. 15, Raid 6) though certainly the Japanese knew of IFF by this time and may have tried some electronic countermeasures other than the window aircraft mentioned in the text, though there is no mention of it in Japanese records.

Fire Control Radar

DESIGNATION	FREQUENCY	RANGE	REMARKS
Mk. 4 (Mk. 4, Mk. 37)	700mc 43cm w/1		Fire control for 5"/38 on all ships. Used in conjunction with Mark 37 Gun Fire Control System. Generally the battleships had four. Carriers and cruisers two, while the destroyers had one. Provided range, bearing and altitude information to fire control computers.
Mk. 8 (Mk 8, Mk. 34)	700mc 43cm w/1		Fire control for main batteries of battleships and cruisers. Used in conjunction with Mark 34 Fire Control System. Excellent for laying main battery weapons to 35000 yards. Substantial improvement over Mark 3 system.

US Airborne Radar

US Naval aircraft carried two types of radar at this time. The night fighters (24 F6F-3(N) and 3 F4U-2) carried the A1A equipment which had 65 mile, 25 mile, 5 mile and one mile scales, with 120° beam ahead (60° either side of dead ahead). Not entirely dependable. Biggest problem with the night fighters in air search was the fact that they were single place machines. Thirty-seven of the TBF/TBM carried the ASB radar which could theoretically detect a ship at 32 miles. Both the ASB and the A1A equipment were installed in wing radomes which resembled large American or Rugby footballs.

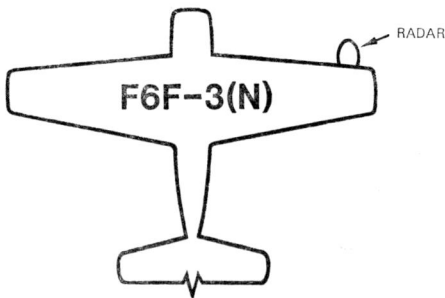

RADAR

F6F-3(N)

Japanese Shipboard Radar

By 1944 Japanese warships were equipped with three radar types, all search sets.

DESIGNATION	FUNCTION	WAVE LENGTH	RANGE	REMARKS
Type 21	Air and Surface Warning	1.5 Metre	1 aircraft 32 miles. Large ship 12.5 miles	Bedspring antenna, power rotated in most cases. Limited height finding capability. MUSASHI sets as installed performed as follows: TARGET — RANGE Seaplane — 20000M Seaplane Form. — 30000M Torpedo Planes — 40000M Battleship — 35000M Sub on Surface — 10000M BEARING ERRORS Maximum Range — 5° Close Range — 10° RANGE ERRORS Range – 25000 less 300M Range – 40000 less 500M A Scope only.
Type 13	Air Warning	1.5 Metre	Similar to 21	'Yagi' array – Ranges only.
Type 22	Surface Warning	10 CM	Large ship 21.5 miles	The Antenna looked like two megaphones, one for transmitting, one for receiving. Sufficient range and bearing discrimination for gunnery though not technically fire control equipment. When fitted MUSASHI's sets got accurate detection at 22000M on a BB. YAMATO's sets obtained 24625M range on a similar target. A-Scope only. First Japanese radar using multi-cavity magnetron.

Japanese Airborne Radar

Details on Japanese Aircraft Radars are sketchy. It is known that some of their aircraft were equipped with radars. The reconnaissance aircraft are mentioned in *Campaigns of the Pacific War*. This would mean that some of the Judys assigned to 1 SF for reconnaissance work, the 18 Kates of 653 NAG and perhaps some of the Jakes assigned to Second Fleet might have had radar capacity.

Mark 6/Model 4/Type 3 was the standard carrier aircraft radar in the Japanese Navy in 1944. It had an estimated range on a BB of 45 miles and 15 miles on a submarine with decks awash. The Japanese operator had not achieved any proficiency and in fact their post mortem says in regard to aircraft radars, '. . . the radars were totally unusable'. Whether this is an overstatement or not is not known but it is true that in the one area of electronics equipment in which the Japanese had seemed to close the technological gap their problems with large scale training had nullified any approach to parity.

The Japanese aircraft radars were fixed 'T' arrays usually on the leading edge of the wing(s) and in the fuselage aft of the wing.

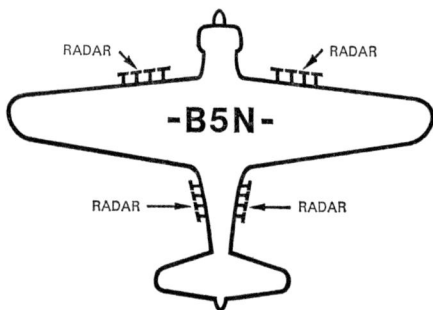

Close Air Defence

A Anti-aircraft Gunnery

Both navies close air defence theory was quite simple: A hail of gunfire would meet any aircraft which penetrated the fleet's fighter defences. The US Navy employed three close air defence weapons: the 5″/38 cal dual purpose gun (cruisers *Indianapolis, New Orleans, Minneapolis* and *San Francisco* carried 5″/25 cal weapons), the 40 mm (in quad, twin and single mounts) and 20 mm (in dual and single mounts) heavy machine guns. With varying degrees of sophistication all of these weapons were director controlled with visual and for the 5″ radar control. Aircraft were tracked by search radar until they were within range of gunfire control equipment (radar or visual). They were then tracked by this equipment and computers trained, elevated and fired the guns (and when appropriate set timed fuzes). The most popular dual purpose weapon in the Japanese Navy was the 5″/40 cal, though various other calibres were employed (5″/50; 4.7″/45; 3.9″/65; 3″/60). The dual purpose weapons were supplemented by the 25 mm heavy machine gun which came in triple, twin and single mounts. The former weapons were usually director controlled and used computers for training, elevating, firing and fuze setting. The Japanese did not have fire control radars at this time and could use radar in air defence for tracking only. The 25 mm was often director controlled though many were fired in local control only. The Japanese used an additional weapon in their AA in June 1944. The main batteries of their battleships and cruisers carried a type projectile called 'sanshiki-dan' (incendiary shrapnel) which employed a bursting charge of up to 10,000 (in *Yamato* class 46 cm guns) smaller charges of 25 mm size. These were fired with timed fuzes at long ranges for AA.

By 1944 the ships of both navies were bristling with heavy machine guns. Any deck space which offered a clear arc of fire was soon occupied by a heavy machine gun mount. It should be pointed out, however, that gunfire regardless of volume and control method was not generally as effective as a well directed fighter defence.

1 Heavy (dual purpose) AA weapons
  a USN 5″/38
      Ammo   projectile wt. 54 lb
                      case assembly 28 lb

Performance	muzzle velocity	2600 ft/sec	
	Horizontal range	18,000 yds	
	Vertical range	12,500 yds	
	Rate of fire	Maximum	22 RPM
		Sustained	15 RPM

      Crew   single mount 17
                     twin mount 27
                     (handling room personnel included)

  b IJN 5″/40
      Ammo   projectile wt. 50.8 lb
                      case assembly

Performance	muzzle velocity	2380 ft/sec	
	Horizontal range	16,200 yds	
	Vertical range		
	Rate of fire	Maximum	
		Sustained	

      Crew   twin mount

2 Heavy Machine Guns
  a USN 40 mm/56 cal

Range	Horizontal	11,000 yds	
	Ceiling	5000 yds	
Muzzle vel		2800 ft/sec	
Max elevation		90°–15°	
Shell wt.		2 lb	
Rate of fire		160 RPM	

      Swedish designed (Bofors) weapon used in practically every Navy in World War II

  b IJN 25 mm/60 cal

Range	Horizontal	6800 metres	
	Ceiling	5000 metres	

Muzzle vel	900 m/sec
Max elevation	80°–10°
Shell wt.	250 g
Rate of fire	220 RPM

Single mount 1943 design
Twin mount 1933 design
Triple mount 1941 design

This weapon was a French design and its performance was considered excellent

c USN 20 mm/72 cal

Range	Horizontal	5000 yds
	Ceiling	
Muzzle vel		2725 ft/sec
Max elevation		87°–5°
Shell wt. (round)		0.5 lb
Rate of fire		Max 450 RPM; effective 250–320 RPM

Commence firing range: High elevation 1000 yards, Horizontal 2000 yards

Swiss design (Oerlikon) weapon used in practically every Navy in World War II

B Formations

Both navies employed the circular AA defence formation with one to four carriers at its centre and battleships, cruisers and destroyers in the outer circle(s).

The American formations contained three or four carriers with a carrier (except Task Group 58.7) at the centre. The remaining carriers were placed on a 2000 yard circle while the cruisers and destroyers were placed on a 4000 yard circle. American formations maintained the course and speed of the guide and manoeuvred independently only when required to avoid immediate threats such as torpedoes in the water etc. This was because of the relative priority the US gave to methods other than manoeuvre for thwarting enemy air attacks. As stated in USF-10A ('Current Tactical Orders and Doctrine, US Fleet') these methods were ranked as follows:

a Most effective fighter direction and coverage.
b Maximum anti-aircraft fire from all weapons.

    c Mutual support between heavy ships and of heavy ships by the screen.

    d Effective avoiding manoeuvres under broad control by the officer in tactical command, with ships at foci of attacks supplementing signalled manoeuvres as required.

Note that manoeuvre was given lowest priority.

The Japanese formations contained one to three carriers with a carrier at the centre as formation guide. The remaining carriers (in A Force and B Force) were placed on each quarter of the guide carrier at 1500 metres. The battleships and heavy cruisers were also on the 1500 metre circle while the light cruisers and destroyers were evenly distributed about a 2000 metre circle. In contrast to the American method however Japanese formations under attack sinuated as soon as enemy aircraft appeared, conforming only to the general movements of the guide. Once an attack was underway they manoeuvred independently, often with little apparent regard for mutual defence. There were two reasons for this divergence from the US method. First Japanese cruiser and destroyer captains had gained great respect for US naval aircraft in the Solomons campaign and felt that skilful helmsmen were the only real defence against American attack aircraft. Second, Japanese doctrine placed a higher emphasis on manoeuvre than US principles stating:

'Evasive action against bomb or torpedo attack when in circular formation will be carried out as follows: The carrier will take individual evasive action, and the other ships will follow it. . . . The carrier with the senior officer aboard will take individual evasive action, and the other ships will follow it. Repeated practice is regarded necessary for executing this action.'

Anti-Submarine — Warfare Equipment and Ships, and Submarines

USN ASW Ships
Escort Aircraft Carriers (CVE)
USS *Hoggatt Bay* (CVE–75) 7800 tons; 512'× 65'× 20'; 19.25 kts; 1–5"/38 gun, 16–40 mm; 28 aircraft; 860 men; radar equipped.

Destroyer Escorts (DE)
USS *England* (DE–635), *George* (DE–697), *Raby* (DE–698), *Spangler* (DE–696) 1400 tons; 306'× 37'× 9.5'; 23.5 kts; 3–3"/50 guns, 6–40 mm; 3–21" torpedo tubes; 220 men; 2 hedgehog throwers, 8 K guns and two depth charge tracks; sonar and radar equipped.

USN Submarines (Fish and Marine Creatures)
T class – *Gar* (SS–206) 1475/2370 tons; 307.25'× 27.25'× 13.75'; 20/8.7 kts; 10–21" Torpedo Tubes (6 bow, 4 stern) 20 torpedoes; 1–5"; 1–40 mm; 85 officers and men; 300' safe depth.
P class – *Plunger* (SS–179) 1330/2005 tons; 300.5'× 25.25'× 14'; 19/8 kts; 6–21" T.T. (4B/2S) 12 torps; 1–4"; 55 men; 300' safe depth.
New S class – 1st group – *Stingray* (SS–186) 1435/2210 tons; 308[1]× 26.5'× 14.25'; 21/9 kts; 8–21" T.T. (4B/4S); 16 torps; 1–4"; 70 men; 300' safe depth.
New S class – 2nd group – *Swordfish* (SS–193), *Seawolf* (SS–197) 1450/2350 tons; 310.5'× 27.25'× 13.75'; 21/9 kts; 8–21" T.T. (4B/4S); 16 torps.; 70 men; 300' safe depth.
Gato class – *Archerfish* (SS–311), *Plaice* (SS–390), *Pintado* (SS–387), *Pilotfish* (SS–386), *Tunny* (SS–282), *Albacore* (SS–218), *Bang* (SS–385), *Finback* (SS–230), *Flying Fish* (SS–229), *Muskallunge* (SS–262), *Seahorse* (SS–304), *Pipefish* (SS–388), *Cavalla* (SS–244), *Growler* (SS–215), *Hake* (SS–256), *Bashaw* (SS–241), *Paddle* (SS–263), *Harder*

(ss–257), *Haddo* (ss–255), *Redfin* (ss–272), *Bluefish* (ss–222), *Jack* (ss–259), *Flier* (ss–250) 1525/2415 tons; 310.5′ × 27.25′ × 13.75′; 20.25/10 kts; 10–21″ T.T. (6B/4S); 20 torps; 1–5″; 1–40 mm; 80 men; 400′ safe depth.

USN ASW Weapons

Depth Charges – usn destroyers and destroyer escorts carried three types of depth charges: Mk 6 (300) and Mk 7 (600) were the familiar 'ash can' while the Mk 9 (600) was 'tear' shaped and had a faster and more uniform sink rate. Set to explode at a given depth.

Hedgehog – A 24 spigot ahead thrown weapon firing 24 contact exploding weapons in a circular pattern about 250–300 yards in front of the firing ship allowing the attacking ship to maintain constant sonar contact throughout an attack.

USN Sonar

World War II sonars were effective up to about 18 knots. They were 'searchlight' sets; i.e. they had to be trained on the bearing sought to be covered (usually about 10°), unlike today's sets which search 360° (less shaft baffles) on each sweep. Normally search was conducted in sweeps through 180° on one side and then 180° to the other, a complete sweep taking several minutes. Effective range was usually about 1000 yards.

IJN Submarines

I–5: 2243/3061 tons; 320′ × 30.25′ × 16.5′; 18/8 kts; 6–21″ T.T. (bow) 20 torpedoes; 2–5.5″; 80 men; 250′ safe depth.

I–10 (*I–9* class) 2919/4150 tons; 372.75′ × 31.3′ × 17.5′; 23.5/8 kts; 6–21″ T.T. (bow) 18 torpedoes; 1–5.5″; 4–25 mm; 1 aircraft; 100 men; 325′ safe depth.

I–38 (*I–15* class) 2584/3654 tons; 356.5′ × 30.5′ × 16.75′; 23.5/8 kts; 6–21″ T.T. (bow) 17 torpedoes; 1–5.5″; 2–25 mm; 1 aircraft; 100 men; 325′ safe depth.

I–41 (*I–40* class) 2624/3700 tons; 356.5′ × 30.5′ × 17′; 23.5/8 kts; 6–21″ T.T. (bow) 17 torpedoes; 1–5.5″; 2–25 mm; 1 aircraft; 100 men; 325′ safe depth.

I–53 (*I–52* class) 2564/3644 tons; 356.5′ × 30.5′ × 16.75′; 17.75/6.5 kts; 6–21″ T.T. (bow) 17 torpedoes; 2–5.5″; 1 aircraft; 100 men; 325′ safe depth.

I–184, *I–185* (*I–176* class) 1833/2602 tons; 346′ × 27′ × 15′; 23/8 kts;

6–21″ T.T. (bow) 12 torpedoes; 1–4.7″; 2–25 mm; 80 officers and men; 260′ safe depth.

Ro–36, Ro–41, Ro–42, Ro–43, Ro–44, Ro–47 (Ro–35 class) 1115/1447 tons; 264′× 23′× 13.25′; 19.75/8 kts; 4–21″ T.T. (bow) 10 torpedoes; 1–3″; 2–25 mm; 80 men; 260′ safe depth.

Ro–68 (Ro–60 class) 996/1322 tons; 250¹× 24.25′× 12.25′; 16/8 kts; 6–21″ T.T. (bow) 10 torpedoes; 1–3″; 1–25 mm; 60 men; 195′ safe depth.

Ro–104, Ro–105, Ro–106, Ro–108, Ro–112, Ro–113, Ro–114, Ro–115, Ro–116, Ro–117 (Ro–100 class) 601/782 tons; 199.75′× 20′× 11.5′; 14/8 kts; 4–21″ T.T. (bow) 5 torpedoes; 1–3″; 75 men; 245′ safe depth.

IJN ASW Weapons
1 The standard Japanese depth charge was a 350 lb weapon with a 230 lb charge.
2 Most Japanese destroyers carried 4 depth charge throwers (Y guns) plus stern tracks. The *Akitsuki* class carried six while *Shimakaze* carried two. They did not carry ahead thrown weapons though they would experiment with the concept before the war ended.

Japanese Echo Ranging Equipment
Japanese destroyers and light cruisers had active echo ranging equipment which 'displayed its greatest effectiveness when the ranging ship was proceeding at ten knots or less with twelve knots as the maximum effective searching speed, and after that it tended to diminish rapidly in effectiveness as the speed increased and that the destroyers and light cruisers equipped with such echo ranging could not have been particularly effective at eighteen or even sixteen knots.'
War College Analysis The Battle of Leyte Gulf.
Some Japanese battleships, cruisers and aircraft carriers had passive hydrophone arrays which gave 'limited detection capability when the ship was making low speed or stopped.'
Battleship, Garzke and Dulin, U.S.N.I.

General comment
The principal defence of a fast carrier task force against submarine attack was its high speed. World War II submarines had very low submerged speeds and could not maintain their maximum speed for more than a few minutes without endangering their ability to

remain submerged because of the great drain high speed had on the batteries, the source of power for submerged running. The high speed prevented a submerged submarine from being able to make an attack approach except from nearly dead ahead. A large number of screening ships was the next defence principally relying on seeing the periscope (visually or on radar) of any submarine attempting to penetrate the screen. Additionally both navies used battleship and cruiser floatplanes and carrier aircraft in anti-submarine patrol ahead of the fleet in an attempt to discover and destroy any submarines along its line of advance and in the event they failed to destroy them to force them to submerge thus reducing the probability that they could approach the formation.

Japanese Naval Air Training 1940-1944

The unique role played by Japanese Naval Air training in this battle is sufficient reason for a concise review of that programme in the war years. The source quoted is *Interrogations of Japanese Officials*.

'Until December 1940, the Japanese Naval Air Force training programme consisted of the following phases:

1 Elementary or basic training of 30 hours in Type-3 trainers or Type-90 seaplane trainers. Following completion candidates went to:
2 Intermediate training using Type-90 land trainers and Type-93 (Willow). After 40 hours, trainees moved to:
3 Advance combat training where combat and obsolete combat type aircraft were employed. 30 hours flight time in Zekes, Claudes, Kates, Vals, Alfs, Petes and Nells was required before candidates were assigned to:
4 Operational units. If selected for shipboard air groups, personnel had another 50 hours training before leaving operational units.

In December 1940, elementary and intermediate training were combined, but total flight time of the two reduced by 10 hours.

When First Air Fleet was being organized during the last half of 1943, approximately 20% of those completing elementary/intermediate training were transferred directly to operational units under that command, skipping the advanced combat training phase. Those selected were the most promising candidates. CinC First Air Fleet preferred to have those assigned to his command trained in combat type aircraft directly under his supervision, believing that this would result ultimately in a better trained and integrated organization.

Frequently crews "got into bad habits" during advanced combat training and the CinC First Air Fleet wanted to avoid this.

In the spring of 1944 the "skipping" of advanced combat training was stopped by the Naval General Staff and restored for all trainees because:

1 Operational losses were excessive.
2 The longer period of training in the newer combat type planes consumed more aviation gasoline than training in the less modern aircraft assigned to advanced combat training units; and
3 Tactical units were then beginning to employ new plane types such as George, Jill, Judy, Myrt and Frances which were "too hot" for any but experienced pilots to fly.'

Principal Characters Involved in the Battle of the Philippine Sea

A United States Navy

Spruance, Raymond Ames; Admiral USN; USNA 1907; CO *Bainbridge*, 1913; New York Navy Yard, Asst. Eng. Off.; CO Destroyers; Bureau of Engineering; Naval War College; CO *Mississippi*, 1938; Commandant 10th Naval District 1940-41; Cruiser Division Commander; Commander Task Force 16 at Midway; Chief of Staff, Cincpac; Deputy Cincpac and Cincpoa; Commander Fifth Fleet.

Mitscher, Marc A.; Vice-Admiral USN: USNA 1910; 1915 Naval Aviator; CO NAS Rockaway and Miami; Pilot NC-1; *Saratoga*, 1926; XO* *Langley*, 1929; BUAER; Chief of Staff Commander Aircraft Base Force; Compatwing 1, 1938; CO *Hornet*, 1941, Doolittle Raid, Midway, Compatwing 2; Commander Fleet Air Wing Noumea; Comairsols; Commander Fleet Air Wing, West Coast; Commander Fast Carrier Forces Pacific Fleet, March 21, 1944.

Reeves, John W.; Rear Admiral USN: USNA 1911; Battleships and destroyers; *Sampson*: XO *Maury*; Flag Secretary to Commander Naval Forces Eastern Mediterranean; *Concord*, Engineer Officer; CO *Worden*; Material Division CNO; CO *Parrott*; Navy Department; *New Orleans*, First Lieutenant**; Naval Aviator 1936; XO *Langley*; XO and CO Fleet Air Base Pearl Harbor; CO *Wasp*; Commander Alaskan sector, NW Sea Frontier; Commander Carrier Division Four.

---

*XO – Executive Officer. Second in command in USN usage.
** First Lieutenant. In USN usage the first lieutenant is the deck officer, not the second in command as in the Royal Navy.

Montgomery, Alfred E.; Rear Admiral USN: USNA 1912; *West Virginia*; Submariner 1915; CO *R-20*; Naval Aviator 1922; XO Observation squadrons; CO VT-1 and VB-1; Repair Officer and XO NAS San Diego; Senior Air Officer *Langley*, *Saratoga*; CO NAS Seattle; Staff Aviation Officer *Chicago*; CO NAS Anacostia; Staff, Plans and Operations Officer, *Saratoga*; XO *Ranger*; CO *Ranger*; Chief of Staff Comairlantflt; Commandant Naval Air Training Center, Corpus Christi; Comcardiv 12; Comcardiv 3.

Clark, Joseph J.; Rear Admiral USN: USNA 1918; Naval Aviator 1925; Aviation Officer *Mississippi*; XO NAS Anacostia; CO *Lexington* VF squadron; Inspection and Survey Board; Air Officer *Lexington* and *Yorktown*; CO *Suwannee*, North Africa; CO *Yorktown*; Commander Carrier Division 13.

Harrill, William K.; Rear Admiral USN: USNA 1914; *Pennsylvania*; Staff Officer, Commander Mine Force Atlantic Fleet; Naval Aviator 1921; Squadron Commander in *Langley* and *Saratoga*; Aide to SecNav for Aeronautics; XO and CO NAS Anacostia; Asst Naval Attache for Air London; CO *Ranger*; Commander Replacement carrier squadron; Commander Carrier Division 1.

Lee, Willis Augustus; Vice-Admiral USN: USNA 1908; Destroyers; CO destroyers *Fairfax*, *W. B. Preston*; *Lardner*, Naval War College; XO *Pennsylvania*; CO *Concord*; Staff of Commander Cruisers Battle Force; Director Fleet Training; Asst Chief of Staff Cominch; Combatdiv 6; Commander Fast Battleships Pacific Fleet.

B Imperial Japanese Navy

Ozawa, Jisaburo; Vice-Admiral IJN; Professor Naval Academy; CO *Maya*, *Haruna*; Chief of Staff, Combined Fleet; Commanding Officer Cruiser Squadron; Director Torpedo School; Commanding Officer, First Air Squadron; Commanding Officer Battle Squadron; Commanding Officer Southern Area Fleet, Borneo and Malaya; Staff Officer, Naval General Headquarters; Commander in Chief Third Fleet; Commander First Mobile Force.

Kurita, Takeo; Vice-Admiral IJN; CO Seventh Squadron (Cruisers); CO Third Squadron (Battleships); Commander in Chief, Second Fleet; Commander First Diversionary Attack Force.

Joshima, Takaji; Rear Admiral IJN; CO *Shokaku*, Pearl Harbor; Commander Seaplane Carrier Division 11, Eastern Solomons; Staff Officer Rabaul; Commander 11th Air Fleet Rabaul; Commander Second Aircraft Carrier Squadron, August 1943.

Obayashi, Sueo; Rear Admiral IJN; CO *Zuiho*; Commander Third Aircraft Carrier Squadron.

Kakuta, Kakuji; Vice-Admiral IJN; Commander Fourth Aircraft Carrier Squadron, Philippines, Malaya; Commander Second Mobile Force (Aleutian portion of Midway operation); Commander Second Aircraft Carrier Squadron, Santa Cruz; Commander Fifth Base Air Force.

APPENDIX NINE

Summary of Air Operations

A UNITED STATES NAVY

INTERCEPTIONS 19 JUNE, 1944

Task Group	Carrier	Missions	Squadron	Sorties
58.1	Hornet	3	VF–2	36
	Bataan	2	VF–50	31
	Yorktown	2	VF–1	30
		1	VF (N) 77	1
	Belleau Wood	2	VF–24	16
58.2	Bunker Hill	3	VF–8	36
	Wasp	2	VF–14	25
	Monterey	3	VF–28	21
	Cabot	5	VF–31	28
58.3	Enterprise	2	VF–10	24
	Lexington	3	VF–16	38
	San Jacinto	5	VF–51	21
	Princeton	2	VF–27	20
58.4	Essex	4	VF–15	42
	Cowpens	2	VF–25	22
	Langley	1	VF–32	12
TOTALS		42		403

★ *Engage Enemy A/C* – Number of fighters engaging enemy aircraft.
★★ *Enemy A/C Engaged* – Number of enemy aircraft engaged. Of course there would be duplication in this category.

SCORES CLAIMED BY FIGHTER SQUADRONS WERE AS FOLLOWS:

	VF–2	VF–50	VF–1	VF (N) 77	VF–24	VF–8	VF–14	VF–28
Destroyed	37	11	32	1	10	18	11	19
Probables	5	2	5		3	2		
Damaged	2				6	1	4	

Abort.	*Engage Enemy A/C	**Enemy A/C Engaged	AA	Losses A/C	Ops
	33	53	1	1	
	7	20			
2	21	46		2	
	1	1			1
	12	35			
	28	33		2	
	16	15			2
	19	22			1
	22	67			
	14	19			
2	32	52			1
	8	10		1	
2	18	45		2	
2	37	115		4	
	17	13		1	1
	2	2			
8	287	548	1	13	6

VF–31	VF–10	VF–16	VF–51	VF–27	VF–15	VF–25	VF–32	TOTALS
25	17	26	8	29	63	9	2	318
1			2	6	12	3	0	45
1							0	14

	Squadron	Number of Sorties	Abortive	Number Attack Enemy Ships	Number Engage Enemy A/c	Number Enemy A/c Engaged	Destroyed	Probable	Damaged	GP Bomb(s)	Other	Torpedo	Lost to AA	Lost to A/c	Oper. Loss
TG 58.1															
Hornet	VF-2	15	1	14	1	1		1			2				7
	VB-2	14	0	14	1	2				6	4		1		11
	VT-2	8	2	6	0	0				2	4	4			1
Bataan	VF-50	10	0	6	4	17	4		3	1				2	1
Yorktown	VF-1	16	1	11	1	1		1	3						1
	VB-1	15	2	13	1	1				6	4				9
	VT-1	9	2	8	5	5			3	5	5	2			4
Belleau	VF-24	8	2	2	3	10	3	3						1	1
Wood	VT-24	4	0	4	2	4			2	4	4	3			
TG 58.2															
Bunker	VF-8	14	0	4	14	10	2	2	1						1
Hill	VB-8	12	0	12	6	5		2	1	6	2			2	9
	VT-8	8	0	8	8	2			1	8					5★
Wasp	VF-14	16	0	16	11	5	5							1	1
	VB-14	12	0	12	5	5			2	5	3			1	10
	VT-14	7	0	7	1	1				7					3
Monterey	VT-28	4	0	4	1	2			1	4					1
Cabot	VT-31	4	0	4	2	2			2	4					2
TG 58.3★★															
Enterprise	VF-10	12	0	8	12	20	7	1	1					1	1
	VB-10	11	0	11	11	10				2	2			1	2
	VT-10	5	0	5	2	12	1	1		4					4
Lexington	VF-16	11	0	11	2	2	1		1	1				1	1
	VB-16	16	1	15	15	21	2	1	2	3	4			1	2
	VT-16	6	1	5	6	11	1		6	5	5			1	2
San Jacinto	VT-51	2	0	2	2	4					2				1
TOTALS		239	12	191	116	153	26	10	25	61	53	13	6	12	80

Breakdown of Total Raiders Launched—VF 102; VB 80; VT 57
Breakdown of Losses Operationally—VF 14; VB 43; VT 23

★ This table shows the *Bunker Hill* VT as carrying 8 GP bombs, 8 'other' (AP or SAP) and 8 torpedoes. Since she only launched 8 planes in the raid and most of the VT participating carried GP bombs they have been shown in that column

★★ *Princeton* of TG 58.3 did not participate in this attack.

B Imperial Japanese Navy

The Air Groups assigned to the Japanese Carrier Squadrons had the following complements:

601 *Kokutai*–81 A6M VF, 81 D4Y VB, 54 B6N VT, 9 D4Y VS–Total 225
652 *Kokutai*–81 A6M VF, 36 D4Y VB, 18 B6N VT   Total 135
653 *Kokutai*–63 A6M VF   27 B6N VT   Total 90
Totals   225   117   99   9   450

Due to operational losses and the non-availability of sufficient numbers of D4Y and B6N type aircraft to fill the complements the number of aircraft on board the Japanese ships on June 19, 1944 was as follows:

601 *Kokutai*–79 A6M VF, 70 D4Y VB, 51 B6N VT, 7 D3A VB–Total 207
652 *Kokutai*–81 A6M VF, 39 D4Y VB, 18 B6N VT, 27 D3A VB–Total 135
653 *Kokutai*–62 A6M VF,   9 B6N VT, 17 B5N VT–Total 88
Totals   222   79   78   24/17   430

OPERATIONS ON JUNE 19, 1944
601 *Kokutai*
a Air Searches – *Shokaku* launched 11 D4Y at 0530.
b Attack on contact 7–*I*.

Number and Type	Lost	Returned
48 A6M	32	16
53 D4Y	42	11
27 B6N	23	4
Totals 128	97	31

c Pathfinder group

2 B6N	2	0

d Window aircraft

1 D4Y	1	0

e Attack on Contact 15–*Ri*

9 A6M	8	1
9 B6N	1	8
Totals 18	9	9

f Sunk with *Taiho*
    5 A6M; 4 D4Y; 1 D3A; 3 B6N=13
g Sunk with *Shokaku*
    5 D4Y; 2 D3A; 2 B6N=9

Recapitulation

Type	No. on board 000, 6–19–44	Lost	No. survived	No. in operational Condition 6–20–44
VF	79	45	34	17
VB	77	55	22	8
VR	51	31	20	7
Totals	207	131	76	32

652 *Kokutai*
a Attack on contact 3–*Ri*

	15 A6M VF	1	14
	25 A6M VFB	5	20
	7 B6N VT	1	6
Totals	47	7 (lost)	40 (returned)

b Attack on contact 15–*Ri*

	18 A6M VF	18	10 (VF and VFB)
	10 A6M VFB	10	0
	27 D3A VB	27	0
	9 D4Y VB	9	0
Totals	64	64★	10★

Recapitulation

Type	No. on board 000, 6–19–44	Lost	No. survived	No. in operational condition 6–20–44
VF	81	29	52	38
VB	36	36	0	0
VT	18	1	17	9
Totals	135	66	69	47

653 *Kokutai*
a Air Searches – 3 ACS launched 13 B5N at 0515
    10 returned.
b Attack on contact 7–*I*

	16 A6M VF	8	8
	45 A6M VFB	32	13
	8 B6N VT	2	6
Totals	69	42 (lost)	28 (returned)

c Pathfinder group
    2 B5N

Recapitulation

Type	No. on board 000, 6–19–44	Lost	No. survived	No. in operational condition 6–20–44
VF	62	40	22	13
VT	26	5	21	9
Totals	88	45	43	22

★ Some of the aircraft of 652 *Kokutai* raid on 15–*Ri* landed on Guam but none were in operational condition.

After the fight of June 20, 1944 First Mobile Force had 35 aircraft of all types in the carriers which were in operational condition.

Japanese War History Office gives a different make up of the Air Groups as of the time of the Japanese sortie, as follows:

601 *Kokutai*–91 A6M VF; 70 D4Y VB; 44 B6N; 9 D3A   214
652 *Kokutai*–80 A6M VF; 11 D4Y VB; 15 B6N; 29 D3A   135
653 *Kokutai*–63 A6M VF;   19 B6N;   18 B5N 90

Totals	234	81	68	18	439

SECOND FLEET AIRCRAFT

The role of Japanese scout seaplanes in the battle was of sufficient importance to give a breakdown of their distribution amongst the Japanese cruisers and battleships. The basis of this table is the US Naval War College Analysis of the Battle for Leyte Gulf.

Other sources have been consulted, but the War College Analysis seems to have the most thoroughly researched list.

Yamato–3 F1M; *Musashi*–4 F1M; *Nagato*–2 F1M; *Kongo*–2 E13A; *Haruna*–2 E13A

Tone–5 E13A; *Chikuma*–5 E13A; *Mogami*–6 E13A; *Kumano*–3 E13A; *Suzuya*–3 E13A; *Chokai*–2 E13A; *Maya*–2 E13A; *Atago*–2 E13A; *Takao*–2 E13A; *Myoko*–2 E13A; *Haguro*–2 E13A; *Noshiro*–2 E13A; *Yahagi*–2 E13A

Totals: 42 E13A; 9 F1M.

On the morning of June 19, 1944 First Mobile Force had a total of 43 Float Planes of all types on board.

On the morning of June 20, 1944 First Mobile Force had a total of 27 Float Planes of all types on board in operational condition.

After the air battle of June 20, First Mobile Force had a total of 12 Float Planes of all types on board in operational condition.

Index

252